Subordinated Development

Studies in Critical Social Sciences Book Series

Haymarket Books is proud to be working with Brill Academic Publishers (www.brill.nl) to republish the *Studies in Critical Social Sciences* book series in paperback editions. This peer-reviewed book series offers insights into our current reality by exploring the content and consequences of power relationships under capitalism, and by considering the spaces of opposition and resistance to these changes that have been defining our new age. Our full catalog of *SCSS* volumes can be viewed at https://www.haymarketbooks.org/series_collections/4-studies-in-critical-social-sciences.

Series Editor
David Fasenfest, Wayne State University

Editorial Board
Eduardo Bonilla-Silva (Duke University)
Chris Chase-Dunn (University of California–Riverside)
William Carroll (University of Victoria)
Raewyn Connell (University of Sydney)
Kimberlé W. Crenshaw (University of California–LA, and Columbia University)
Heidi Gottfried (Wayne State University)
Karin Gottschall (University of Bremen)
Alfredo Saad Filho (King's College London)
Chizuko Ueno (University of Tokyo)
Sylvia Walby (Lancaster University)
Raju Das (York University)

SUBORDINATED DEVELOPMENT

Transnational Capital in the Process of
Accumulation of Latin America and Brazil

RUBENS R. SAWAYA

TRANSLATED BY
JOHN KOLODZIEJSKI

Haymarket Books
Chicago, IL

First published in 2018 by Brill Academic Publishers, The Netherlands.
© 2018 Koninklijke Brill NV, Leiden, The Netherlands

Published in paperback in 2019 by
Haymarket Books
P.O. Box 180165
Chicago, IL 60618
773-583-7884
www.haymarketbooks.org

ISBN: 978-1-64259-066-1

Distributed to the trade in the US through Consortium Book Sales and Distribution (www.cbsd.com) and internationally through Ingram Publisher Services International (www.ingramcontent.com).

This book was published with the generous support of Lannan Foundation and Wallace Action Fund.

Special discounts are available for bulk purchases by organizations and institutions. Please call 773-583-7884 or email info@haymarketbooks.org for more information.

Cover design by Jamie Kerry and Ragina Johnson.

Printed in United States.

10 9 8 7 6 5 4 3 2 1

Library of Congress Cataloging-in-Publication Data is available.

To all those who have contributed, in varying degrees, to this book. It would be impossible to list them all, and perhaps unfair to some I may have left off that list.

∴

Contents

Introduction   1

1 Capital Accumulation, Concentration and Centralisation   9
   1.1   Introduction   9
   1.2   The Commodity as a Process Cell   11
   1.3   The Process of Capital Accumulation   21
   1.4   Productivity and the Concentration of Capital   27
   1.5   Realisation of Value, the Condition for Accumulation, Concentration and Centralisation   34
   1.6   The Centralisation of Capital   42

2 Capital Accumulation, Transnational Capital and the Exclusion of the Periphery   54
   2.1   Introduction   54
   2.2   The Question of Space for Accumulation   57
   2.3   Globalisation: Accumulation and Concentration   59
   2.4   Concentration   63
   2.5   Accumulation and Concentration: The Question of Political-Geographic Space   65
   2.6   Internationalisation as the Realisation of Value   67
   2.7   Realisation, Internationalisation and the Political-Geographic Space   71
   2.8   Capital Centralisation   72
   2.9   The Centralisation of Space: The Exclusion of the Periphery   78

3 The Inclusion of the Periphery in the Process of Global Accumulation   82
   3.1   Introduction   82
   3.2   The Logic of Development through Import Substitution   85
   3.3   State Participation   94
   3.4   The Participation of Transnational Capital   98
   3.5   Transnational Capital as Dynamic Centre   101
   3.6   Materialisation of the New Dependency   104
   3.7   The Development of Submission to the Movement of Globalised Capital   111

4 Brazil in Capital's Globalisation   115
   4.1 Introduction   115
   4.2 Vargas – The Institutional Apparatus for Development   121
   4.3 National Associated Development – The Targets Plan (Plano de Metas)   125
   4.4 The Attempt to Recreate a National Policy and the Resumption of Associated Development – 1960–64   131
   4.5 The Strengthening of Transnational Capital – The "Economic Miracle"   136
   4.6 Brazil as a Power – II PND   143
   4.7 Scrapping the National State – The 1980s   149
   4.8 The 1990s – Growing Subordination to Globalised Capital   155
   4.9 The Lula Government Facing the Power Structure: Conciliation or Confrontation?   170

5 The Possibility of a Forced Disconnection   176
   5.1 Accumulation, Subordination and Disconnection   176
   5.2 The Question of Centralisation   185
   5.3 The Centralisation of the 1980s and 1990s   188
   5.4 Centralisation between Countries   193
   5.5 Centralisation and Financial Flows   195
   5.6 Centralisation and the Periphery   197
   5.7 The Forced Disconnection   199
   5.8 Final Considerations   204

   Bibliography   209
   Index   217

Introduction

There has been a great deal of discussion in recent years regarding Brazil's inclusion in the world economy in the accumulation process of globalised capital. A series of policies were adopted through the 1990s with the explicit aim of creating an environment favourable to the attraction and strengthening of large foreign capital in the Brazilian economy. This was seen as a necessary means for promoting development, or to definitively leave underdevelopment behind, as the way out of backwardness and towards the modern. The aim was to raise the level of the country's integration in the world economy. Brazil, along with other Latin American countries, engaged with this idea. They supported and undertook a series of policies requested by large transnational capital, submitting themselves voluntarily to the movement of world capital. This is nothing new in the country's history. The strategy of import substitution by the Economic Commission for the Development of Latin America and the Caribbean – CEPAL had already advocated a kind of alliance with transnational capital in an effort to develop Latin America. In Brazil, since President Juscelino Kubitschek with his Target Plan ("Plano de Metas" 1956–1960), or similarly during the military government's "Economic Miracle" (1968–1973), the strategy had always been associated with foreign capital, submitting itself directly to the process of global capital accumulation led by the countries at the centre. This association defined the way industrialisation was implemented in some Latin American countries – as well as in Brazil – leaving transnational companies in control of the most dynamic sectors of the economy. A number of authors have shown how this submission to the movement of world capital was constructed, based on the nation states of the periphery, through pacts of interests with their elites, as much in the Target Plan as well as in CEPAL's strategy. In the 1990s, a new pact was created in the same vein again, but at a new stage of world capital movement, enhancing and creating new contradictions to this model.

So, partly seeking to revive the analysis of this process, what one verifies is that Brazil as well as other Latin American countries that adopted this industrialising strategy in their development processes, ended up by submitting themselves in their history to the movement of world capital in its different periods of expansion over the world. Despite this, or as a result of this, they have remained peripheral countries still. They are very far from the countries at the centre, if not moving increasingly away from the condition of being developed.[1] In the face of this strategy that involved a series of peripheral economies, the question that is posed here is: What is the significance of submitting to the movement of global capital? How is this movement of capital? What does it mean to seek the development of the periphery?

In analysing the movement of capital in its processes of global accumulation, concentration and centralisation, one may infer that the historic strategy of submission through import substitution policies with foreign capital – that in spite of being responsible for the formation of the industrial structure of the Latin American countries, led to an increase and not a reduction in dependency. One may also infer that submission was enhanced in the 1990s by the adoption of a number of liberalising policies, resulting in a tendency, not of the periphery's inclusion in the movement of globalised capital, but in its exclusion. Or, at best, in the maintenance of its condition as being on the periphery, moving continually away from the countries of the centre.

Understanding the process of world capital accumulation consists in analysing how this movement occurs. Marx explains the movement of capital as a process that involves the accumulation, concentration and centralisation of capital. Within this logic is contained the idea of expansion, of movement, of continuous valorisation in value, capital accumulation. The process of capital accumulation, as a more general movement, is characterised by the requirement that each individual capital has to keep itself in permanent valorisation on an extended scale in order to exist as capital. It is the need, embodied in the action of each individual capital, of maintaining the surplus value created (excess value created) in a growing cycle of valorisation; it is the requirement for the existence of individual capital as a specific agent of capital valorisation on an increasing scale, to always keep itself growing upon the risk of perishing in the presence of other capitals, succumbing to competition. Related to this movement is the process of capital concentration. In so far that capital expands, it constantly increases the surplus value in search of valorisation that obligatorily has to be reinvested. This movement of concentration enlarges the need for space in which each individual capital moves for the continuity of accumulation. Finally, also linked to the logic of capital accumulation is the process of capital centralisation that consists in the expropriation of the capitalist himself by capital. This is a process which at the same time propels capital towards expansion and holds it back by the elimination of other individual capitals, strengthening capitals that remain in the process of appreciation.

---

[1] "Close to the start of WWI, Argentina's income per capita ... was higher than that of France, Germany, Italy and Spain. The incomer per capita of the region [Latin America] exceeded that of Japan and three and half times the rest of Asia" (UNCTAD 2003:127).

The latter case is a process which shows itself with all its force when the space for accumulation becomes restricted as in moments of crises in which companies go bankrupt, close or are acquired by others.

The movement of capital described above is specifically embodied in the process of the formation and strengthening of large economic groups, the direct representatives of capital, that find a natural ally in their national states of origin, but that also seek new allies in peripheral states in their growth process. These economic groups are the specific social subjects (but not individuals) responsible for the process of accumulation in their places of origin and through their expansion (and not transference) to the periphery as an obligatory mechanism of capital maintenance in the process of valorisation. Thus, the processes of accumulation, concentration and centralisation of capital that occur in the local space, transcend frontiers, occupying a global space by the action of the large groups that have become transnationals. These are strengthened and supported by their states, and transport the contradictions of the process of accumulation which was previously restricted to a local space to a global space. The expansion of the area of accumulation, that is in part responsible for the industrialisation of a portion of the periphery through productive investments, ends up by subordinating that same periphery to their specific interests, submitting it to the condition of "junior partner" of foreign capital at best. However, at the same time, it becomes vulnerable to the movement of global capital, to the point of its being able to exclude it from global accumulation itself based on the wide-ranging processes of restructuring and re-engineering of these large corporations. These processes are assured by the wave of liberalisation and deregulation requested by its own capital in its process of global centralisation.

In order to explain this movement, one needs to analyse how the process of capital valorisation occurs on a global scale. Its stages of commercial and productive internationalisation have already been widely studied by a number of authors (Chapter 2) following the logic described by Marx. But how does one explain the more recent times of the process of global accumulation in which the periphery, the industrialised parts of Latin America, experiences the tendency to increasingly move away from the central countries or of becoming de-industrialised? Would this movement also have some adherence to the logic of the process of capital accumulation as described by Marx? Would this logic have explanatory capacity for what has been occurring on the periphery of the system?

Taking as a basis the "World Investment Report" (UNCTAD 2000 and others), a United Nations publication on the global investments of large transnational groups, the data is clear. In the 1990s, the most important investments of large corporations were not made in expanding (productive) capacity, but largely consisted of mergers, acquisitions and the purchasing of existing companies, in a broad process that appears to fit perfectly under the designation "capital centralisation" coined by Marx. So, the central hypothesis is that this process, extensively studied by Marx as an element of the process of accumulation, could be an explanation for the re-ordering of the world economy towards the centre, which ends up by pointing to a possible tendency to the exclusion of the periphery, in a movement of "forced disconnection" (Chesnais, 1986).

The process of capital centralisation, a movement realised with transnational capital as the leading actor, occurs from the centre (as is explicit in the concept centralisation). On reorganising the global productive structure by the restructuring of each individual capital, it may remove part of this productive structure from part of the periphery in so far that the contradictions of the process of capital accumulation itself implanted there makes these peripheries less attractive to transnational capital itself. This would result in the exclusion of at least part of the periphery from the process of global accumulation of capital conducted from the centre or, as in Brazil's case that has significant portion of its industrial base occupied by foreign capital; it makes the "included" periphery (Michalet, 2001) much more subordinated and vulnerable to the process of accumulation at the centre. This point is only reached when the accumulation of capital reaches a global scale and extends its contradictions beyond its frontiers in a hierarchical structure between the centre and periphery, the "included" periphery.

The logic of this movement is in the transposition of the contradictions of capital accumulation that were previously restricted to the local space to the world-space. The basis is in fact that capital, free to accumulate according to its nature, to engender intrinsic contradictions to accumulation ends up by creating a wide contingent of the excluded in each space in which it establishes itself. The internationalisation of capital itself, starting from the centre was due in part to establishing these contradictions in its local space, an element that, on increasing the volume of the excluded, made it difficult to realise value in this restricted space; and, on the other hand, owing to the expansive nature of capital that obligatorily has to provide valorisation for an increasingly larger mass of surplus value, at the risk of placing the process in crisis. These factors impose on capital the search for new spaces to continue its process of valorisation.

Apart from this, the tendency of capital towards centralisation – resulting from its own contradictions as outlined above – catalysed by temporary crises characteristic of its own accumulation, contributes to increase even more the potential for exclusion within each space where capital freely operates. Capital thus leaves its local space to ensure the continuity of the process of accumulation on an increasing scale, its valorisation and existence as capital. But, in so far as it expands the accumulation to other places, it takes with it the mechanisms that generate its contradictions that are established in the most radical way in this new space, at the same time that these same contradictions also extend themselves into the global space. The manifestation of these contradictions at the periphery results in reducing the basis for capital accumulation in this new place and also now on a world scale. It does not leave it any other alternative to ensure the continuity of accumulation apart from the destruction of superfluous individual capital, "by the partial destruction of fixed capital that is found in operation" (Aglietta, 1979:194), by the productive restructuring of large capitals, embodied in a process of global centralisation, a process of reordering the global productive process. In the process of centralisation, capital destroys itself to make the individual capital that survives stronger. Capital centralisation is a mechanism "through which, the movement of general accumulation finds new conditions for its future development" (Aglietta, 1979:196).

The centralisation of world capital is thus a process of withdrawal from capital's cross-frontier expansion, while the processes of accumulation and concentration demarcated the expansion of capital occupying the geographical spaces that interest it. The process of capital globalisation in the 1990s is the materialisation of the centralisation of capital in the global context, with the tendency to "deindustrialise" entire countries and regions, centralising production in specific clusters, excluding not only parts of the centre but also of the periphery. The basis for accumulation, the mass of capital in valorisation, is reduced at the same time in which those that participate in the process are reduced. It marks a process of exclusion on a global scale.

Faced with this scenario, undertaking liberalisation policies on the periphery in order to be integrated in the movement of capital implies being subordinated to the apparently abstract rules of the "market". It means letting oneself be carried by the movement of capital along the road to possible exclusion, or at best, increasing submission. The global centralisation of capital was not a central characteristic when policies of import substitution were implemented, these were present in the Brazilian case in the Target Plan ("Plano de Metas") as well as during the "Economic Miracle", given the period of expansion in which capital found itself in search of new spaces for accumulation. These two phases in the history of capital accumulation in Brazil made the country more industrialised, but at the same time, left it in a more vulnerable situation, given that it allowed the construction of a structure subordinated by growing subsumption to foreign capital, one of the central agents of this industrialisation. But, occupying this world-space by capital embodied in various individual capitals (large transnational corporations), is the process of centralisation, now global, that has taken place. So to implement it, as was done in the 1990s in various industrialised countries of Latin America, with Brazil in the forefront, a policy of engagement in this new phase of accumulation with measures that give more freedom to the movement of capital, in fact contributes to accelerating the process of the de-industrialisation of this periphery, perhaps as far as exclusion; or, as in fact has happened, resulting in increased vulnerability and subordination of this periphery to the centre.

The analysis that is proposed here, about the action of the process of capital accumulation on a world scale and its impact on the periphery, is connected, mainly to what Milton Santos defines as the "space of verticality", in which macro-enterprises and corporate interests play the central role in the rationale of the functioning of these spaces. The aim here is not to analyse what this author defines as "horizontalities", the "banal space", in which all agents are involved in their search for survival in a solid network of local production (Santos, 2000:105–111). So, one does not have the aim here of discussing the possibilities of inclusion, perhaps marginal, of the social groups that belong and survive outside of the established relations in the vertical space and are excluded from this specific space. Making an analogy, one could say that this space in which the verticalities are manifested constitutes the space for the performance of capital, mainly of world capital, occupied specifically by large transnational corporations.

In the same way, it is also not proposed here a specific discussion of the nation state as regards its relationship with the movement of capital. Arrighi brings the discussion about the autonomy of the state in relation to capital and demonstrates, analysing various authors, that there is not much evidence that individual capital (the large corporations) would be dominating the state and vice-versa (Arrighi and Silver, 2011). Here one assumes that the concept of capital cannot be disassociated, as far as being social, from the forms of social organisation manifested in the state. Individual capital does, very often appear as disassociated from the state given that it represents the more specific interests of a social class or a group of individuals that have a strong connection, perhaps a growing one, with the nation state forming a power bloc.

The idea is thus assumed that there exists a relative autonomy between the state and individual capital which allows, sometimes, the state to act in the sense of those social interests of other classes that are not the class of capital's representatives. Although this relative autonomy is recognised, one cannot imagine it equal to the power and the relation that the states of the countries of the centre have with their national capitals with the power and the relation that peripheral states have with the transnational capitals that are established and dominate dynamic sectors of the periphery, the aim of this book. At any event, we start here with the assumption that there exist nation states on the periphery and these have an important role in decisions about the form of inclusion of these countries in global capitalism and in their "alliance" with transnational capital. Different states face this in different ways, according to the degree of power, the forms of inclusion in the movement of capital.

From these considerations, what seems to become clear, in the light of the way some Latin American countries and Brazil were inserted in the process of global capital accumulation, is that the peripheral state and its elites in power historically acted much more as partners of this capital, an action that was embodied in the way the process of import substitution was implemented, broadly concentrated in foreign capitals. Thus the result is the leveraging of the contradictions of the periphery based on its form of insertion in world capitalism, a phenomenon that tends to be aggravated when transnational capital undergoes the process of centralisation in its logic of global accumulation.

Thus, this book is divided into five large blocks. In the first one, based on Marx, is analysed what the logic of the processes of accumulation, concentration and centralisation of capital is, seeking to demonstrate how it functions. One is also aware of the power that capital gains based on the exacerbation of these processes, a power that is embodied in a relative gain of autonomy vis à vis the forms of social control over its movement, a power that will be represented in the transnational corporation and will be dramatic in the periphery.

Following this, in the second block, the movement of capital is related to its process of internationalisation, it is sought to demonstrate the degree of adherence to what was described by Marx as the globalisation of capital. This process is seen as an expansion of the logic of accumulation from the local space to the global space, with different relations of control over it at the centre and in the periphery.

In the third block, the same process is analysed from the point of view of the form of insertion of Latin-American countries in this movement of capital starting from its strategy of implanting capitalism by import substitution with foreign capital. Far from aiming to analyse the different types of periphery, the analysis is focussed on those that, like Brazil, constitute countries that were industrialised in the wake of the process of global accumulation of capital having their industrial structural foundations created by transnational capital, (which differentiates the industrialised peripheral economies based on national capital, and the enclave economies based on natural resources). Hence it is sought to demonstrate how the degree of subordination has grown, almost always by consent, of the peripheral economy in its development strategy, in line with the process of global capital accumulation.

In the fourth block the specific form of Brazil's insertion is analysed in the global accumulation of capital through its process of industrialisation in alliance with foreign capital. It is sought to demonstrate how, throughout history, Brazil through this alliance, has been submitting itself to the movement of global capital, a submission crowned by liberalisation policies of the 1990s that established a scenario of total freedom for transnational corporations at the peak of the process of global centralisation of capital.

Finally, in the fifth block, by way of conclusion, it is sought to demonstrate, based on the way the process of global centralisation arose in the 1990s, what the position of this periphery is in the logic of submission to the movement of the process of global accumulation.

CHAPTER 1

Capital Accumulation, Concentration and Centralisation

1.1 Introduction

Marx describes the dynamic of capital as value in constant valorisation, based on his analysis of the processes of accumulation, concentration and centralisation. These processes describe how capital in its own movement tends to gain autonomy in relation to those who apparently have control over it. For Marx, the more the process of accumulation advances in capitalism, the more concentrated and centralised capital becomes, and the more independent in its own movement it tends to become according to the nature of its valorisation, and the more acute do the contradictions resulting from this movement present themselves.

The freedom of movement of capital in a "free market" is the condition that, on the one hand, ensures the process of accumulation, but on the other, and at the same time, creates contradictions that threaten the continuity of this accumulation. The more autonomous in its process of accumulation capital becomes, an autonomy that is increased as a result of the processes of concentration and centralisation that are embodied in the formation of the large capitalist corporations, the more freedom capital will demand for its movement to continue its accumulation in order to maintain its valorisation and not perish as capital, not stop being it. Continuous valorisation is its condition for existence and, to break barriers that may impede this movement, a tendency of its nature. At the same time, the process itself of free accumulation is responsible for the creation of the contradictions that may undermine its continuity and result in cyclical and structural crises.

The "impersonality" that the movement of capital gains over those that participate in its process of valorisation is in the way it uses these individuals who act through it. On the one side, is the worker that depends, as a condition for his existence as a worker, of being included in the process of accumulation as the workforce, the way he is inserted in the production process. He only manages to ensure his existence as a social being by submitting this way to the process of capital valorisation. On the other side, appears the capitalist, who has control over the valorisation process, but who only exists as such with the primary function of ensuring accumulation on an expanded scale; he only exists as a capitalist in so far as he works for the valorisation of capital, a task which involves appropriating another's labour, that of the worker. But, as capital advances in the processes of concentration and centralisation, capital itself tends to expropriate the capitalist, demonstrating clearly that it is not "the individual capitalist" that is in command of the process, but capital itself, which uses the capitalist or contracts an "executive" tasked with the valorisation. That is why Marx states that "...the behaviour of men in the social process of production is purely atomic. Hence their relations to each other in production assume a material character independent of their control and conscious individual action..." (Marx 1, 1887a:53). In this way, in the context of the logic of capital movement, the only possible freedom appears to be for capital itself, with individuals as isolated beings subordinated to it.

What gives a rationale to this idea of the autonomy of capital, that gives substance to its constantly seeking freedom, is the concept of commodity. In capitalism the commodity becomes the centre of social relations. It takes for itself, it incorporates what might have been relations between people and submits them to its form of capital, a commodity in the process of valorisation, the form most completely assumed by the commodity under capitalism. The commodity takes the place of people by this mechanism and projects itself into the market as the representative of people, as the centre of social relations. People only exist as such as the representatives of commodities. They are what they have. It is from this logic of capitalism described by Marx that the process of commodity production comes to dominate, as much the workers – that only exist as commodity labour force, as commodity producers – as the capitalists, making itself autonomous of both, submitting them under capitalism to the movement of capital, commodities in the process of valorisation.

The centralisation of capital embodied in the large corporation makes this movement of the commodity in detaching itself real, as far as being from that which gave origin to it. The higher the degree of capital centralisation, the more autonomy this gains through the action of the large corporation, submitting all those involved to its continuous process of valorisation. Capitalism has always passed through wide-ranging and important processes of capital centralisation as mergers, acquisitions and joint-ventures that companies undertake in their expansion. Today this process has acquired a worldwide character, as will be described below, in a worldwide movement of capital centralisation as shown in the United Nations report (UNCTAD 2000) commonly approached as part of what is known as "globalisation" (Chesnais, 1996). The aim of this chapter is to demonstrate how Marx described this process of centralisation as a result of the nature of capital accumulation already in his *Capital*, to afterwards show how this same process occurs worldwide (Chapter 2).

1.2 The Commodity as a Process Cell

For Marx, the basic elements that describe capitalism's character is in the set of social relations that define it as a mode of production – how a society organises itself to produce and reproduce its existence. Economic relations often do not appear as a result of specific social relations, but the character of capitalism is determined in the context of social relations, in this case, the social relations of production, that define the processes of production, distribution and accumulation of wealth, at the same time in which they are defined by them. The relations are social although they appear as material, economic relations.

This happens because the real social relations are hidden in their specific material appearance in the form of the commodity. The commodity in capitalism acts as the representative of social relations, a representative of individuals. It hides for this reason the real movement of capital, this movement that defines and is defined by the way society is organised in the production and accumulation of wealth. In so far as the commodity occupies this place, the place of individuals, the possibility is posed of its separation in relation to those that give it form and substance.

"A commodity is therefore a mysterious thing, simply because in it the social character of men's labour appears to them as an objective character stamped upon the product of that labour, because the relation of the producers to the sum total of their own labour is presented to them as a social relation, existing not between themselves, but between the products of their labour. This is the reason why the products of labour become commodities, social things whose qualities are at the same time perceptible and imperceptible by the senses" (Marx I, 1887a:44).

In appearance the economic relations are relations between commodities – that is why so much importance is given to the market – but, in reality, they are relations between people mediated by commodities, people representing commodities. People are what they possess. Therefore, they are social relations, but on taking on the form of commodities they come to have a movement independent of the people who created them. This makes commodities capable of submitting their creators to their movement. "A definite social relation between men, that assumes, in their eyes, the fantastic form of a relation between things." (Marx I, 1887a:45). "This fact simply means that the object that labour produces, its product, stands opposed to it as *something alien*, as a power independent of the producer … and beings to confront him as an autonomous power; that the life which he has bestowed on the object confronts him as hostile and alien." (Marx, Economic and Philosophic Manuscripts of 1844 in Marx-Engels collected works volume 3, p. 272). That is why under capitalism the "market" has become the centre of social relations, a place where commodities, through people, relate to each other.

Abstracting from appearances, therefore, the relation between things is a relation between people. For Marx these relations are, under capitalism, masked as if between things (commodities). This is the result of the fetishistic character of capitalism that transforms things into what they are not. "Money, capital and other economic categories are not things, but (social) relations of production" (Rubin, 1980:72). These social relations are obscured by the form of commodities and by the relations of the market, a place where commodities are hegemonic, where people, as owners of commodities, appear the same as if they were their representatives, exchanging what they possess. Thus, in Marx's statement, "The persons exist for one another merely as representatives of, and, therefore, as owners of, commodities." (Marx I, 1887a:50). That is why the social relation in capitalism does not occur as a relation between people, but through the commodities that take their place; people come to be merely vehicles for commodities.

Faced with this, man cannot be free because he is in this way bound to commodities. In capitalism, they are what give him social existence. Man is that which owns and that is why he has become the hostage of commodities and has a tendency to be controlled by them. "...In the place of *all* physical and mental senses there has therefore come the sheer estrangement of all these senses, the sense of *having*. The human being had to be reduced to this absolute poverty..." (Marx, Marx, Economic and Philosophic Manuscripts of 1844 in Marx-Engels collected works volume 3, p. 300, author's italics). In this sense, social relations condition and are conditioned by relations of property over commodities, the material form of wealth, over money, the representative of wealth, over capital, commodity in the process of valorisation. It is commodities that define the position of each one in society; they define the form of relations between people, the form which it submits them to its movement, as owners of commodities. It is commodities that define people.

"We have seen that the capitalist process of production is a historically determined form of the social process of production in general. The latter is as much a production process of material conditions of human life as a process taking place under specific historical and economic production relations, producing and reproducing these production relations themselves, and thereby also the bearers of this process, their material conditions of existence and their mutual relations, i.e., their particular socio-economic form." (Marx III, 1894:558)

Given the fact social relations are represented by what people own, and this is what determines the place of each in society, the way how each one is included in it. But, at the same time, the placing of commodities as the centre is the result of the social relation as an historic process. That is why the place that the people occupy in society, the way how they are included in it defines in turn what they own. Therefore, social and material relations are mutually defined and define the subject that acts on them, as its subject or as its object, defining them, and at the same time being defined by them.

Through the idea of "commodity fetishism" Marx shows the movement of detachment that the commodity, as a social relation, assumes from those that give origin and existence to it, but do not appear as such. This is due to the fact that the commodity, in its form of existence in capitalism, as value, hides its origin, the human labour that creates wealth, showing itself as wealth itself, given that it incorporates within itself the value created by labour. Thus, in its appearance it loses the characteristic of being labour, a social relation. It stops being human labour to become a commodity and value, obscuring its origin, human labour, the only thing able to create it, of creating therefore, value: "...we bear in mind that the value of commodities has a purely social reality, and that they acquire this reality only in so far as they are expressions or embodiments of one identical social substance, viz., human labour...." (Marx I, 1887a:31) Thus the value is social, the fruit of a social relation, defined on material bases: human labour, as commodity itself, submitted to the process of capitalist production. The commodity serves as a vehicle for these social relations; it constitutes itself in the representative element of the value produced by society, assuming for itself this characteristic it acquires from the other, making possible its separation from those who created it. The value appears as being from the commodity itself and not from the labour that created it.

This separation of the commodity from that which gives origin to it – human labour – is what allows it to be appropriated in the way that it occurs in capitalism. This obscuring of reality in the form of the independent commodity manages to cover up the true social relation. It thus presents people as representatives of commodities, of that which they own, and not as people themselves. This condition ends up by defining how a capitalist society is organised in individual owners of commodities, in which the accumulation of wealth becomes possible by the appropriation of the work of others, a process that is only possible by the separation between labour and commodity. It is that which in capitalism permits that the process of wealth accumulation may occur in such an efficient way in extracting the surplus from labour. It is this relation that an economy that places the commodity as its centre, covers up. It "...conceals, instead of disclosing, the social character of private labour, and the social relations between the individual producers." (Marx I, 1887a:46). Individual action, the act of producing wealth, manifested socially through another entity, as if it were something else, the commodity, losing the relationship with its origin, labour. The commodity possesses value, but this value appears as belonging to itself and not originating in the labour that created it, so, it may be easily appropriable by another. It is worth underlining that this form of appropriation is what guarantees the efficiency of the process of capitalist accumulation.

That is why, through this social status that the commodity acquires, that the place people occupy in society depends on the commodity and not on them as people, it depends on the type of commodity they have to sell. The worker only owns his labour force and this commodity defines his position in society. The capitalist owns the means of production and buys the labour force, depending on it to put them into operation. To belong to society and to be included in it, which means to take part in production, it is necessary to own something (a commodity), that only has social value as something that can be exchanged (has exchange value). Thus to be excluded is to be outside this set of relations, it is not to own anything to exchange. The social place of people is defined not by the people themselves but by what they possess, by things. "In the first place, all appear only as the owners of commodities … As owners of commodities, they are all on an equal footing…" (Sweezy, 1973:67), they appear as free and equal human beings, as the exchangers of commodities.

It is the material relation that is determined and determines the true social relation in capitalism. The form of private appropriation of the means of production, the material relation, defines the economic functioning, the process of production and distribution of wealth, the inclusion and exclusion of each one of the individuals.[1] Private property in capitalism has a primary function: it is based on this social relation that the material basis rests in order that the wealth of some is the result of the work of others, a fact that ensures the process of capitalist accumulation. It is ownership over other's labour that specifies the character of capitalist relations and allows its efficient expansion. Work has a social character, it produces social wealth that in reality takes on the appearance of a commodity separate from labour, thus being able to be appropriated in a private way for the accumulation of capital. The capitalist corporation is the place where this occurs.

---

1 This question about inclusion or exclusion seems a high abstraction in Marx but it is not. "Joan Robinson said once: there exists only one thing that is worse than being exploited by the capitalists: it is not being exploited by the capitalists. Much of this could be said about globalisation, to which may in fact exclude a significant portion of people. The market may exclude them as consumes or buyers if they have no income … it may also exclude them as producers or sellers if they do not have physical or financial assets…" (Nayyar, 2003:75). There is also a difference between exclusion and impoverishment. The second term refers to underemployment, lower remuneration, etc., which is not exactly exclusion.

It is important to make it clear that what characterises capitalism is not its ownership over whichever commodity. It is not the possession of different physical objects that is the essence of capitalism, but ownership over somebody else's labour, which is only possible based on the transformation of labour into a commodity, the work force, thus making it capable of being appropriated by another. "Political economy confuses on principle two very different kinds of private property, of which one rests on the producers' own labour, the other on the employment of the labour of others. It forgets that the latter not only is the direct antithesis of the former, but absolutely grows on its tomb only" (Marx 1, 1887a:385). The form of capitalist appropriation is thus the negation of individual property over his own labour, over the results of his labour, of labour that generates wealth for himself. This form of property is developed by the negation of individual labour, by the separation between the individual and labour. Thus wealth in capitalism is not the fruit of the individual labour of thousands of disperse producers that employ their own labour (as Adam Smith and liberal thought would wish), but the appropriation of someone else's labour with the aim of ensuring accumulation. This is only possible in capitalism, in which the means of production and the surplus are appropriated in a private form. It is the monopoly over these means of production that permits the private appropriation of surplus value produced by someone else's labour, turning it into capital (Marx 1, 1887a:387). It is this form of appropriation that ensures control over this excess value and the accumulation of capital in an "efficient" way; that gives capital the possibility of its appropriating this surplus for itself through its representative (the capitalist) in order to maintain itself in constant valorisation.

The question of seeing private property this way is important because it denies ownership as something linked to isolated individuals, to affirm it as a form of capital control over individuals and their labours. Capital becomes the owner of individual workers. In this framework the capitalist personified is only someone useful for this process. Only thus is it possible to understand what a large capitalist enterprise is, as the personification of capital, as individual capital, but not linked to an apparently autonomous individual himself, but "with all the attributes of capital in general" (Aglietta, 1979:189). Only in this way is it possible to understand its distancing in relation to those through which it acts as a form of ensuring the process of its constant and autonomous valorisation.

Capital is thus a commodity in the process of valorisation, a process that creates value through the labour of others, by using labour force as commodity itself, privately appropriated. Value in the process of valorisation is the most abstract and most complete form that capital assumes. Invisible, value is manifest most generally in its apparent forms as a commodity, taking on the forms of money capital, productive capital and commodity capital, which, if they are decontextualised from the social process of production, from the process of valorisation, they seem not to be forms of capital. On the other hand, they only take on these forms in capitalism (analogously to the worker and capitalist). "Capital is not a thing, but rather a definite social production relation, belonging to a definite historical formation of society, which is manifested in a thing and lends this thing a specific social character." (Marx III, 1894:555). Reframing the question from the point of view of the fetish of the commodity on new bases, at the end of Volume I, Marx states that "...capital is not a thing, but a social relation between persons, established by the instrumentality of things" (Marx I, 1887a:385).

Thus, capital as value is movement. Its concept presupposes the process of valorisation. It is in this process that it takes on the form of productive capital, money and commodity. Capital in so far as value "...can be understood only as a motion, not as a thing at rest. Those who regard the gaining by value of independent existence as a mere abstraction forget that the movement of industrial capital is this abstraction in *actu*.... Value here passes through various forms, various movements in which it maintains itself and at the same time expands, augments." (Marx II, 1887b:61). Capital is the materialisation of this movement and stops being a mere abstraction when it is concretely personified in individual capitals, large capitalist corporations, engaged in the process of valorisation of capital in general. This is not a process that happens in the abstract, but has as its real mechanism various processes of valorisation realised by individual capitals in flows M-C-M' (money-commodity-money with added value) uninterrupted "...capital is found, by its nature, divided into capitals that constitute centres of individual autonomous decisions from the point of view of its valorisation ... the autonomous capitals possess all the attributes of capital in general" (Aglietta, 1979:189). The autonomous individual capitals, the large corporations, are specific agents of this valorisation.

In the same way that commodities become independent from those that create them and assume the social space of people, capital as a commodity that is value in the process of valorisation, also takes on an autonomous independent form, "...capital, into value big with value, a live monster that is fruitful and multiplies." (Marx I, 1887a:102) Its existence depends on its guaranteed continuous valorisation by the impersonality of the large corporations. Thus, capital, as if other, also makes itself autonomous in relation to the capitalist as well as the worker, despite being the fruit of a specific social relation of production in that these, those that give it existence, are inserted as people apparently independent and free, but submitted to a social historical relationship

CAPITAL ACCUMULATION, CONCENTRATION AND CENTRALISATION

established between them, with the overriding function of ensuring the existence of capital, the valorisation. Capital acquires its own movement that, in its constant expansion, seeks to submit places and people to its movement of valorisation. It becomes independent of the people who act for it, but, contradictorily, it cannot do without them, given that they are what ensure the process.

Hence, it emphasises how for Marx capitalism is characterised by a form of societal organisation in which the process of commodity production, the process of capital accumulation, has come to dominate man, instead of the opposite, of being controlled by him: "To them, their own social action takes the form of the action of objects, which rule the producers instead of being ruled by them" (Marx I, 1887a:46). In this sense, the worker and the capitalist, as individuals, appear as subject to the same process although not in the same way. Both end up working for capital. The capitalist owns and controls the means of production whilst the worker creates the value that puts the capital in movement, in the process of accumulation. "…That's why, the owners of commodities therefore find out, that the same division of labour that turns them into independent private producers, also frees the social process of production and the relations of the individual producers to each other within that process and from all dependence on the will of those producers, that the seeming mutual independence of the individuals is supplemented by a system of general and mutual dependence." (Marx I, 1887a:60).

Thus, capital as the social relationship that it is, comes to be, in a certain way, the controller of people. This aspect becomes clearer when, not only the worker, but the capitalist, appears as an employee of capital, capital appears in control of social relations and not as a simple commodity, but as a commodity inserted in the process of production, thus going beyond the idea of a commodity. "Capital is, therefore, not a personal, it is a social power" (Marx, Manifesto of the Communist Party p. 499 – in Marx-Engels collective works volume 6) that seeks to submit individuals to it, to its own movement.

The worker, the one that only owns himself as a commodity, is clearly an employee of capital given that his existence depends on managing to sell himself as a commodity with the function of putting into movement the means of production and to create value. "Within the process of production, as we have seen, capital acquired the command over labour, i.e., over functioning labour-power or the labourer himself." (Marx I, 1887a:155). On the other side is the capitalist, "capital personified," who has the role of acting as an intermediary of capital in the acquisition of the workforce apart from "taking care so the worker undertakes his task," ensuring the accumulation of capital, ensuring the process of valorisation in an efficient way. The capitalist has no other function than to guarantee his existence as such. That is why Marx compares capital to an orchestra conductor that prompts and decides the aim of capitalist production to the greatest possible expansion of its own capital, submitting the individuals engaged in it, be they capitalist or worker. "Their union into one single productive body and the establishment of a connection between their individual functions, are matters foreign and external to them, are not their own act, but the act of the capital that brings and keeps them together." (Marx I, 1887a:166). Therefore, it is the logic of capital that imposes on the people involved constant growth and the expansion of accumulation that tends to involve different places, different spaces.

Given capital is a social relationship that takes shape independently from those that act for it, the action of the individual capitalist is in large part determined by capital. The capitalist embodies capital as if he were capital itself. In the end, only in this way does he have an existence guaranteed as capitalist (or "executive," contracted by capital). He defines himself and is defined by this form of relationship with capital. This is his form of existence as far as being a social being, his form of social inclusion. But the movement of capital is superior to him, it is outside of him and that is why it may make itself independent of the individual, sometimes, it may even eliminate him from the process. "… As capitalist, he is only capital personified. His soul is the soul of capital. But capital has one single life impulse, the tendency to create value and surplus value, to make its constant factor, the means of production, absorb the greatest possible amount of surplus labour." (Marx I, 1887a:120).

The capitalist thus becomes a mere representative of capital "…the capitalist is merely capital personified and functions in the process of production solely as the agent of capital" (Marx III, 1894:558). If he wishes to exist as such, he must work through and for capital. If he does not act satisfactorily, he loses his position, he is excluded from the process by the logic of capital accumulation itself. He is thus obliged to maintain the capital that he has under his command in continuous valorisation and expansion, on pain of losing it, "The constant augmentation of his capital becomes a condition of its preservation." (Marx II, 1887b:45). The capitalist, as a representative of capital although independent of it, may be swallowed up by the movement of capital in its process of valorisation. That is the contradiction: capital eliminating those that fight for it, even those that have the role of preserving and expanding it. The process of centralisation manifests this independence that capital in general has, in relation to the capitalist-person and to individual fragmented capitals, despite it being these capitals that give it social existence.

Mészáros in "Beyond Capital" describes this process in which capital becomes the orchestra conductor as the "socio-metabolical reproduction of capital". He defines it as "a totalising framework of control into which everything else, including human beings, must be fitted and prove thereby their 'productive viability,' or perish if they fail to do.... This applies not only to the workers, in whose case the loss of control – whether in paid employment or out of it – is quite obvious, ... but even the richest capitalists. For no matter how many controlling shares the latter might be able to boast in the company ... their power of control within the framework of the capital system as a whole is quite negligible" (Mészáros, 1995:41–42).

In this context, Marx concludes that nobody is free from the movement of capital, from its intrinsic need to valorisation. "It is an enchanted, perverted, topsy-turvy world, in which Monsieur le Capital ... do [Its] ghost-walking as social characters and at the same time directly as mere things." (Marx III, 1894:564) Thus, the commodity appears, a thing, as mistress of the process, in its most complex form: capital.

This idea of the autonomy of capital, as a social entity, independent of its representative, the capitalist, is the fundamental outcome of the fetishism of the commodity. Capital is in its abstract form (value in valorisation) the entity of a whole social relationship, its essence. That is what explains the intrinsic movement of continuous expansion that the capital has and stamps itself on the people involved in it. Despite being a social relationship, created historically by real people, it tends to become autonomous in relation to its own creators "Men make their own history, but they do not make it as they please" (Marx 1977b: 203).

That is why capital clamours for freedom of movement and for a "free market." That is the place desired by capital, where it is allowed the full realisation of its autonomy. Capital needs freedom in order to submit everything and everyone, which is only possible in a place in which it may move itself freely, based on its "impersonal laws." The free market is, therefore, the subjection of society itself to the movement of capital that, of course, in this context, also manifests its contradictions in its most radical form to the point of constructing its own destruction, as Keynes well understood in his "The End of Laissezfaire" (Keynes, 1978).

The importance of these questions is in the relative autonomy that capital tends to conquer. Autonomy in relation to the workers as much as in relation to the individual capitalist. Capital as a social relation assumes and defines the roles of each one in the process, in its movement, despite the latent contradiction in inverting the roles between subject (man) that becomes an object and the object (capital) that becomes the subject. It manages this by the apparent separation of the individuals from everything they are involved in, presenting them as free individuals, but in reality, submitted in everything.

To understand the autonomy of capital in its process of accumulation it is vital to understand the processes of concentration and centralisation as autonomous movements of the capital that, in its process of valorisation, continuously destroys individual capitals, mainly in its cyclical crises. As Giannotti observed well, "it little matters the disappearance of an individual capitalist, given that his functions will be fulfilled right away by another; what is of interest is the way each singular movement of valorisation is integrated in the movement of social capital as a whole" (Giannotti, 1983:256).

"The movements of capital appear as the action of some individual industrial capitalist who performs the functions of a buyer of commodities and labour, a seller of commodities, and an owner of productive capital, who therefore promotes the circuit by this activity. If social capital experiences a revolution in value, it may happen that the capital of the individual capitalist succumbs to it and fails, because it cannot adapt itself to the conditions of this movement of values. The more acute and frequent such revolutions in value become, the more does the automatic movement of the now independent value operate with the elemental force of a natural process, against the foresight and calculation of the individual capitalist, the more does the course of normal production become subservient to abnormal speculation, and the greater is the danger that threatens the existence of the individual capitals. These periodical revolutions in value therefore corroborate what they are supposed to refute, namely, that value as capital acquires independent existence, which it maintains and accentuates through its movement." (Marx II, 1887b:25).

Thus, as the processes of accumulation, concentration and centralisation are the forms how capital moves itself, the "revolutions in value"[2] which leave the weakest capital obsolete and generate crises, are a characteristic of this movement. The process of internationalisation, which as will be seen, is related to the expansion of capital over places, as well as the globalisation related to the world centralisation of capital, both are the results of this movement of capital, consequences of the autonomy of capital in its process of valorisation realised by the hands of individual fragmented capitals (large corporations), each one "making the cycle possible" (Marx, as quoted above), or rather, carrying within itself the "…circular flow, whose form is a circular process of transformations in the forms of value…" (Aglietta, 1979:193), the capitalist production on a progressive increasing scale. Internationalisation and globalisation are manifestations of a movement that seeks to submit to capital not only people but also the spaces that compose what is called the "market," the space

---

2 The concept of "revolution of value" will be explained where productivity and capital concentration is dealt with.

in which capital moves according to its characteristics in its process of reproduction on an extended scale.

1.3 The Process of Capital Accumulation

In a society ruled by commodities such as the capitalist one, the exchanges appear as the central element in social and economic relations given that people relate to each other by what they have: they are what they possess. The market, the place where these commodities, as commodity capital, realise their value in the form of money capital, assumes the appearance of the place where this value occurs. This appearance, taken by some as the essence of economic relations, makes the market a central place for them.

In Marx's view, the market as a place, is only where commodities realise the value incorporated in them that originated in the process of production on changing its form of capital from commodity capital into money capital. The "market" is important for the social realisation of value derived from the labour incorporated in the commodity, but not for the creation of this value. This surplus arises from a relation of exchange, but it is not from this exchange that is apparent in the market, the exchange of commodity – use-value by commodity.

In capitalism, in so far that relations of exchange are relations between commodities and everything is transformed into commodities, the real relationship of exchange becomes obscured, the relationship responsible for the creation of the surplus value that permits the accumulation of capital. The relevant exchange in capitalism is not the exchange of commodities, products of human labour; the central exchange, that remains opaque in this world ruled by commodities, is the exchange that the capitalist conducts with the worker on buying his labour-power as commodity; it is in the market that the latter sells the only commodity he has, his labour-power. This exchange is what makes capitalism a specific mode of production and is always masked in the apparent exchanges of commodities produced by labour. This obscuring of what is essential to the process of creating wealth is only possible because everything takes the form of commodity.

The first, the simple exchange of commodities, Marx calls C-M-C (commodity-money-commodity), commodity is exchanged for commodity. This is the exchange that is in the appearance of the capitalist relation, but it is not the essential exchange of the system. This is the mercantile exchange that does not create value given that commodities already possessed it beforehand. It is an exchange in which the commodities exchanged have the same value and that is why nothing is added. In it, money appears simply as a facilitator, therefore, it is without any real importance.

"The simple circulation of commodities – selling in order to buy – is a means of carrying out a purpose unconnected with circulation, namely, the appropriation of use-values, the satisfaction of wants. The circulation of money as capital is, on the contrary, an end in itself, for the expansion of value takes place only within this constantly renewed movement. The circulation of capital has therefore no limits." (Marx I, 1887a:79)

The relevant exchange is the buying of labour as commodity by the capitalist with money transformed by this act into capital, placing this specific commodity in the process of production, with the overriding aim of creating a greater value than that which began this exchange. The money that he gave him at the beginning added to the surplus value created in this process. The capitalist, on acquiring labour-power in the "market" by its exchange value as a commodity, manages to extract and appropriate from the resulting surplus from the capacity of this work force to produce value beyond that he paid him as a commodity. This occurs because the labour-power is a specific commodity that on being used has the capacity to generate more value than that which it needs for its social existence, its value of exchange. This is the relevant exchange that characterises capitalism, M-C-M', money that buys commodities means of production (living labour and dead labour – machines and raw materials), that acquire value by the new labour incorporated in them, transforming them in new commodities that reassume the form of money on realising themselves in the market, on being sold.

"In order to be able to extract value from the consumption of a commodity, our friend, Moneybags, must be so lucky as to find, within the sphere of circulation, in the market, a commodity, whose use-value possesses the peculiar property of being a source of value, whose actual consumption, therefore, is itself an embodiment of labour, and, consequently, a creation of value. The possessor of money does find on the market such a special commodity in capacity for labour or labour-power." (Marx I, 1887a:88)

This is the real capitalist exchange, realised through the mediation of various individual fragmented capitals, permitting the process of capital accumulation in general. The capital through which its representative holder of money acquires the labour commodity and other means of production (he makes an investment) with the intention of gaining a greater amount of money. It is in this exchange that surplus value is produced. It is this that transforms money and commodity into capital, value anticipated that gains value in the process of production that adds surplus value. "The value originally advanced, therefore, not only remains intact while in circulation, but adds to itself a surplus value or expands itself. It is this movement that converts it into capital." (Marx I, 1887a:79).

It is this constant process of valorisation of capital realised through the process of production, through labour and the form of extraction and appropriation of the surplus by the separation of labour that creates value from the commodity, which permits its functioning incrementally: the valorisation of capital and the accumulation of capital; its continuous process of expansion by the reinvestment of the surplus value generated in new capital. It thus takes on the characteristic of an automatic process that passes through a variety of forms. The valorisation of capital by this process is what guarantees the continuity and existence of it and of those that act through it. In so far as it creates new value and this value is appropriated by capital, a greater value must be put into action so as to ensure the continuity of the process, in a circular, incremental flow that characterises the reproduction on an extended scale, the accumulation of capital.

"It is constantly changing from one form to the other without thereby becoming lost, and thus assumes an automatically active character. If now we take in turn each of the two different forms which self-expanding value successively assumes in the course of its life, we then arrive at these two propositions: Capital is money: Capital is commodities. In truth, however, value is here the active factor in a process, in which, while constantly assuming the form in turn of money and commodities, it at the same time changes in magnitude, differentiates itself by throwing off surplus value from itself; the original value, in other words, expands spontaneously. For the movement, in the course of which it adds surplus value, is its own movement, its expansion, therefore, is automatic expansion. Because it is value, it has acquired the occult quality of being able to add value to itself." (Marx I, 1887a:80)

Thus, the capitalist process of production has for an intrinsic characteristic the generation of a surplus in the form of value as the result of labour. But labour always, by its nature, generated a surplus. What makes capitalism different from other modes of production is its form of appropriation of this surplus which is integrated inside the process of production that separates labour and commodity (what the worker produces is not his), this surplus is what remains obscured by the form of value and it only appears in the commodity in a new form, money, when the realisation of its value occurs in the market, giving the impression that it arose from the commodity itself.

This mechanism is what permits the process of specifically capitalist reproduction on an extended scale, expanded accumulation. It is through it that the holder of capital may appropriate for himself the surplus and reinvest it in a continuous and incremental form. It defines the laws of capital movement, acting as a continuous engine that ends up by becoming relatively autonomous as value, taking the form of exchange value, apparently a substratum of the commodity and of the labour that creates it. This mechanism defines the position of the worker and the capitalist, and it is this relation manifest in a specific form of extraction and appropriation of the surplus to create more surplus is what transforms capitalism into an efficient machine for accumulation that cannot stop, and, when it stops, it enters into crisis.

The continuous reinvestment of the surplus extracted from labour, in the process of production, as money that is constantly reconverted into constant (dead labour) and live (live labour) commodity capital, the reinvestment of the surplus value, is what allows the process of capital accumulation. In the words of Marx "Employing surplus value as capital, reconverting it into capital, is called accumulation of capital." (Marx I, 1887a:288)

It is through this mechanism that the principle of private property, as ownership over the means of production, becomes central. It is through this form of property that it is possible the appropriation by capital of the value created by others' labour in an "efficient" form, ensuring the efficiency of capital accumulation which means the extraction of a greater surplus per unit of labour (greater productivity – a non-Marxist concept). And, it is because of this form of appropriation of this surplus that makes possible the process of expanded capital accumulation, supplying content and form for this process. That is why one may say that capitalism is, in fact, extremely efficient in the creation of wealth, but that is not appropriated by people (individuals) themselves.

Therefore, accumulation is the reproduction of capital on an expanded scale by the continuous reinvestment of the surplus generated in each cycle of capital turnover in new means of production. "From a concrete point of view, accumulation resolves itself into the reproduction of capital on a progressively increasing scale. The circle in which simple reproduction moves, alters its form, and, to use Sismondi's expression, changes into a spiral." (Marx I, 1887a:289). Money capital that is converted into productive capital resulting in capital commodity that, on being sold, it reconverts itself into capital money greater than that which started it, being the surplus reinvested as capital, in a continuous flow.

The process of accumulation is an intrinsic necessity of capital that is imposed on the capitalist, its representative. The impetus of value appreciating itself in a growing and continuous form is imposed by the nature of the process itself. The capitalist is as if obliged to replace the surplus extracted from labour in the form of surplus value in the expansion of his business. According to Marx the capitalist "…is but one of the wheels of this social mechanism. Moreover, the development of capitalist production makes it constantly necessary to keep increasing the amount of the capital laid out in a given industrial undertaking, and competition makes the immanent laws of capitalist production to be felt by each individual capitalist, as external coercive laws. It compels him to keep constantly extending his capital, in order to preserve it, but extend it he cannot, except by means of progressive accumulation." (Marx I, 1887a:295). Ownership over the means of production and over the surplus value is what ensures the capitalist the possibility of executing this role. And the more capital remains under his control, the greater will be the capacity for accumulation and the greater will be the need for accumulation to maintain the flow.

This question is central here. The movement described above is what impels capitalism in its continuous expansion. It originates in the natural need capital has of expanding itself to guarantee its existence, also always seeking new spaces and places to ensure its expansion to guarantee reinvestment of the surplus generated in a new cycle of accumulation, to maintain itself in valorisation. The process of capital accumulation thus leads to its expansion and the occupation of the periphery as we will see.

The capitalist as an individual representative of capital is therefore compelled to accumulation at the same time in that this process involves his wish to obtain and increase the value of his individual wealth. But, there is a contradiction. The real interest of the capitalist as an individual is the money that results at the end of the process of valorisation (M-C-M') On the other hand, for capital, the real aim is its continual valorisation. In so far that the main aim of the capitalist is obtaining more money, if it were possible to manage it without going through the hardships of the process of production, he would do it[3] (Marx II, 1887b:32) The contradiction is that, at the same time in that he desires as an individual, hoarder or consumer, to withdraw the surplus value generated from the process of valorisation, he sees himself obliged to place it and replace it in operation to ensure his existence as a capitalist by the preservation of his capital. "But along with this growth, there is at the same time developed in his breast, a Faustian conflict between the passion for accumulation, and the desire for enjoyment." (Marx I, 1887a:295) That is why, it seems clear, that one cannot say that the process of capital accumulation is the fruit of the desire of the capitalist, of an individual, despite his being the agent of the process by the place he occupies within it.

It is important to remember that the process of accumulation is an intrinsic need of capital in its mechanism of expanded valorisation and it uses individuals for this. The increase in the productive forces themselves leads to this

---

[3] This would thus result in what today is called "a speculative bubble" that results in financial crises.

continuous need for expanded accumulation. Thus, in Marx's words "It must never be forgotten that the production of this surplus value – and the reconversion of a portion of it into capital, or the accumulation, forms an integral part of this production of surplus value – is the immediate purpose and compelling motive of capitalist production. It will never do, therefore, to represent capitalist production as something which it is not, namely as production whose immediate purpose is enjoyment or the manufacture of the means of enjoyment for the capitalist. This would be overlooking its specific character, which is revealed in all its inner essence." (Marx III, 1894:168) Surplus value is increased. Any increase in this is capital's natural aim. At the same time, it is embodied as an objective attitude by its representative, the capitalist, who if he were not to do it would simply be excluded (or dismissed in the case of an executive).

Thus, the process of capital accumulation has, as a given, a specific form of extraction and continuous appropriation of the surplus, ensuring its existence as capital. In this way, in providing the process the basis for its movement (the appropriation by the capitalist of the surplus), it imposes on this movement a continuous rhythm of growing capital valorisation, dictating that the excess is always transformed in capital to increase its value. This is the result of making capital autonomous as value that is obliged to keep itself increasing in value by the constant extraction of surplus value.

It is, at the same time, this drive of capital towards valorisation, the only way of perpetuating itself as capital, that leads it to internationalisation as we shall see in Chapter 2. The growing need to transform masses of money created in the process of valorisation into new capital, in a permanent way – in conjunction with the need for control over markets in order to ensure realisation of value (this will be seen further below) – is what obliges the productive internationalisation of capital, the export of capitals in the form of direct investment, removing industry from its national base, destroying old national industries in the new places that "...are dislodged by new industries". (Marx, Manifesto of the Communist Party p. 488 – in Marx-Engels collective works volume 6)

Competition, on pressuring an individual capital against another, also transforms itself in the form of pressure to the continuous expansion of capital. It also leads them to seek new markets, new techniques that "revolutionise value," elements that act in addition to, and leverage the natural need of capital to expand itself as pointed out earlier. It acts as a catalysing element for accumulation, thus with an expansive effect, of occupying new spaces, constantly impelling individual capital to intensify its productive force as a "...law which again and again throws bourgeois production out of its old course and which compels capital to intensify the productive forces of labour, *because* it has intensified them – the law which gives capital no rest and continually whispers in its ear: 'Go on! Go on!' ... If now we picture to ourselves this feverish *simultaneous* agitation on the *whole world market,* it will be comprehensible how the growth, accumulation and concentration of capital results in an uninterrupted division of labour, and in the application of new and the perfecting of old machinery precipitately and on an ever more gigantic scale." (Marx Wage Labor and Capital in Marx-Engels Collected works volume 9, pp. 224–225)

At any event, it is important to remember that for Marx the process of accumulation is an intrinsic need for capital in its described mechanism of expanded valorisation that goes beyond competition. The need for continuous valorisation as much as competition are forces that lead capital to its expansion and occupation of new geographic spaces in the world, manifesting itself in internationalisation, which makes it impose its rationality throughout the world. It stands out from the outset that these elements go far beyond the problem of the realisation of value that will be broached below, the focus of the expansive logic of Rosa Luxemburg. It is now stressed that realisation is just a part of the process of capital accumulation.

Additionally, given that it is as much the intrinsic need of capital to accumulate as competition are elements that impose on individual capitals their continuous expansion, the fight that results from this for new spaces of accumulation leads it to another process that will be defined later on, the process of centralisation, in which the strongest individual capitals destroy and occupy the place of the weakest capitals. "Centralisation is a qualitative change that remodels the autonomy of individual capitals and creates new relations of competition..." (Aglietta, 1979:194).

1.4 Productivity and the Concentration of Capital

What impels the movement of capital and defines its essence is its intrinsic need to increase the surplus that it extracts in the process of production for the process of its own accumulation in a continuous and growing movement. This mechanism ends up by constantly increasing the value that each individual capital has in its hands and must obligatorily replace in the process, a condition for its existence. This movement is the stronger the more surplus is extracted from labour. "The directing motive, the end and aim of capitalist production, is to extract the greatest possible amount of surplus value and consequently to exploit labour-power to the greatest possible extent..." (Marx I, 1887a:166)

This search moves each individual capital in the direction of its technological modernisation and expansion of productive scale to increase its capacity for extracting the surplus. The aim of capital is to cheapen the product so as to manage to sell it, even if temporarily, above its market value,[4] by the price defined socially. Gains in scale and technological improvement are the mechanisms used in the process Marx called "revolution in value". They are the result of the need for capital accumulation, driven by competition. It is these actions that result in the concentration of capital, which permits a single individual capital to continuously expand its base of extraction of surplus value in its growing process. The corporation must grow without cease, moved by accumulation itself. As will be seen below, this process differs from the centralisation of capital that consists in the growth of an individual capital over the ruin of another.

"Concentration ... is an immediate effect caused by the unequal development of the fractioning of capitals, whose cause ... is in the increase of labour productivity. Each individual capital is a centre of concentration because it brings together a growing level of the means for its valorisation ... that finds itself subject to the law of capital accumulation" and that, in turn, constantly increases the value it must replace in valorisation, "the complete cycle of valorisation.... Thus, the concentration ... is a phenomenon that derives from accumulation..." and that occurs in the sphere of each individual capital (Aglietta, 1979:194–195).

The concentration of capital is, then, a need imposed by capital itself that implies a continuous transformation of the process of production in search of new forms for increasing surplus value. For the capitalist as an individual, this increase has as its aim the increase of his wealth; for capital it is just feed to make itself larger and stronger, expanding the value to be replaced in the process of accumulation, refuelling the process. "...As capitalist, he is only capital personified. His soul is the soul of capital. But capital has one single life impulse, the tendency to create value and surplus value, to make its constant factor, the means of production, absorb the greatest possible amount of surplus labour. Capital is dead labour, that, vampire-like, only lives by sucking living labour, and lives the more, the more labour it sucks." (Marx I, 1887a:120)

The increase of the extraction of excess labour itself, the surplus value, on making available a greater value that must return to the process to allow expanded accumulation, it obliges each individual capital to increase its

---

4 Market value is determined as the amount of average (or majority) social labour employed in a segment given the average organic composition of capital in the segment (Marx III, 1894:121).

productive capacity. This it does through new forms of the organisation of production that provide it with gains in scale and cheapens its products. Accumulation on an extended scale itself continually obliges each individual capital to expand its business, always seeking new ways to increase the capacity of extraction of the surplus from labour, gaining efficiency and resulting in a concentration of capital.

As already pointed out, competition is the catalysing element of this process. "The law of the determination of value by labour-time, a law which brings under its sway the individual capitalist who applies the new method of production, by compelling him to sell his goods under their social value, this same law, acting as a coercive law of competition, forces his competitors to adopt the new method." (Marx I, 1887a:160). It functions as a form of pressure on the capitalist, faced with the movement of other individual capitals, to increase productivity and cheapen his products below their social value. This may give him an increase of his market share in a movement of expansion,[5] or even the removal of his competitors, in a movement occupying the space of someone else (in this second case one is speaking about concentration with centralisation, which will be broached further on).

These pressures – accumulation itself and competition – oblige capital to always be focussed on an incessant search to increase the surplus that it extracts from labour. Labour is the source of all the surplus generated in the economy; it is the only commodity that simultaneously replaces its value as a commodity, make possible to preserve of the values of the materials employed in the process of production, and generate surplus (Marx I, 1887a:104). The increase in labour productivity, by lowering market value of wage commodities, is what permits the extraction of a greater surplus value for accumulation that, in turn, provides the concentration. "Given the general basis of the capitalistic system, then, in the course of accumulation, a point is reached at which the development of the productivity of social labour becomes the most powerful lever of accumulation" (Marx I, 1887a:308) With the growth in the capacity for accumulation, there is an ascending flow of concentration and accumulation, "Every accumulation becomes the means of new accumulation. With the increasing mass of wealth which functions as capital, accumulation increases the concentration of wealth in the hands of individual capitalists, and thereby

---

5 It is an expansion in the micro-economic sense. If other companies go out of business, one could say that the micro-economic expansions of individual capital arose on the retraction of the space in the macro-economic sense by the partial destruction of capital that was in operation (the closure of productive units).

widens the basis of production on a large scale and of the specific methods of capitalist production" (Marx I, 1887a:310).

This increase in the excess extracted from labour – the central element of concentration that is appropriated by the capitalist – can only occur through the increase in working time, of absolute surplus value, or through the growth in the capacity of the labour generating surplus by lowering the value of labour-power via increasing productivity, the relative surplus value. "The automaton, as capital, and because it is capital, is endowed, in the person of the capitalist, with intelligence and will; it is therefore animated by the longing to reduce to a minimum the resistance offered by that repellent yet elastic natural barrier, man." (Marx I, 1887a:198). As the first form of increasing the surplus is physically limited by human capacity, capital, personalised in the capitalist has historically expanded the relative surplus value.

The increase in absolute surplus value has, apart from legal barriers by the definition of a maximum working day, a natural limit, physically supportable, given the time needed for the reproduction of the labour force, recovery of energy etc. (Marx I, 1887a:153). The limit for the expansion of absolute surplus value is given by the law of value itself.

The expansion of relative surplus value, on the other hand, does not have such defined limits. Through seeking gains in productivity, each individual capital seeks to expand it anyway. This fact pressures them towards technical improvement, with new machines, technology and new forms of the organisation of production that give them gains in scale or a reduction in the turnover time of capital, altering the organic and technical composition of capital.

The rise in productivity increases the extraction of surplus labour by the reduction of the necessary working-time for the reproduction of the labour-power (what the worker gains) increasing what the worker produces of surplus value. For Marx, this occurs, on the one hand, by cheapening the products that make up the cost of reproduction of the labour force, reducing the cost of labour, the socially necessary work for the reproduction of the labour force, as proposed by David Ricardo (1985).[6] This is one of the factors that allows capital to extract a greater surplus in various branches to "shorten that part of the working day, during which the workman must labour for his own benefit, and by that very shortening, to lengthen the other part of the day, during which he is at liberty to work gratis for the capitalist." (Marx I, 1887a:161).

---

6   Ricardo proposes that cheapening farm products is the solution to increasing the profits given that it lowers the cost of labour.

On the other hand, the introduction of new methods of production and new machines in a certain sector raises labour productivity and increases its intensity. "Generally speaking, the mode of producing relative surplus value consists in raising the productive power of the workman, so as to enable him to produce more in a given time with the same expenditure of labour." (Marx I, 1887a:201). The form of organisation of labour within the process of production is one of the legs of this movement. In his chapter on cooperation, Marx evaluates the increase in productivity that arises from it, stating that "As co-operators, as members of a working organism, they are but special modes of existence of capital. Hence, the productive power developed by the labourer when working in co-operation, is the productive power of capital ... it appears as a power with which capital is endowed by Nature a productive power that is immanent in capital." (Marx I, 1887a:167) In this sense, the form of organisation of labour provides gains in scale for capital, contributing to the expansion of capacity of capital valorisation (Marx I, 1887a:163). "The combined working day produces, relatively to an equal sum of isolated working days, a greater quantity of use-values, and, consequently, diminishes the labour-time necessary for the production of a given useful effect. Whether the combined working day, in a given case, acquires this increased productive power." (Marx I, 1887a:165)

The constant introduction of more modern machinery also acts on the intensity of labour, raising productivity. "Like every other increase in the productiveness of labour, machinery is intended to cheapen commodities, and, by shortening that portion of the working day, in which the labourer works for himself, to lengthen the other portion that he gives, without an equivalent, to the capitalist. In short, it is a means for producing surplus value." (Marx I, 1887a:184). The machine is not the source of surplus value but it increases the power of generating the surplus for the one that manages it. In the same way that the worker in cooperation (division of labour – assembly line), raises productivity, several machines driven by only one engine also act in this way. Apart from this, the revolution in a certain branch of industry provided with the introduction of a more modern machine radiates throughout the whole economy, increasing productivity (Marx I, 1887a:189–190) The introduction of new machines imposes on the economy, on individual capitals, a new intensity of labour, raising productivity.

"Machinery produces relative surplus value; not only by directly depreciating the value of labour-power, and by indirectly cheapening the same through cheapening the commodities that enter into its reproduction, but also, when it is first introduced sporadically into an industry, by converting the labour employed by the owner of that machinery, into labour of a higher degree and greater efficacy, by raising the social value of the article produced above its individual value, and thus enabling the capitalist to replace the value of a day's labour-power by a smaller portion of the value of a day's product. During this transition period, when the use of machinery is a sort of monopoly, the profits are therefore exceptional, and the capitalist endeavours to exploit thoroughly 'the sunny time of this his first love,' by prolonging the working day as much as possible." (Marx I, 1887a:199)

If on the one hand these mechanisms raise the extraction of the surplus from labour, the microeconomic efficiency for each individual capital, on the other hand it creates an enormous macroeconomic contradiction. The constant growth of productivity implies the substitution of living labour by dead labour, of workers by machines. This is "a tendency of capital, …to reduce as much as possible the number of labourers employed by it, or its variable constituent transformed into labour-power, in contradiction to its other tendency to produce the greatest possible mass of surplus value" (Marx I, 1887a:153). Capital, in its hunger for valorisation by raising productivity, eliminates its basis for the creation of the surplus value: labour. Thus the process generates by its own nature an enormous "industrial reserve army," when not, "relative surplus-population" (Marx I, 1887: Chapter 25, Sections 3 and 4; Marx III, 1894: Chapter 15, Section 3), in a process of exclusion of the labourer from the process.

The exclusion of labour, the term being employed here as described in Item 2 of this chapter, is one of the main contradictions of the process of accumulation and concentration of capital. It is emphasised here just to show that the process of accumulation itself, the creation of mechanisms for its expansion and the concentration of capital that results from it, generates the impoverishment of some of the people, and this will be one of the elements that will explain the crises of realisation or super-production that will be dealt with further on. It is highlighted as being one of the central contradictions because, as we shall see, the crises of realisation and super-production will be related to the expansion of the value itself that occurs almost in an independent way from its capacity of realisation, generating temporary crises.

The obligatory raising of productivity to ensure continuity of the process and of the existence of each individual capital in particular, presupposes constant change in the industrial structure. The nature of the process of accumulation on an extended scale itself that presupposes an always growing need for reinvesting the surplus value generated, thus results in a growing concentration of capital. This concentration of capital provides each individual capital with an increase in its gains in scale and, therefore, results in a need for realisation and the replacement of a greater value in movement, in the flow of valorisation, which becomes a contradiction faced with the alteration of the industrial structure that replaces lively labour by dead labour.

"The development of the productiveness of social labour presupposes cooperation on a large scale; how it is only upon this supposition that division and combination of labour can be organised, and the means of production economised by its concentration on a vast scale; how instruments of labour which, from their very nature, are only fit for use in common, such as a system of machinery, can be called into being; how huge natural forces can be pressed into the service of production, and how the transformation can be effected of the process of production into a technological application of science.... The basis of the production of commodities can admit of production on a large scale in the capitalistic form alone.... With the accumulation of capital, therefore, the specifically capitalist mode of production develops and with the specifically capitalist mode of production capital accumulation. Both these economic factors bring about, in the compound ratio of the impulses they reciprocally give one another, that change the technical composition of capital by which the variable constituent becomes always smaller and smaller as compared with the constant" (Marx I, 1887a:309–310)

Emphasising these capital movements is central to what here one wishes to understand: their seeking new spaces for accumulation. The process of capital concentration is a direct consequence of the need for accumulation on an extended scale that, like a snowball, increases the surplus constantly to be placed in valorisation, raising the mass of functioning capital of each individual capitalist. The productivity (efficiency) leverages and permits this process. That is why, faced with the mass of value that each individual capitalist has to constantly place in valorisation, the search for new spaces for it becomes imperative. Therefore, the process of concentration, the result of the accumulation and that at the same time enhances it, pressures each individual capital towards expansion, to search for new spaces of valorisation for the mass of surplus value that they have. On the other hand, the growth of productivity occurs by the reduction of the variable capital (labour-power), creating contradictions for the maintenance of the flow of accumulation on an extended scale in a given place, contributing even more to the expansion of capital to other spaces. Thus they are several processes acting together in this direction.

At any event, the concentration of capital is still only part of the movement of capital, but that allows the understanding of the other part: the centralisation of capitals that strengthen it. In the latter, individual capitalists are eliminated during the process of capital valorisation, increasing the concentration of the part of those that survive. "The tendency of capitalism to distance itself from free competition between producers and in the direction of forming monopolies, is intimately linked to a greater mixture of capital ... Two aspects must be considered: first, the growth of constant capital in relation to variable; and, second, the growth of the fixed part of constant capital ... The result of these two tendencies is an increase in the average volume of the productive unit..." (Sweezy, 1973:284).

1.5 Realisation of Value, the Condition for Accumulation, Concentration and Centralisation

The process of accumulation, that has as a starting point the process of production, the creator of value, and its reinvestment on an expanded scale depends, for the social realisation of this value, on the transformation of commodity capital in exchange value, being converted in the market into the form of money. This is the process of realisation of the value embodied in the commodity that needs to be sold to realise itself as far as social value. This is what Marx calls "the *salto mortale* of the commodity" (Marx I, 1887a:59). Only in this way is its social existence recognised as commodity-value. Only the realisation of the commodity as money by its sale does it make possible the reconversion of this in capital: money that will buy the means of production (Marx I, 1887a:281). Value, only under this new form, means of production, can it restart the process permitting valorisation of capital on an expanded scale, accumulating itself in an incremental flow. "...as the act consists precisely in giving away money, the individual can remain the owner of money only in so far as the act of giving away implies a return of money. But money can return to him only through the sale of commodities." (Marx I, 1887a:21)

Capital in its valorisation must pass through different stages to guarantee it, a process Marx called capital turnover: money capital that is transformed into productive capital resulting in commodity capital to, with its sale, reconvert itself into money capital, allowing the process to restart (M-C-M' ... M'-C-M" ... etc.). The passage through these stages is what ensures capital accumulation, its valorisation on an expanded scale, with the reconversion of the value created in means of production, of surplus value created in new means of production. This process of valorisation functions as an ascending spiral, in which the money that appears from the realisation of the commodities must, in order to maintain the process of valorisation, must return as capital through the purchase of new commodities, means of production, in an ascending flow. This flow makes sense in relation to capital in general (in macroeconomic logic) as for each individual capital[7] (microeconomic logic). But, if capital is considered in general, the purchase of the means of production is what ensures the realisation itself of the commodities produced, permitting the accumulation on an extended scale.

On this point, one may trace a parallel with Keynes theory (1982) that ascribes to investment (the purchase of capital goods and labour – means of production) the dynamic factor in the process of wealth generation that is only realised as such if new cycles of investment are begun, one after another, also in an ascending spiral, in which the new value which begins the process is always obligatorily larger than the previous one, an indispensable condition for realisation, in order that all that was produced may be sold or, in Marx's parlance, realised as value (Palloix vol. 1, 1971:86). Here, there are no disagreements in relation to the movement of the flow of accumulation that is the responsibility of each individual capital to realise, in order that the process of capital accumulation in general occur.

In this sense the non-realisation of the commodity through its sale paralyses the process of production and capital valorisation, given that it impedes the reconversion of the value created into new capital. In capitalism one must sell to be able to buy. The commodity to be sold in this case is the product and the commodity to be bought, productive capital, constant capital (machinery etc.) and variable (labour), the generator of value. Part of this realisation is in the hands of individual capital itself that must buy new means of production, and the other part is in the consumption of the workers that must be included in this new cycle of production in order to dispose of income to consume the new commodity created. Only in this way may the flow of accumulation on an extended scale be realised, even knowing that the sale of commodities produced is only a specific part of the flow and is not where the value is created, but realised.

The turnover of capital in all these stages thus becomes an important issue for the process of accumulation, being responsible by definition for its movement and rhythm. This may be faster, the greater the speed of realisation of the commodity as value in the market. "A given capital-value will serve, in

---

7 Individual capital in the sense used here is the agent of capital, it is that which makes the process of capital accumulation real. "To say that each individual capital has the characteristics of social capital ... means that it constitutes a centre in which a circular flow is inserted [flow of accumulation], whose form is a circular process of transformation in the forms of value [M-C-M']" (Aglietta, 1979:193).

widely different degrees, as a creator of products and value, and the scale of reproduction will be extended or reduced commensurate with the particular speed with which that capital throws off its commodity-form and assumes that of money, or with the rapidity of the sale." (Marx II, 1887b:24). The faster the time of capital turnover, the more accelerated will be the accumulation (Marx II, 1887b:73). The faster the capital passes through its various forms in the period of turnover, money capital, productive capital, commodity capital and, again money capital, the more intense will be the process of accumulation, or of the valorisation of the value. The search for new markets and new spaces for accumulation, or control over them, functions as a guarantee for the process as well as contributing to enhancing it.

The duration of the period of capital turnover determines the rhythm of accumulation. This duration or, paralysation in some of the stages, depends on how the capital is distributed in each stage for each branch of production, varying according to circumstantial factors as well as technical ones. "The continuity of the reproduction is at times more or less interrupted so far as individual capitals are concerned. In the first place the masses of value are frequently distributed at various periods in unequal portions over the various stages and functional forms. In the second place these portions may be differently distributed, according to the character of the commodity to be produced, hence according to the particular sphere of production in which the capital is invested. In the third place the continuity may be more or less broken in those branches of production which are dependent on the seasons, either on account of natural conditions (agriculture, herring catch, etc.) or on account of conventional circumstances, as for instance in so-called seasonal work." (Marx II, 1887b:60)

As the turnover time of capital implies its journeys through three successive stages, money capital, productive capital and commodity capital, if this gets blocked in any one of them, it interrupts or slows down the process of accumulation. Paralysations of the capital may occur in the commodity or money form; or the commodity is not sold, or the money is not converted into productive capital (through a new investment) becoming, for example, speculative money, a typical aspect of financial crises, in which, there occurs a shift of the valorisation from concrete assets to financial ones. In both the commodity form as money form, the process of capital valorisation is paralysed and, as a result there occurs crisis and unemployment. "Capital describes its circuit normally only so long as its various phases pass uninterruptedly into one another. If capital stops short in the first phase M-C, money-capital assumes the rigid form of a hoard; if it stops in the phase of production, the means of production lie without functioning on the one side, while labour-power remains unemployed on the other; and if capital stops short in the last phase C'-M', piles of unsold commodities accumulate and clog the flow of circulation." (Marx II, 1887b:29)

In order that the process is not paralysed as commodity capital, or in the transformation of this into money capital, the commodities produced to be sold, need simultaneously to be bought, ensuring the realisation of the value and the flow. In order for this to happen the capitalists, as much as the workers, need to acquire these commodities produced that consist as much as the means of production – machinery, raw materials etc. exclusively for capitalists' spending – as well as the final consumer goods – consumed by the workers as well as the capitalist as an individual. "In the form C' ... C' the consumption of the entire commodity-product is assumed as the condition of the normal course of the circuit of capital itself. The individual consumption of the labourer and the individual consumption of the un-accumulated part of the surplus-product comprise the entire individual consumption. Hence consumption in its totality – individual as well as productive – enters into circuit C' as a condition of it. Productive consumption (which essentially includes the individual consumption of the labourer, since labour-power is a continuous product, with certain limits, of the labourer's individual consumption) is carried on by every individual capital. Individual consumption, except in so far as it is required for the existence of the individual capitalist." (Marx II, 1887b:54)

Faced with this statement, given that the workers' consumption is important for the process of the realisation of the commodities, an important contradiction raised by Marx himself remains latent, as far as these "as sellers of their commodity, the labour-power," (Marx II, 1887b:193) have their value constantly lowered in relation to total value created. It is worth pointing out that the worker's consumption is important, but he is only given this capacity in so far as he is transformed into variable capital, selling himself as labour-power, only thus can he become a consumer.[8] Now, by the rationale of the process of accumulation, concentration and centralisation of capital, this becomes increasingly more difficult given the tendency to the exclusion of the worker or of the reducing of his share in the wealth created in the process of accumulation, making clear the contradiction commented previously, embodied in the concept of efficiency. An economy is considered efficient when productivity increases, which means greater value produced per worker, or rather, a smaller

---

[8] On this point Keynes goes further. The capacity for consumption of the non-capitalists depends on the decision of individual capital in acquiring them as the labour force by the transformation of his money into capital.

share for the worker in the product, or the value produced grows more than the value appropriated by labour.

On the other hand, the process of turnover may be paralysed in the form of money capital. From a certain view point, the paralysation of the process in this form is a characteristic of capitalism in so far as money is the object of desire of the individual capitalist. He places it in the process in order to afterwards take it back in a larger amount, using it in the process of production for such. "The process of production appears merely as an unavoidable intermediate link, as a necessary evil for the sake of money-making. All nations with a capitalist mode of production are therefore seized periodically by a feverish attempt to make money without the intervention of the process of production" (Marx II, 1887b:32), that lead to financial crises in speculative cycles. If it were possible the increase of wealth in a financial way, the individual capitalist would see no reason to invest his money in a productive form. In this case he would stop acting as such ceasing to value the capital under his control. This fact is important only to reaffirm that the capitalist only invests his money as capital because he is compelled to do so and not simply by his desire. The problem is that in capitalism money carries the magical power of wealth hiding the reality and inverting it, taking the place of the real commodity without being it (Marx, Economic and Philosophic Manuscripts of 1844 in Marx-Engels collected works volume 3, pp. 322–325).

The factor that impels the paralysation of the process in the form of money capital is not only related to the desire of the capitalist but the form how the system is organised in isolated autonomous capitals. Different productive sectors at different times and with various fixed/circulating capital relation, retain money capital by dint of the various characteristics of their periods of turnover. Hoarding may thus be related to the need of each individual capital as much as the replenishment of fixed capital vis a vis the form that this fixed capital transfers its value to the product. It may also result from the time that capital remains in a productive form which differs for each individual capital. Both these factors oblige the individual capitalist to retain more or less capital in the form of money for a certain period, which may result in problems of realisation depending on whether this retention occurs at the same time for the majority of individual capitals. Here, the economy as a whole will have problems of realisation, or rather, production will not be sold.

The period that capital remains as productive capital may be defined by the type of commodity that each industry has as a product. The fact that some sectors of the economy will have longer production periods than others, leads them, from the individual point of view, to need greater working capital, which means to say for Marx, that they are obliged to preserve capital in the form of money for periods that are more or less long, awaiting the moment to restart the production process, or to replace the money in the form of capital. This hoarded money that is the result of a sale unaccompanied by the purchase of commodities, interferes in the process of realisation. From the point of view of capital in general, this difference of rhythms of production interferes in the "interweaving of capitals". Various sectors follow various rhythms of how they use their surplus value in its valorisation. "In order to accumulate capital he [individual capital] must first withdraw in money-form from circulation a part of the surplus value which he obtained from that circulation, and must hoard it until it has increased sufficiently for the extension of his old business or the opening of a side-line. So long as the formation of the hoard continues, it does not increase the demand of the capitalist. The money is immobilised. It does not withdraw from the commodity-market any equivalent in commodities for the money equivalent withdrawn from it for commodities supplied." (Marx II, 1887b:70)

Given the diverse nature of individual capitals, there is an inter-relationship between them, through their simultaneous acts of buying and selling. The interweaving between the various capitals does not always match, given that the difference in time that capital remains in each stage results in problems of realisation, apparent in the volume of sales of each individual capital."...however it is not at all required for the discharge of the functionally determined role played by every metamorphosis occurring within the process of circulation of some individual capital that this metamorphosis should represent the corresponding opposite metamorphosis in the circuit of the other capital, provided we assume that the entire production of the world-market is carried on capitalistically." (Marx II, 1887b:66)

This problem of realisation is related to the renewal time of fixed capital and of working capital that must remain in the form of money, hoarded. This is also related to the form how fixed capital has its return in the form of money through the sale of commodities in time (Marx II, 1887b:96). This returns to the hands of the capitalist in the form of money in parts, before the need for its renewal as fixed capital. One may say that after each period of acquisition of new fixed capital, the transformation of money capital into productive capital, appears a period of hoarding, in that it does not acquire new fixed capital. This is an important factor in crises of realisation and in the temporary cycle of business.

"This much is evident: the cycle of interconnected turnovers embracing a number of years, in which capital is held fast by its fixed constituent part, furnishes a material basis for the periodic crises. During this cycle business undergoes successive periods of depression, medium activity, precipitancy and crisis. True, periods in which capital is invested differ greatly and far from coincide in time. But a crisis always forms the starting-point of large new investments. Therefore, from the point of view of society as a whole, more or less, a new material basis for the next turnover cycle." (Marx II, 1887b:47–48)

Thus is the crisis of realisation configured that results in over-production or under-consumption as an intrinsic consequence of the process of capital turnover. The commodities that cannot be realised in a balanced and simultaneous way due to their own characteristics of the process of production, in the way how production is structured between the sectors, between the different individual capitals in capitalism. It is worth remembering, as previously described, the crises of realisation are also sparked by the exclusion of the worker from the process of production and by the reduction of his share in the income created. The difference between these two mechanisms for causing the crisis of realisation is that the first is circumstantial, whilst the second, dealt with previously, is structural, the result of the evolution of the process of accumulation and concentration of capital.

Apart from this, it is worth highlighting that the problems of realisation are related to the inherent need for capital to increase in value in an independent way and in an incremental process that overtakes its possibility for realisation. As Marx states, "With the development of capitalist production, the scale of production is determined less and less by the direct demand for the product and more and more by the amount of capital available in the hands of the individual capitalist, by the urge of self-expansion inherent in his capital and by the need of continuity and expansion of the process of production. Thus in each particular branch of production there is a necessary increase in the mass of products available in the market in the shape of commodities, i.e., in search of buyers. The amount of capital fixed for a shorter or longer period in the form of commodity-capital grows. Hence the commodity-supply also grows." (Marx II, 1887b:84). This means to say that the process of capital accumulation does not follow the rationale of demand, but its intrinsic need to replace the surplus value created in valorisation, the role of each individual capital.

These problems have been widely debated by various authors in discussions about demand and problems of realisation (Palloix I, 1971:86). Keynes (1982) proposed the administration of demand as a form of reaching a balance with supply, while Luxemburg (1983) demonstrated the need for the internationalisation of the process of accumulation. But, both solutions are fragile in the face of the problem that is related to the fact that capital accumulation is a process that occurs in an incremental flow, on one side, and at the same time is an excluding process, on the other. This causes in each turnover cycle, the capital to be placed in movement is always greater, and it increases the risk of crises of realisation that may paralyse the process of accumulation. For Boccara the problem of realisation is much more related to the over-accumulation of Marx.[9] He states that "In reality, as the theory of over-accumulation shows, it is the progress of productive forces in the context of the capitalist structure, with the decisive aim of the valorisation of capitals, growing accumulation ... that explains the difficulties of over-accumulation and of unemployment" (Boccara, 1978:329–330). This idea goes beyond theories of under-consumption, that does not cease being present and materialising in problems of realisation, but is configured as a problem of accumulation on an extended scale itself. At any rate, the problems that result therefrom lead capital to constantly expand its space for accumulation. "The need of a constantly expanding market for its products chases the bourgeoisie over the whole surface of the globe. It must nestle everywhere, settle everywhere, establish connections everywhere. ... through its exploitation of the world market given a cosmopolitan character to production and consumption in every country" (Marx, Manifesto of the Communist Party – in Marx-Engels collective works volume 6, p. 487).

The process of accumulation may accelerate or deaccelerate in a crisis, or even, be paralysed, when the commodity does not realise its value. As pointed out, this may occur through differences in the cycles of turnover of different capitals, through the excluding character that reduces the share of labour, or by its own need for accumulation on an extended scale that pushes each individual capital to new valorisations independently of the capacity of realisation that results in over-accumulation and in over-production. For whichever of these reasons, these movements cause breaks in the process of accumulation in which part of the working capital does not find space to maintain itself in the process of valorisation. Part of the capital will therefore be destroyed in a crisis, which is manifested in the closing of factories, bankruptcies etc. As Aglietta points out, the real significance of the crisis is "the partial destruction of fixed capital that finds itself operating in production ... factories are closed ... the means of production are materially destroyed ... of one part of industrial capital [that] reduces the total mass of capital employed in production" (Aglietta, 1979:194). This means to say that crises reduce the mass of capital as a result of the reduction in the space of accumulation, be it as a consequence of circumstantial questions (disproportionalities in the rhythms of accumulation

---

9   Described in Capital, Book III, Chapter 15 – "The internal contradictions of the law of falling rates of profits" (1985).

or over-production) or be it by structural problems (reduction of the share of labour in income and over-accumulation).

The crises therefore stimulate movements of productive restructuring that are the only form for capital to resume the accumulation process. "Accumulation returns to be undertaken thanks to the qualitative transformation of the productive forces..." (Aglietta, 1979:84–85). This restructuring occurs through mergers, acquisitions or simply suppression of individual capitals, a process called the centralisation of capital. "With centralisation, innumerable individual capitals disappear through absorption whilst others are regrouped through mergers..." (Aglietta, 1979:195). This means to say that crisis is one of the catalysing elements of the process of capital centralisation. And, the opposite of destroying the process of accumulation, because of the centralisations that it stimulates, it restores the process of accumulation in a new productive structure. Therefore, the centralisation of capital is the factor that replaces the flow of accumulation on an extended scale on a new level.

"The centralisation of capitals ... is an effect of the general process of depreciation of capital over the fractioned capitals, through which, the movement of general accumulation finds new conditions for its future development" (Aglietta, 1979:196). Thus, one may say that the movement of centralisation of capitals functions as a counterbalancing factor to the crises of capitalism, permitting capital to continue its process of accumulation, now more strengthened, in a defined space.

In this sense, it is also worth commenting that internationalisation, by the occupation and control of other markets in other places, in the sense of expanding the horizon for realisation, in fact may ensure the continuity of the process of expanded accumulation, as well as contributing to leveraging it. On the other hand, this process of internationalisation, despite historically proven, only projects the "solution" of the problem further ahead, in so far that, within limits, it creates circumstantial crises of international realisation. The problem of realisation is simply transferred from the local to the world, reinstating these contradictions in the global domain that will have as a solution the restructuring of capital in the world sphere in a process of global centralisation.

1.6 The Centralisation of Capital

Concentration and centralisation are two different processes, although at times they may be confused. This occurs because the process of capital centralisation almost always results in greater concentration. On the other hand, the more concentrated individual capital is, the greater tends to be its power in relation to other capitals (depending, of course, on the types of sectors), that may move it in the direction of centralisation by the absorption of other minor capitals. Concentration and centralisation are two interlinked processes that mutually reinforce each other.

Concentration is the expansion of appropriation over the value created in the process of accumulation on an extended scale of each individual capital, of the mass of surplus value that each capitalist extracts from labour and must replace in the process of valorisation. In it, "Every accumulation becomes the means of new accumulation.... the growth of social capital is effected through the growth of many individual capitals" (Marx I, 1887a:310) therefore being part of a movement of capital expansion by the hands of a variety of individual capitals.

Centralisation, on the contrary, is not a movement of expansion, it is the expropriation of the individual capitalist by capital in general, a process in which individual capitals are excluded from the process of accumulation or are absorbed by other individual capitals in a process of qualitative transformation in the productive structure (Aglietta, 1979:192–197). From the point of view of each individual capital, centralisation is a process of concentration, but from the point of view of capital in general, centralisation does not imply an increase in the mass of functioning capital, on the contrary, it feeds itself from its reduction mainly when it is the result of crises. It does not depend on the expansion of the base of accumulation of capital in general.

At any rate they are two processes interlinked to each other and both are the result of the process of the accumulation on an extended scale of capital, with the difference that in centralisation, capital, in its incessant flow of valorisation, comes to expropriate, not only labour (that characterises concentration), but the capitalists themselves. Thus, capital centralisation is, in a more general sense, a movement resulting from the processes of accumulation and concentration, given that the more concentrated an individual capital is, the greater its tendency to suppress or occupy the space of other capitals. In this aspect it is almost a natural result of accumulation and concentration, it is strictly linked to them.

On the other hand, the centralisation of capital, unlike the process of concentration, causes a qualitative change in the process of accumulation in so far as it changes the way how individual capitals relate to each other. It is the result of the dispute between individual capitals for the restricted space of accumulation where only one of them wins. Moreover, it is a process that apart from being related to competition between individual capitals, it is the result mainly of the struggle for space in the process of accumulation, a struggle that becomes more entrenched at the times when that space is reduced in the face of the mass of capital in movement in search of valorisation. That is why the centralisation of capitals is manifested as a rearrangement of the space of accumulation as the result of cyclical crises or not. Marx relates these crises mainly to what he calls over-accumulation (Marx III, 1894:172). That is why it is a process that normally occurs in waves.[10] In this context, centralisation is a process in which the conditions for the continuity of the process of general accumulation are reinstated on a new level, realised on new bases through the individual capitals that survive and are fortified in the process of centralisation. "The antagonism between each individual capitalist's interests and those of the capitalist class as a whole" (Marx III, 1894:174). Some capitals must be destroyed so that others are strengthened.

The process of centralisation may appear as something abstract, given its being a movement of capital in general, a movement that destroys individual capitals at the same time that it strengthens other individual capitals. But this sense of abstraction is soon undone when one observes that this process is materialised in acquisitions, mergers or simple failures of individual capitals that normally take place in times of productive restructuring. They are real processes demonstrated by the historic tendency of capital that, through the intermediation of individual capitals, tend to form oligopolies and monopolies, to centralise itself in the form of large groups, conglomerates of companies or not, corporations (a web of contracts involving property or not, see Chesnais 1995 and Williamson, 1985) that come to control the process of accumulation.

"This last does not mean that simple concentration of the means of production and of the command over labour, which is identical with accumulation. It is concentration of capitals already formed, destruction of their individual independence, expropriation of capitalist by capitalist, transformation of many small into few large capitals. This process differs from the former in this, that it only presupposes a change in the distribution of capital already to hand, and functioning; *its field of action is therefore not limited by the absolute growth of social wealth, by the absolute limits of accumulation.* Capital grows in one place to a huge mass in a single hand, because it has in another place been lost by many. This is centralisation proper, as distinct from accumulation and concentration." (Marx I, 1887a:310 – my emphasis)

---

10 Aglietta, analysing this process in North American history, notes that movements of centralisation tend to be stronger in peak periods, "when the rate of surplus value begins to fall and the struggle against this fall begins an intensification of obsolescence," and also at the end of a recession, when centralisation reorganises the productive structure (Aglietta, 1979:196).

The centralisation of capital is not subject to the constraints of the process of the creation of surplus, of the "increase in social wealth". It does not depend on its expansion to place itself in movement, on the contrary, it is characterised by the acquisition of part of the existing economic wealth or simply the removal of other individual capitals from the space of accumulation. An individual capital is strengthened on the tomb of another. It is affected mainly through the elimination of individual capitals but it does not limit itself to reducing the number of autonomous capitals and to increasing its size. The destruction of a part of the capital reduces the total mass of working capital and provides new opportunities for valorisation of all the capitals that remain. "The masses of capital fused together overnight by the centralisation reproduce and multiply as the others do, only more rapidly, thereby becoming new and powerful levers in social accumulation." (Marx I, 1887a:312) That is why, as Marx says, it is a process that is not restricted to the absolute limits of accumulation imposed on each individual capital.

"This is law for capitalist production, imposed by incessant revolutions in the methods of production themselves, by the depreciation of existing capital always bound up with them, by the general competitive struggle and the need to improve production and expand its scale merely as a means of self-preservation and under penalty of ruin. The market must, therefore, be continually extended, so that its interrelations and the conditions regulating them assume more and more the form of a natural law working independently of the producer, and become ever more uncontrollable. This internal contradiction seeks to resolve itself through expansion of the outlying field of production. But the more productiveness develops, the more it finds itself at variance with the narrow basis on which the conditions of consumption rest." (Marx III, 1894:168).

In more general terms, the process of centralisation is the result of the movement of capital itself. Its incessant search for valorisation and its need to be accumulated on an extended scale, always reinvesting the surplus value in new productive capital, it is guaranteed only if there is space for its continuity, which does not occur given the tendency that capital has for accumulating itself independently of the "narrow base on which the relationships of consumption rest," from these conditions of realisation. Marx calls this overproduction and over-accumulation, related to the excess of capital (Marx III, 1894:172). This means that for the continuity of the process the removal of individual functioning capitals, the devaluing and elimination of the weakest individual capitals. Boccara (1978) points out how this happens in his analysis of this over-accumulation. For the author, this process results from accumulation itself that obliges capital constantly to return to the form of productive capital and consists in the incapacity of additional capital invested to obtain profit. According to Boccara. "In the case of the over-accumulation of capital, the attempt at valorisation of additional capital, in consequence of seeking accumulation by different individual capitals, needs a part of the social capital not to appreciate, but that it may be, so to speak, devalued" (Boccara, 1978:52). This means to say that part of the social capital cannot continue to increase in value in order that others may do so, a "devaluation of a part of the total capital that allows, as a rule, the continuity of valorisation of other capitals and of global capital" (Boccara, 1978:53). Therefore, those individual capitals that are not capable of continuing their trajectory of valorisation must succumb in detriment of others that are stronger.

"Although, as the description of this conflict shows, the loss is by no means equally distributed among individual capitals, its distribution being rather decided through a competitive struggle in which the loss is distributed in very different proportions and forms, depending on special advantages or previously captured positions, so that one capital is left unused, another is destroyed, and a third suffers but a relative loss, or is just temporarily depreciated, etc. ... But the equilibrium would be restored under all circumstances through the withdrawal or even the destruction of more or less capital." (Marx III, 1894:174). This capital destruction is characterised by "violent and acute crises ... of a real falling off in reproduction..." (Marx III, 1894:174) "The crises are always but momentary and forcible solutions of the existing contradictions. They are violent eruptions which for a time restore the disturbed equilibrium." (Marx III, 1894:171)

Thus, centralisation, as a qualitative change in the structure of capital through the elimination of individual capitals, functions as counteract factor to crises, at the same time in that it feeds upon them. As Aglietta pointed out in agreement with Marx, centralisation is an effect of the process of devaluation of capital in general, materialised on individual capitals by destroying some and strengthening others, movement through which the process of accumulation finds new conditions for its development (Aglietta, 1979:196). It thus functions as a contradictory factor in relation to the fall in the rate of surplus value (Marx III, 1894:169). Going a little further, taking into consideration that the movement of capital is not restricted to geographic spaces as will be seen in Chapter 2, one may add that this is the same mechanism acting nationally and internationally. Taking the words of Marx: "...how does the bourgeoisie get over these crises? On the one hand by enforced destruction of a mass of productive forces; on the other, by the conquest of new markets, and by the more thorough exploitation of the old ones." (Marx, Manifesto of the Communist Party – in Marx-Engels collective works volume 6, p. 490)

The way how the process of centralisation occurs, which capitals will be eliminated or will lose space to others, is connected, as pointed out by Marx above, to the constant "revolutions of value" employed by the new capital that enters in operation. The catalysing elements are competition and the credit that contributes to accelerate and define the process that arises from the very laws of capital movement. It is from these mechanisms that the large capitals crush the small ones. "...with the development of capitalist production and accumulation there develop the two most powerful levers of centralisation – competition and credit." (Marx I, 1887a:311). The battle of competition always ends up with the defeat of many small capitals, "The competitive struggle would decide what part of it [capital] would be particularly affected," which individual capital would be destroyed (Marx III, 1894:173). In this sense, the size of each individual capital is also a determinant in this struggle, given that centralisation itself increases the size of the capitals that survive, structuring them in large economic groups, reinforcing the concentration and centralisation. Credit, along with competition, performs the role of facilitating the financial resources needed for the process of centralisation. Credit is an essential arm for competition and, thus "in an enormous social mechanism of the centralisation of capitals" (Marx I, 1887a:311) given that the processes of centralisation that is manifest in operations for the transfer of property demand important masses of finance capital for their realisation.[11]

On the other hand, the more productive capitals, the newer ones, or innovating individual capital, have advantages in this struggle for survival. For example, they have the capacity to take the value of their product below its social value, providing it with a temporary increase in profits, imposing losses on other capitals, exercising a kind of "temporary" monopoly. Other individual capitals must accompany the movement of "revolution in value" (innovations) to keep themselves in the game and not perish. This movement also can be related to the cyclical crises that contribute to the elimination of various individual capitals in operation that do not accompany the process, resulting in the centralisation of capital. The new productive capital that destroys the old always comes incorporated with new technology that depreciates and contributes to eliminating other capitals. "Capital ... in its new shape, incorporates gratis the social advance made while its old shape was being used up. Of course, this development of productive power is accompanied by a partial

---

11   As we will see in the following chapters, this is the reason capital seeks international financial freedom when the process of centralisation takes the form of globalisation.

depreciation of functioning capitals ... this depreciation makes itself acutely felt in competition..." (Marx I, 1887a:301).

Thus, the centralisation of capital destroys and eliminates the individual capitalist himself, in a demonstration that it is capital in general that controls the process of expanded accumulation. That is why Marx defines centralisation as the result of the historic capitalist process of disassociating labour from the means of production. This process is the essence of the capitalist concept, it is capital and not the capitalist that defines the logic of the process. This for Marx can be understood only when one assumes the concept of private property that entails the disassociation of labour and the labour-power, of labour as a commodity and commodity as a product of labour. This separation is what permits the process of accumulation in the capitalist form, and its most complete form is, apart from the expropriation of the worker, the expropriation of capital of the capitalist himself: the centralisation of capital. This completes and permits one to learn the true nature of capitalism. Marx says, "It is this same severance of the conditions of production; on the one hand, from the producers, on the other, that forms the conception of capital. It begins with primitive accumulation (Marx I, 1887a: Chapter XXIV, Part 8), appears as a permanent process in the accumulation and concentration of capital, and expresses itself finally as centralisation of existing capitals in a few hands and a deprivation of many of their capital." (Marx III, 1894:169). Hence, one may say that centralised capitalism is the manifestation of this disassociation taken to its limit, it is capital in its purest state; it marks the idea of separation between the individual and the process of accumulation. Centralisation is qualitatively different from concentration because it changes the autonomy of individual capitals; with it individual capitals disappear (Aglietta, 1979:195) as central agents and places them in their real place as representatives of capital in general, being able, moreover, to be suppressed individually in the process.

Thus, centralisation characterises capital in its purest state because it denies the form of individual capitalist property in so far as it expropriates him. It denies the classic concept of enrichment through individual work to reaffirm capital as an entity that controls the process, a fact that is reinforced the more centralised capital is. The mode of capitalist production is controlled by capital and not by the individual capitalist. The capitalist participates in the process as agent, but, contradictorily, capital may do without him or eliminate him as an individual or individual capital. The capitalist mode denies the individual private property based on one's own work,[12] it denies the individual to

---

[12] That is why Marx notes in his "Economic and Philosophic Manuscripts of 1844" that the real problem about the question of ownership is not the ownership over objects obtained

affirm capital.[13] The corporation form or capitalist group is the place in which this characteristic is manifest in its purest form, where capital manifests its essence, its autonomy.

In the corporation or group of companies acting in the form of an oligopoly or monopoly, characteristics of centralised capital, the traditional figure of the individual capitalist that experiences the "Faustian" conflict of accumulating or spending the surplus value generated in the process of production, stops existing. In the corporation all of its administrators are in fact officials of capital. They are contracted by "it" with the exclusive function of maintaining its continuous and growing process of valorisation, of ensuring accumulation on an extended scale, or rather, of ensuring that all the surplus value generated in the process of production is reconverted into new productive capital. Thus, centralised capital tends to eliminate the figure of the traditional capitalist. The existence of this comes to occur only at the margin of the process. The tendency is to remove him or leave him aside, replacing him really by an official of capital a "contracted executive,"[14] a "chief executive officer".

This tendency was proposed in a very clear way some time ago by Baran and Sweezy in their *Monopoly Capitalism*. They state that "the leader today is a very different type of magnate from 50 years ago (...) he is the antithesis of entrepreneur and of the magnate at the same time: these were individualists *par excellence*, while he is a main species of a genus known as organisation man. ...The leader is a man on the inside, dominated by it. The loyalty of the former is for himself and his family...; the loyalty of the latter is to the organisation to which he belongs and through which he expresses himself. For the first, the company was only a means of enrichment; for the second, the good of the company becomes an end in itself at the same time economically and ethically" (Baran and Sweezy, 1978:39).

In so far as capital conquers its "autonomy" in relation to the individual capitalist, to control of the capitalist, submitting him to the obligation of constantly increasing surplus value, capital is free to manifest its movement in the sense of valorisation. The more it is centralised, the more capital has at its disposal elements that ensure its expansion of accumulation, of extraction of the surplus. The more it is concentrated and centralised, the greater its capacity for

---

from one's own work, but the ownership over someone else's work (Marx, Economic and Philosophic Manuscripts of 1844, in Marx-Engels collected works, volume 3, pp. 293–294).
13   This fact makes the idea of isolated company or "dot firm" (Coriat & Weinstein,1995:15) or of methodological individualism of traditional microeconomics mere abstractions.
14   A much deeper and interesting discussion on the theories of what a big company is undertaken by Coriat & Weinstein (1995) in a didactic way.

control over markets and technology that make possible increased productivity and extraction of surplus value.

Centralised capital is capital walking on its own feet. It itself comes to have more autonomy to organise its movement, submitting individuals to its movement. As an autonomous entity, it comes to have power – or to exert pressure in order to have it, in a growing form – to organise its markets and ensure its level of accumulation over individuals and societies. This centralised capital is not an abstraction. It is manifest in large monopolies and oligopolies that act globally, managed by officials of capital that seek to obtain domination and control over the process of accumulation. The centralisation of capital characterises a capitalism in which capital itself comes to organise its movement of continuous valorisation. "The old society decomposed, (…) the capitalist mode of production stands on its own feet … takes a new form, (…), the expropriation of the private proprietors" (Marx I, 1887a:383–384)

The importance of pointing out this fact is due to the need to qualify what a large corporation comes to be for Marx, the central aim of this work. The large conglomerate, originating from successive processes of centralisation, and that is given substance as a large transnational company, becomes the most pure representation of the interest of capital in its process of accumulation on an extended scale. It is this corporation or group that, with these characteristics, manifests the movement of capital in its process of local or global accumulation. What Marx is pointing out by the process of centralisation and concentration is the nature of capital in taking the form of monopolies or oligopolies, in centralising itself in large groups, conglomerates or not, that come to dominate and control the process of accumulation. On the other hand, he also points to the elimination of individual capitalists in this process in the sense of a new form of organisation of large corporations, now commanded by executives, the officials of capitalism, with the only function of giving unceasing continuity to the process of accumulation and hence to make the company "world leader," a key catchphrase of company management "gurus."

At the same time, if the characteristic of the large corporation – as individual capital that is the material agent of the movement of capital in general – is to incorporate, now in a more "impersonal" way the movement of capital, the contradictions that this movement creates by its own nature of accumulation find the open space to flourish in a more radical form, exacerbating its own conditions that result in crises and that always lead to new waves of centralisation in a permanent flow.[15] In so far as the large corporation occupies the

---

15 "In any given branch of industry centralisation would reach its extreme limit if all the individual capitals invested in it were fused into a single capital.12 In a given society the

centre of the process of accumulation with capacity to expand its productive scale and dominion over technology, beyond its power – that is a power of capital, now more autonomous, of control over production and over markets – the conditions are given to make the contradictions of the process of accumulation itself more acute. In this sense, capital moving itself in freedom is much more subject to crises of over-accumulation, to crises of realisation, as well as the expansion of the contingent of excluded, be they workers who lose their jobs, be they capitalists that stop being so by the process of expulsion imposed by centralisation, reducing also the basis for the realisation of value.

"Whilst centralisation thus intensifies and accelerates the effects of accumulation, it simultaneously extends and speeds those revolutions in the technical composition of capital which raise its constant portion at the expense of its variable portion, thus diminishing the relative demand for labour." (Marx I, 1887a:311). In so far as the processes of accumulation, concentration and centralisation are at the centre of the movement seeking to increase the surplus extracted by the increase in labour productivity and, that is why it constantly eliminates labour, contradictorily they replace that which creates value, live labour, by that which just transfers its value to the final product, dead labour. At the same time, in the same processes, capital reduces through this its own capacity to realise the surplus value created. By dismissing live labour, it makes its realisation more difficult, the necessary basis for the continuity of the valorisation process. By eliminating live labour, it loses its capacity to generate surplus value in the same proportion.

Authors such as Schumpeter advocate the idea that capital centralisation would increase the planning capacity of the individual corporation, imagining, moreover, that this type of control would imply greater rationality for the whole system (Schumpeter, 1961). But, the individual control of the movement does not result in the control of capital in general, given that corporation personifies the movement of capital and therefore exacerbates the contradictions. "The giant company removes from the market sphere large portions of economic activity, subjecting them to planned scientific management. This change represents a continuous increase in the rationality of parts of the system, but it is not accompanied by any rationalisation of the whole" (Baran & Sweezy, 1978:334). On the contrary, the individual company, even with wide powers of control over the markets, global market, in so far that it is the personification of capital without intermediaries, is much more subject to the movement of capital in general and, therefore, to its contradictions that are exacerbated and

---

limit would be reached only when the entire social capital was united in the hands of either a single capitalist or a single capitalist company " (Marx I, 1887a:311).

are not reduced because of this. The more capital is centralised, the less will be the possibility of organisation of anything other than that of capital, given that the manager keeps himself to his obligation as an instrument of valorisation, providing it with the ways that ensure valorisation on an extended scale and its position in the market in search of leadership. A professional administration has greater chances of ensuring these elements. It has as a rule, in so far that the manager is the official of capital, to maintain the movement of the company in line with the movement of capital valorisation in general. He is obliged to do it to keep his position and his job, as the official of capital that he is.

Therefore, given that the rationality of the large corporation is the rationality of capital, the contradictions of the system pointed to by Marx, the contrary of dissolving themselves, are strengthened, spreading the instability of the system, be it by the growing social exclusion it wishes to create, be it by the inequality of income, be it by the cyclical crises inherent in the process of accumulation or over-accumulation. One may add one more point to this: as one expands the power of capital embodied in the large corporation that has now become transnational, the tendency is for the weakening of the social and institutional counter-powers that could counteract the movement of capital. Capital gains autonomy or greater power to conquer it.

Accumulation, concentration and centralisation of capital are processes that describe the movement of capital in its search for valorisation. They describe the movement of capital in the direction of greater autonomy in relation to those that act through it. It is an autonomy burdened with contradictions in so far that the processes destroy those that created it. It destroys labour, the source of surplus value and responsible for the transfer of the value of capital in operation, the means of production. It destroys the individual capitalist as an agent that has control of production, separating him from control of production, replacing him by one, in fact, an official of capital, who looks after its maintenance and valorisation. It also removes various individual capitals in the process of centralisation. That is why, to think about the large corporation in capitalism as an individual does not make sense.

Thus capital conquers its autonomy. It conquers the power to walk on its own feet, in an almost independent way, occupying, as the commodity that it is, the social space, controlling social relations, defining the forms of functioning that ensure it and do not obstruct its process of valorisation, be it on a national or international scale. Thus, concentration and centralisation have in themselves a sense of power. Power of control over markets, of control over the process of production and reproduction of capital and finally, expansion of the power of control over others' labour, this power although exercised by people, is, as one has tried to demonstrate, in a certain impersonal way in so far that it is from capital, therefore given substance as a social power materialised in a large corporation or group action. This power in capitalism since its origin has always been related or supported by the political power of the state. Capitalism was born within mercantilism, having the state as its large capital partner, as an absolutist state allied to commercial capital in its global venture. In capitalism, this state allies itself to industrial and financial capital and born from this alliance are imperialism and the globalisation of capital.

In this sense, the more autonomous the movement of capital becomes, the stronger is this tendency which for contradictory reasons may perhaps not apparently reduce the rate of profit because of the process of centralisation but it certainly increases exclusion. The more autonomous it is, the greater, by its own nature, is its incessant search for valorisation. Centralised, capital seeks to uncouple itself from practically all restraints that are able to impede it from continuing its search for expansion. At the same time, contradictorily, as it eliminates them, it destroys the basis for the continuity of the process. The extremely centralised economy, also internationally, marks out the autonomy of capital, relatively free to act according to its nature.

The processes of concentration and centralisation of capital en route to "monopoly capital" or to the establishment of large oligopolies, is an historic process manifested in large corporations and transnational groups today. Several authors have described and restated this condition of capitalist development, and there is also various data providing proof of this movement, as will be seen in Chapter 2. Different corporations from different sectors are organised in different ways in search of mastery over spaces throughout history. What there is that is new, despite this natural process of capitalism having been discussed since Lenin (1987), is it comes transforming itself in its characteristics but not in its essence, in so far as capital internationalises itself. From domestic spaces where this oligopolistic capital gains strength to, in a first stage, to conquer new spaces, in a second stage to take control over these new spaces occupying them with their productive structures in its process of expansion and, in a third stage, in an expanded process of global centralisation, it retracts itself and is restructured by the elimination of individual capital that becomes superfluous. Seemingly the 1990s marked this last stage, verified by the global process of mergers and acquisitions in a global scenario of ample freedom for the movement of capital, manifested in the restructuring of large economic groups. The new contradictions that rise from this process would appear in 2008 crises.

CHAPTER 2

Capital Accumulation, Transnational Capital and the Exclusion of the Periphery

2.1   Introduction

The aim of this chapter is to show how effective the logic of capital accumulation on an extended scale is, as approached in Chapter 1, to explain the movement of accumulation on a global scale and its contradictions and impacts upon the periphery.[1] It starts from the idea that the processes of accumulation, concentration and centralisation of capital, intrinsic to the nature of functioning capital, often viewed as being restricted to national economies, are, in so far as they describe the movements of capital, processes that do not respect national spaces; are mechanisms for the transmission of the contradictions of the capitalist mode of production and its consequent inequalities. They begin, firstly, in the local environment and then expand themselves on a global scale, starting from their original centres formed around the countries that compose the Triad.

The specific agent of this movement is capital embodied in increasingly concentrated and centralised individual capitals. Today, they are large transnational corporations acting in oligopolised markets, controlled by professionals, having long ago separated from the individual capitalist – who personified capital –, from his control. The transnational corporation, as if devoid of personality, is what directs the process of accumulation, now on a global scale, in a professional way.[2]

The process of accumulation on a global scale is the result of the specific nature of capital accumulation that does not consider geographical-political

---

[1] The term peripheral will be used to designate the set of countries at the margin of those composing the Triad (USA, Europe & Japan/Asia). This term is used because it describes a determined situation, a position of countries relative to the centre, while the term underdevelopment conveys the idea of relative backwardness and a stage of development. "Peripheralisation is an economic, social and political process through which a country loses part of its autonomy in detriment to a centre" (Nagels, 1993:85).

[2] The oligopolist multinational frees itself from the individual capitalist to professionalise its structure of control (see Sweezy & Baran, 1978:39, and Mészáros, 2002:103), it remains free from the contradictory interest of individual capital in his "Faustian conflict between the passion for accumulation, and the desire for enjoyment" (Marx I, 1887a:295).

limits in its expansion. Capitalism was born and was strengthened having as one of its seeds the processes of European unification and the formation of the state, establishing and constituting itself always starting from localised hierarchical relationships of power and domination in hegemonic centres.[3] These centres of domination are today made up of the countries that compose the Triad under the leadership of North America (Palloix, 1971:14; Carroll, 2010). From these central clusters, capital expanded itself between the Triad countries, and between them and the peripheral countries.

In this movement, capital reproduces its contradictory characteristics of accumulation, constantly occupying local, regional, national and global spaces. It reproduces not only those conditions that constantly create inequalities, its excluding character[4] and as creator of poverty, but also the contradictions embedded in its own process of accumulation on an extended scale which result in crises (Chapter 1), in each space that it occupies from the centre, as well as globally. In this sense, the expansion of capital not only establishes the exploitation of new markets, the inclusion of new places to ensure the reproduction of capital, but also, of the disintegration of different places, of exclusion and, finally, linked mainly to centralisation – understood not only as the expropriation of the capitalist by capital, but as a return to the centre – of the exclusion of entire regions from the map of accumulation, by the restructuring of global capital in operation. These movements become stronger as the more autonomous and free is the movement of capital, when it becomes subject to accumulation.

In the first place, it thus highlights, the process itself of capital accumulation on an extended scale. In it is contained the logic of expansion embodied in the nature of capital itself. In a sense, this more general movement of capital does not depend necessarily on concentration and centralisation, the specific consequences of the process of accumulation. It is characterised by the obligation each individual capital has to maintain the process of valorisation, that makes it more dramatic the more concentrated and centralised (oligopolies) capitalism is. It is the need to constantly replace the surplus value created anew in the process of valorisation. This in itself impels capital to seek new spaces.

Besides this movement – and related to it – is the process of capital concentration that constantly expands the amount of surplus value in the hands of

---

3 Giovanni Arrighi, for example, seeks historic standards in the varied configurations of global hegemony (see Arrighi, 1996, and Arrighi & Silver, 2001).
4 The term exclusion is here employed from the point of view of participation in the accumulation of capital. Given that the social relationship in capitalism transforms everything into commodities, for an individual to belong to society and be included in it, he needs to perform his role as far as being a commodity, a role that is only realised as the work force or as the controller of another's labour (see Chapter 1, Item 2).

each individual capital in search of valorisation, increasing and making more critical the need for capital to seek new spaces. It is a movement of capital expansion. As an essential and more apparent part of this need for the expansion of the basis of capital accumulation, is the search for new spaces to realise the surplus value which is expanded in line with the increased concentration in large individual capitals, as well as and mainly, for spaces for the continuity of the process of valorisation in an extended scale, for the realisation of new productive investments.

Completing the manner and the contradictions that the process of accumulation entails is the process of capital centralisation, the expropriation of the capitalist by capital itself, a process that impels each individual capital to expansion by the retraction of the mass of functioning capital in processes of productive restructuring (see Chapter 1). It is a process in this sense different from previous ones that, as Samir Amin states (2002:89), were "constructive and integrating", these were productive investments that the Triad countries made in the periphery, despite their shaping "an asymmetric dependent and unequal development" on a global scale. Differently, the process of global centralisation is one of disintegration, of retraction. Enlarged accumulation and concentration expand capital taking the contradictions to all the spaces. While centralisation is a response to the establishment of these contradictions, in a movement of retraction and exclusion. The main characteristic of the capital globalisation that occurred throughout the 1980s and 1990s is the centralisation of capitals on a global scale.

It is worth emphasising that these processes described above, in respect of their relationship with the internationalisation and globalisation of capital that will be detailed further on, are not arranged in a clearly separated or sequential order. They are dimensions of the same process. They are in a kind of spiral movement related to the territorial expansion of capital; they are produced and reproduced in each new space occupied by capital, reaching and occupying the whole world-space; they take the contradictions of the process to all the spaces, creating expansion and exclusion in this movement, growth and crisis, in each new place that it occupies, as much as on a global scale. They are movements of autonomous capital, free from any control.

The fact that some processes might not have been directly commented on in their international or global aspect in Marx, may raise the question whether this approach is relevant. But, when one bears in mind the nature of these processes in the form described by him, it becomes difficult not to relate them to accumulation on a global scale. Rosa Luxemburg, Lenin, Bukharin, Sweezy, Baran, Magdoff and, more recently, Palloix, Hobsbawn, Chesnais, Michalet and many others have worked on these relations starting from Marx, from his logic of accumulation, expounded in these terms. Perhaps, the only aspect less emphasised might be the impact of the process of capital centralisation on a global scale in what refers to its excluding aspect. This is perhaps because this has appeared more recently and with more dramatic impact on the periphery (Latin America), strengthened by the policies of deregulation and liberalisation, allowing the autonomy of capital.

2.2   The Question of Space for Accumulation

This form of approach also brings into discussion the geographic and political space. It tables extremely contradictory questions given that there does not exist capital without a frontier and without a state. Capital continues, in history, related to political frontiers. Even transnational, it needs the support of local and central states.

Capital fights to overcome the space and of state frontiers and, for this, contradictorily, uses frontiers and states; it destroys spaces to reconstruct them hierarchically around certain hegemonic centres within North-Atlantic area (Carroll, 2010). In this sense, at the same time in that capital denies space it reaffirms it. This contradiction is at the foundations of its unequal logic of expansion. It seeks to control and weaken the states and frontiers that impede free expansion and, simultaneously, strengthens the states and frontiers that give it protection and power,[5] thus defining the relationship of hegemony and domination. Really, it strengthens the central states on the hegemonic scale and seeks to control or weaken the peripheral states, centralising power in an analogous way to the centralisation of capital. "If there is some place in the world – beyond the dramatic decomposition of some African 'nearly-countries' – where one may speak about weak states or those made vulnerable by the process of globalisation, (...) this is the territory of the so-called emerging markets, in particular Latin America" (Fiori, 2001:66). This movement is part of the logic of accumulation and is present, today, in the establishment of the clusters around the Triad countries and in the formation of the periphery that takes part in the process.[6]

Frontiers and states influence the movement of accumulation, concentration and centralisation, at times positively and at others negatively, but little

---

5 Poulantzas, dealing with the central states says that "...to maintain ... that, as much as economic power increases and is concentrated, the more it takes power from the state, is to deny not only that the state possesses its own powers, but also that it intervenes in a decisive way in this concentration". (Poulantzas, 1975:86).
6 It deals here with the periphery included in the process that, according to Michalet, is made up of some 15 countries, among them Brazil. Argentina appears as an unknown (Michalet, 2002:147).

do they modify the logic of the nature of capital accumulation, unless when social pressures could impose themselves on the process of accumulation, as occurred in the golden years of the welfare state at the centre, or when the peripheral states imposed protectionist policies. At the same time that the political institution, on the one side, adds power to the process of accumulation through the protection it offers capital, at another time it appears as an obstacle to its freedom. At the same time that capital protects itself behind the nation state, strengthening itself by this veneer, it seeks to break the geographic and political barriers in its process of accumulation on an extended scale. If on the one hand it feeds upon it, on the other, it seeks to destroy it.

This de-territorialisation that characterises the movement of capital has the tendency to occupy all geographic spaces in an uneven way (Ianni, 1999:179). Inequality is not a new outcome of the process of accumulation given that it was always present, even when capital was more restricted to the national space. "If the Free Traders cannot understand how one nation can grow rich at the expense of another, we need not wonder, since these same gentlemen also refuse to understand how in the same country one class can enrich itself at the expense of another". (Marx, "Speech on the Question of Free Trade" in Marx-Engels collected works volume 6: pp. 464–465). The process of global accumulation reproduces this inequality, as well as reproducing and expanding exclusion on a global scale. "Globalisation tends to the polarisation of the global space. A large part of national economies are excluded from the movement and, in their majority, they are less developed countries" (Michalet, 2002:146). As it could not be otherwise, this polarisation has roots in the global movement of capital. Capital expands itself taking its form of existence and its contradictions to all spaces, in a process of creation and destruction, of integration and disintegration, of inclusion and exclusion.

If the occupation of geographic spaces is uneven, the way how capital frees itself from both geographic and political limitations defined by the state also differs. It is not the state itself that is undermined, but some states: the peripheral ones.

"The decisive criteria by which one classifies societies in the global capitalist system as 'central' and 'peripheral' ones is the character of its state. The central societies of capitalism are characterised by the crystallisation of a national bourgeois state, whose central role (apart from simply keeping the dominion of capital) is to control the conditions of accumulation through the national control that it exercises over the reproduction of the work force, the market, the centralisation of the surplus, the natural resources and the technology. The state here fulfils the conditions that allow a 'self-centred accumulation', that is, subjection of the (in most cases aggressively) external relations to the logic of accumulation. In contrast, the peripheral state (which like any other state performs the role of maintaining the internal domination of class) does not control local accumulation. Thus becoming – objectively – the instrument of 'adjustment' of the local society to the global demands of accumulation, for which changes of direction are determined by changes that occur at the centre" (Amin, 1990: Chapter 6).

Capital, by the logic expounded by Marx, could never be restricted to a geographic area and when it bursts into space it is not changing its nature. Historically it has come bursting into spaces, by its movements of accumulation, concentration and centralisation. In this movement, capital free from any control, leads to inclusion as much as exclusion, nowadays on a global scale and not only in each place where it is. It thus separates the centre from the periphery; when it occupies the global-space it makes exclusion not only a local phenomenon, but a world one, excluding entire countries in its movement of centralisation.

"The need of a constantly expanding market for its products chases the bourgeoisie over the whole surface of the globe. It must nestle everywhere, settle everywhere, establish connections everywhere. The bourgeoisie has through its exploitation of the world market given a cosmopolitan character to production and consumption in every country it has drawn from under the feet of industry the national ground on which it stood. All old-established national industries have been destroyed or are daily being destroyed. In place of the old wants, satisfied by the productions of the country, we find new wants, requiring for their satisfaction the products of distant lands..." (Marx, Manifesto of the Communist Party p. 488 – in Marx-Engels collective works volume 6)

2.3 Globalisation: Accumulation and Concentration

Capital has a tendency to occupy global spaces owing to its own nature, its own movement in a permanent and obligatory search for valorisation of value. This movement is manifest in the direct investment of transnational companies seeking their existence and continuity as capital.

It might perhaps be pertinent to ask why highlight capital accumulation, given that this is the synthesis of the process that characterises the mode of capitalist production and leads, at least historically, to concentration and centralisation. Accumulation is the movement that ensures the existence of value as capital that "...can be understood only as a motion, not as a thing at rest. Those who regard the gaining by value of independent existence as a mere abstraction forget that the movement of industrial capital is this abstraction in *actu...*" (Marx II, 1887b:61). In a way, that is why accumulation is independent of the concentration and centralisation of capital, but is strengthened and leveraged by them.

Authors such as Sweezy and Baran (1978), and Lenin himself[7] (1987), strongly relate the process of capital globalisation[8] to monopoly capital, clearly identifying the formation of monopolies in certain places to the expansion of capital, the movement of occupying new places in the world. Certainly the degree of concentration and centralisation of capital drives its movement in the direction of occupying new spaces in a much more dramatic form given the exacerbating contradictions that capital finds in its original space of accumulation, as much as its own need for expansion for the continuity of valorisation. Monopoly capital leverages a process that is already present in its accumulating nature. But, it is here emphasised that the process of capital accumulation embodies in itself an intrinsic characteristic that imposes expansion, independent of its degree of monopolisation. The search for new spaces for the accumulation of capital leveraged by monopolisation demonstrates that in capitalism there exists no alternative apart from accumulation on an extended, growing scale, at the risk of perishing, of stopping existing as capital. That is the constant pressure that individual capital suffers to transform the surplus value created into new capital, restarting the process of valorisation of value. "Employing surplus value as capital, reconverting it into capital, is called accumulation of capital" (Marx I, 1887a:288). This process leads capital to expand its spaces from the local to the national and global.

It is worth emphasising that this is not exclusively a process depicted by Marx. Keynes in his "General Theory" (1982), far from being a Marxist, on analysing the logic of capitalism, demonstrated the pre-eminent need for investment, of the reinvestment of the value created in the process of production into new capital, to use Marx's terms, always on a growing scale, to permit the flow of accumulation is realised and for the system not to enter into crisis (Keynes, 1982:95; see also Chick, 1993:27). For Keynes, the investment decision of companies is the central element for maintaining the dynamic of accumulation, ensuring also the realisation of the value created. Keynes starts from the viewpoint of the problem of realisation, of the obligatory demand for

---

7 For Lenin, monopoly capital is what embodies the movement of internationalisation (Lenin, 1987:60).
8 In fact they termed the process of internationalisation. Despite using the terms globalisation and internationalisation they will be strongly linked, their specificity is almost a semantic question for what is here proposed. The use of internationalisation is linked to the idea of capital crossing frontiers, and globalisation, conveys more the idea of occupation of the global space (see Chesnais, 1996, Michalet, 1983 & 2002).

continuity in the process, which is not that of consumers in general, but that of the capitalists, investment, that must be always growing to maintain the flow and guarantee the employment of resources. While for Marx, the question of expansion of the process of accumulation on an extended scale is not only related to realisation itself, but in the growing need for capital valorisation imposed on each individual capitalist, reinforced by the process of capital concentration and centralisation.

On the other hand, for Keynes, differing from Marx, as the problem is related exclusively to realisation, the constant need for growing investment does not obligatorily imply the globalisation of capital. It may be realised within a nation as long as the growing circular flow occurs, being restricted to the size of income, the income distribution, to the level of employment and to the size of the population. That is why, for Keynes, it is a process that can be managed by the state[9] to control the havoc that it provokes (unemployment and crisis, natural in a free market economy). For Marx, on the contrary, capital cannot be restricted by these elements; the process of accumulation would in fact enter into crisis, because, apart from being blocked from its expanded accumulation, it creates in the restricted space of accumulation contradictions that also entail problems of realisation. Thus, the central problem identified by Marx is that capital accumulation in its dynamic cannot be restricted to a single space, or, in other words, the restricted space limits expanded accumulation. The main reason for this is, partly, in the contradictions (unemployment, exclusion) created by the movement of accumulation itself that makes it difficult to realise value; on the other hand, it is in the possibility of increasing the rhythm and the breadth of accumulation freeing itself from these local constraints. Restricted space limits accumulation, a limitation that is overcome by the expansion of capital throughout the world, globalisation, and by centralisation in the local space in a process of removing the excess functioning capitals (see Chapter 1) compensating in part the spatial limit. A limit that will reappear on a global scale when the world-space useful to accumulation also becomes restricted.

"The development of capitalist production makes it constantly necessary to keep increasing the amount of the capital laid out in a given industrial undertaking, and competition makes the immanent laws of capitalist production to be felt by each individual capitalist, as external coercive laws. It compels him to keep constantly extending his capital, in order to preserve it, but extend it he cannot, except by means of progressive accumulation". (Marx I, 1887a:295) "It must never be forgotten that the production of this surplus value – and the

---

9 See Robinson, 1964:92.

reconversion of a portion of it into capital, or the accumulation, forms an integrated part of this production of surplus value – is the immediate purpose and compelling motive of capitalist production". (Marx III, 1894:168)

Thus, one could say that to ensure the movement of capital on an increasingly scale – in line with what the process itself demands to maintain capital as capital, value in the process of valorisation, that guarantees the constant transformation of money into capital – presupposes the search for new spaces in order that new investments occur. In this sense, it is implicit in the movement itself of accumulation in an increasing scale the irrelevance of any kind of restriction, be it political or geographical, to the process of accumulation. These restrictions would be external factors to the movement of capital itself that could imply impediments to its accumulation on an increasing scale. The only restriction to this expansion will be the world-space itself useful for accumulation.

This process of capital accumulation on a global scale is realised by the action of individual capitals. Thus, as they embody increasing scale capital accumulation in general, it is they who also go out to seek the occupation of global space. Each individual capital is obliged to move itself, to grow not only in scale, but in control over markets and over the spaces available for accumulation to ensure its existence. The corporation, as individual real capital, is required to maintain its surplus value in the appreciation process, a condition for its existence. "...The constant augmentation of his capital becomes a condition of its preservation" (Marx II, 1887b:45). The expiry of a company in capitalism is linked to its inaction in relation to the movement of capital in general, that is the movement as a whole, embodied, as social capital (not individual) in its rivals or competitors.

Michael E. Porter, far from being a Marxist, on analysing how companies moving to seek competitive advantage works, puts this need of capital embodied in the operation of the company in the following way: "The nascent global industrial leaders always begin with some advantage created internally, be it a preferred product model, a higher level of product quality, a new concept of business or cost advantage factors. *But, the continuation of success generally demands that the firm does not stop there.* The advantage obtained in the base country becomes, then, the lever for entry in foreign markets. Once there, the successful global competitor complements the initial internal advantage with economies of scale..." (Porter, 1989:76 – my italics).

So clearly this movement of capital expansion in its process of increased accumulation is what guarantees the continuity of the "success" of the corporation. It ends up by extrapolating frontiers in search of new places to continue the process of valorisation of value or, of maintaining the existence of individual capital as such. It is a process driven by concrete microeconomic actions undertaken by specific agents, realised in movements of global foreign direct investment – FDI. These microeconomic agents are transnational companies that are obliged to act in this way so as not to be crushed by the movement of capital itself, which, in fact, is to succumb to competition or see their rates of profit reduced.

The intrinsic need of capital to maintain the process of accumulation on an increasing scale explains the centre's investment in the periphery as much as that between the countries of the centre.

"In this new and continuously evolving environment, the key strategic issue for firms becomes how to survive and prosper, knowing that there is a market for firms and that sanctions await them if they fail to deliver growth and profits ... All the basic motivations for firms to undertake cross-border mergers and acquisitions then combine to become key elements in the overarching strategic goal to defend and develop competitive positions" (UNCTAD 2000:153).

2.4 Concentration

The concentration of capital that results from the process of accumulation on an increasing scale itself strengthens and complements this movement. It is characterised by the expansion of the basis of accumulation of an individual capital, the increase of its capacity to extract the surplus value (see Chapter 1). Normally this process is confused with the centralisation of capital because the latter results nearly always in greater concentration, in the expansion of the basis of accumulation of an individual capital, although, at the same time it may be linked to a reduction in the mass of functioning capital in general. In crises, centralisation occurs because the basis of accumulation was reduced, making the stronger capitals remove the weaker in the contest for the remaining space for accumulation. But, an individual capital does not need centralisation in order to be concentrated. Concentration is the result of capital accumulation itself in which "Every accumulation becomes the means of new accumulation. With the increasing mass of wealth which functions as capital, accumulation increases the concentration of wealth in the hands of individual capitalists, and thereby widens the basis of production on a large scale and of the specific methods of capitalist production" (Marx I, 1887a:310)

This process contributes to increasing the need to seek new spaces of accumulation, exerting pressure for an even greater globalisation, given the growing mass of surplus value that it placed in the hands of individual capitals and obliges them to maintain the process of valorisation, in order not to perish. It forces them to seek other spaces for accumulation, independently of local limits. Abroad becomes a "spillway for the investible excess created in the sector of large companies of the system" (Sweezy and Baran, 1978:110), and this excess is what grows the greater the degree of concentration of capitalist production in the hands of large capitals. It is the leveraging of the nature of accumulation that now impels capital beyond frontiers.

Charles-Albert Michalet (1983 and 2002) and François Chesnais (1996), going further than the form expounded by Sweezy and Baran – that related excess much more to its financial component (as did Lenin, 1987) – , are authors that call this capital movement in the sense of occupying all the spaces, of expansion of capital beyond frontiers, the process of "capital globalisation". Globalisation transforms individual capital into transnational capital that, in acting as a transnational corporation, experiences constant pressure to expand its basis of accumulation "denying the local space (national or regional) through the movement of the transfer of the place of value formation" (Michalet,1983:127). It exports capital through productive investments, creating productive structures in relevant areas that leverage accumulation and strengthen it. This movement follows the logic of competitiveness and of oligopolistic competition by transnational firms in a process of expansion throughout the world (Michalet, 2002:27–57). Historically, according to Michalet, Hobsbawn (1995), or Chesnais too, this capital movement takes shape and becomes predominant on a global scale between the 1960s and the 1980s in the form of productive foreign direct investment – FDI.

"In fact, in the 1970s, observers began to call attention to a new 'international division of labour', or rather, a massive transfer of industries ... of industrial economies, that previously monopolised them, to other parts of the world. This is due ... to ... the move, by companies from the old industrial world, of part of ... its production to the second and third worlds..." (Hobsbawn, 1995:354).

Despite expansion across the world characterised by an intrinsic need for the continuity of accumulation, the motives that lead transnational corporations to choose other places to invest are related to control of the market and competition: distance, protectionism, financial systems, habits of consumption and risks of losing competitiveness (Michalet, 1983:147–149, and also Michalet, 2002). The multinational company aims to reduce uncertainty and the risk of expiring as individual capital manifested in the loss of competitiveness, in the difficulty of realisation of value, involving the loss of control over markets where it operates and where its competitor acts. Integration on a global scale through verticalisation or horizontalisation is the way of maintaining control over markets and minimising risks from disrupting the process of expanded accumulation; the road is to globalise through direct investment. This set of motives is linked to the pressure that capital experiences in order to always accumulate on an increasing scale; it is this that moves the individual capitalist and that allows his existence as capital. The pressure for constant valorisation of value which is in the nature of capital is manifested, for the individual capitalist, as competition and competiveness (see also Hymer, 1978, Chapter 3).

According to Palloix (1971), this process, which he calls productive internationalisation, is characterised by the consolidation of multinational (transnational) companies as centres of global capital accumulation from productive investments around the world. And, as one will seek to demonstrate, the centralisation of capital on a global scale is the result of this occupation, following what occurred previously in the local space, only that it does not carry within itself a movement of expansion as concentration movement but of retraction.

2.5 Accumulation and Concentration: The Question of Political-Geographic Space

In this movement, the company or corporation that is created and is strengthened under the protection of a specific state expands its operations to other places in the world occupying, in these new places, productive processes that it already dominated in its area of origin. There are various ways to exercise this type of control over productive processes outside the original area, and these forms are modified according to the industrial sector, technology, inputs used etc. Some of them are generalised for production in other places: the installation of subsidiaries, partnerships with local companies, acquisitions, mergers, joint-ventures or outsourcing.[10]

At any rate, this search by capital to surpass the local space (the word "search" in this context is important because recent history has still not seen any suppression of frontiers) is not homogenous for each state. In the central powerful states, capital enjoys a certain historic "protection" that ensures its strengthening and wards off the idea of the weakening of this state in that which affects

---

10 Outsourcing is characterised as a more modern form in some sectors, in which the multinational or transnational company transfers a certain onus of the production process – management of personnel, unexpected circumstantial, local costs and risks – to third party firms (Chesnais, 1996:35) by contract without losing control over the production process and without appearing as the local producer. Depending on the relation of power between the leading company and the outsourced, not even a contract is necessary, as is traditional between car assemblers in Brazil and parts suppliers.

its role in stopping the process of accumulation. The change that occurs in this centre-state has as its basis its relationship with transnational capital, "passing from a system in which the networks of accumulation were embedded in the networks of power and subordinated to it, to a system that the networks of power are included in the networks of accumulation and subordinated to these" (Arrighi, 1996:88), but without losing its symbiotic relationship.

"Even though the stronger nation states continue to perform imperialist tasks, to formulate geo-economies and geo-policies, their prerogatives are no longer those of 'classic' imperialism. At the side of nation states, even the strongest, transnational corporations are already positioned and impose themselves. These have also been transformed into global structures of power. In so far as the corporations acquire the strength, the versatility and the generality that is manifest with the globalisation of capitalism, by the same measure they are reduced or subordinated to the possibilities of the nation states, that were the representatives par excellence of imperialism and of interdependency" (Ianni, 1999:186).

This is not exactly what occurs in less powerful or peripheral states. The tendency for capital in its movement of globalisation is to seek to weaken and control these weaker states, with at times military help, of the stronger states, in the sense of subordinating these weaker states to the movement of globalised capital, according to the interests of capitals of the central states. Thus appears the idea that the pressure for the suppression of states or frontiers brings with it an unequal character. Capital undertakes this enterprise not destroying the institutional structure that supplies support to it, but weakening or co-opting those that block its road to accumulation. "In monopoly capitalism, the creation and realisation of surplus value passes obligatorily through political domination, as well as economic" (Palloix I, 1971:22). That is a tendency that acts as much on the central state as that of the periphery. The difference is that the peripheral state is weakened under pressure from the hegemonic states as well as globalised capital.

Apart from this, the process of capital expansion is not generalised in the regions of the world. Globalisation is a process related only to a set of regions/countries where there are resources or markets. This strengthens even more their exclusion and poverty creation aspects. Some regions are, from the beginning, excluded from the process (Chesnais, 1996:32), there is a tendency to the hierarchal polarisation of the world (Michalet, 2002:147). Thus, the process of capital expansion is organised starting from the hegemonic centres formed around the countries of the Triad or are North-Atlantic centred, starting from which capital projects itself across the world. This polarisation will be radicalised by the process of centralisation of global capital in a movement of return to the centre based on the greater relative autonomy of transnational capital.

As Chesnais states, in one thing the authors Rosa Luxemburg, Trotsky, Hilferding, Bukharin and Lenin agree: "the unity of the global economy, its integration is increasingly closer ... in a system of relations moulded by capital dominated by the central countries" (Chesnais, 1996:48). Despite these authors being situated at the beginning of the last century, they are, as Chesnais demonstrates, still very current in explaining this reality.

2.6 Internationalisation as the Realisation of Value

Commercial internationalisation as a component that seeks to ensure the realisation of value is, historically, the point of the spear of capital's occupation of geographical spaces. It is worth remembering that capitalism was born from the growth of trade that gradually occupied from the regional spaces to the global space, a movement which always involved mechanisms of domination and political control over markets and regions.

This means that it was already born as a world-system. Productive internationalisation, globalisation, comes as a consequence of this movement, it modifies it, but very far from suppressing it, it maintains it. "The notion of the global economy encompasses simultaneously the phenomena relating to circulation and production. This transfer from the field of the traditional analysis of circulation to the process of production must be accompanied by the supremacy of this over that" (Michalet, 1983:11)[11]

Despite realisation (a trade problem) having been approached always as the central phenomenon of the internationalisation of capital, it is only one of the parts that make up the process of capital accumulation. It is about a part of the turnover of capital, the sale of the commodity, the realisation of value as commodity. That is why, despite its importance in the process of accumulation, given that without realisation, the process may be paralysed and enter into crisis, it is only a part of the process. The valorisation of capital does not occur in exchange for commodities, finished goods, but in the specific exchange that occurs between capital and labour, the real source of value. It is not in an exchange of commodities that value is created. Realisation is responsible for economic crises that normally appear as circumstantial crises and not as structural crises of the mode of capitalist production. They alter the structure only

---

11   Despite this fact, the manuals of international economy are still extremely focussed on the trade relations between countries.

in so far that these crises become catalysing factors for centralisation. It is not that realisation is a minor aspect in the turnover of capital, but it deals only in the transformation of the commodity into money and not in valorisation itself. The realisation of the commodity as value, "salto mortale of the commodity" (Marx I, 1887a:59), may, accelerate, brake or paralyse the process of capital accumulation (Marx II, 1887b:60), interfering directly in the rotation of capital, but not its centre.

At any rate, realisation is one of the aspects that had already been directly focussed by Marx as one of the reasons for the internationalisation of capital. "The tendency to create the world market is directly given in the concept of capital itself. Every limit appears as a barrier to be overcome" (Marx, p. 341, Grundrisse From http://www.marxists.org/archive/marx/works/1857/grundrisse/index.html Converted to eBook by Andrew Lannan.). Thus, the search for new markets surpassing the local area is an intrinsic characteristic of the movement of capital in its process of accumulation on an increasing scale.

Realisation extrapolating the local, regional and national space is related to the contradictions embodied in the process of accumulation itself. In the first place, it is the result of the over-accumulation of capital resulting from the inherent need each individual capital has in replacing the surplus value created in the new process of accumulation. In second place, it is a consequence of the differences in the turnover periods of the various individual capitals that result in circumstantial cycles of realisation, often unconnected, that may temporarily interrupt the cycle, resulting in crises of realisation. In third place, it results from its own excluding nature inherent in the process of accumulation that excludes the worker in so far that it replaces live work by constant capital and (dead work), apart from this, excludes the capitalists themselves, in so far that capital is centralised.

These crises of realisation that result from the accumulation on an extended scale may result in crises of over-production (Luxemburg, 1983) or of under-consumption (Sweezy & Baran, 1978). According to these authors, they may be overcome by exporting excess commodities, leading to commercial internationalisation. Luxemburg is the principal theorist of the logic of capital internationalisation through the export of commodities. She has a clear understanding of the functioning of capitalism when she states that "the reproductive process becomes a requirement, a condition of economic existence, unavoidable for individual capitalists" (Luxemburg, 1983:19).But she sees the main incongruence of accumulation, the problem of realisation that impedes the system from maintaining reproduction. Internationalisation for her, therefore, is linked to disruptions to the turnover of capital that result from the need for capital expansion that does not find within its frontiers the possibility of realising the surplus value produced. It therefore needs, according to her, internationalisation not only as a condition to maintain accumulation on an extended scale, but, as a way of increasing the extraction of surplus value, which it does by the destruction of traditional local forms. It is interesting to note the destructive aspect that this process of internationalisation entails on traditional economies, eliminating local production, a movement that opens up space for transnational corporation occupation, a fact not stressed by the authoress but entailed as a logical result.

Thus, for her, the limits to realisation in the local space are what impede the continuity of valorisation to the point of stating that there is no possibility for the accumulation of capital in an isolated society (Luxemburg, 1983:298). Apart from this, for her, these elements impose an international relationship of the centre-periphery type.

It is important to underline certain aspects resulting from her analysis. The contradiction present in the process of accumulation that results in exclusion and reduction of the capacity of realisation in fact impedes the continuity of accumulation when restricted to the local market. This is because the excess to be realised, at each cycle of capital turnover, is growing by the nature of the process of creation and recreation of value itself. This imposes on capital the search for new places for realisation of value. On the other hand, on occupying new areas, capital finds not only potential for the realisation of the surplus that stopped being realised in its place of origin, but, mainly, it expands the capacity of capital expansion given that it widens the potential for consumption, the possibility of realisation, on conquering new markets. This is a complementary factor that is independent of the crises of realisation at the original centre. Overcoming frontiers in the field of realisation expands the potential for capital accumulation. This, which has been happening throughout history is embodied in the logic developed by Luxemburg.

Thus, it involves the idea that capital in fact seeks new markets to ensure its growth, and the more markets it controls, the greater will be its potential for growth and greater will be its capacity to have under its dominion a significant mass of surplus value. Capital historically widens its basis for realisation, be it, in the past, by the conquest of colonies based on the military power of their states of origin, be it today by direct control over these markets, by its actual presence in the area of global accumulation that interests to it. Through direct investment in the periphery, a consequence of the growth in sales of certain companies in distant markets, it will end up by occupying the space left by the destruction of local production, strengthening its activity as transnational capital. The supply of loans or political pressures on the periphery to place certain products in a potential market are other means of control (also noted by Luxemburg), that also become central when the aim is direct investment. The need to search for new areas for realisation is, therefore, an integral part of the process of capital accumulation in that which affects the expansion of capacity or speed of capital turnover; it is also the point of the spear of the contradictions of the process of accumulation for the world-space that will result in the occupation of the periphery by the productive apparatus of the centre itself.

On the other hand, some elements that push capital beyond its local spaces are modified in history starting from the globalisation of capital itself that only had its beginning in the problems of realisation. It is important to highlight that today, the logic of capital in seeking markets outside of its frontiers, in the lack of capacity for realisation in the local place as proposed by Luxemburg, seems to assume an inverted format in relation to the centre-periphery. Regions, mainly formed by peripheral industrialised countries based on foreign direct investment – FDI that have enormous internal inequality of income (brought the contradiction to within their frontiers) and, thus, have internal realisation impaired, they help their strategies of development in exports, in the realisation of surplus value abroad, as mechanisms of capital valorisation.

Hence, the mode of submission of the periphery is also altered given that today what defines the flow of commodities in the world is the pre-existent flow of FDI. It is the decision of productive localisation of companies in their various types that define the flow of commodities in the world. "It is FDI and the strategies of localisation chosen by multinational companies that command a very important part of the cross-frontier flows of commodities and services, contributing strongly to modelling the structure of the system of interchange ... Its organisation is the result of the combined interaction of states and the main agents of the capitalist economy, that are today industrial groups and large banks, acting in response to the pressure of a set of opportunities (of profit) and of economic, political and technological obligations". (Chesnais, 1996:212). Therefore, the question of realisation of surplus value in the global market continues to be present, but the dislocation of production, a movement of capital itself manifest in the FDI of transnational companies is what comes to orchestrate global realisation (trade). They thus alter the characteristics of submission of the periphery in relation to the way posited by Luxemburg. The periphery (most Latin-American one) continues with a subordinate role, but part of it has become quite industrialised. Another part of the periphery, is simply abandoned not containing even space for realisation. Going a little further, as will be highlighted below, even the industrialised portion has its future threatened by new relations that are imposed based on the process of global centralisation accelerated by the policies of liberalisation and deregulation, mainly on the periphery.

In this way a new problem is posed. If before the global market, in the "unoccupied" periphery, served to ensure the realisation of the excess produced in the centre, today, this peripheral space has been occupied by the expansion of capital. The question that is raised then is where will it continue this expansion or occupation? For Luxemburg, capitalism would enter into crisis. For what one intends to demonstrate here, capitalism can adjust itself, as in fact has been occurring historically, but not by a movement of expansion, but by its opposite, the movement of centralisation of capitals that had always occurred in local spaces (as Marx noted) as a counter-balancing factor to temporary crises, alongside the previously possible expansion of capital worldwide. This adjustment to the process of accumulation arises through the qualitative reorganisation of individual capitals in the world with the removal of part of them in a global process of capital centralisation. This point will be taken up again further on.

2.7 Realisation, Internationalisation and the Political-Geographic Space

In the logic of commercial internationalisation, the form of action of capital, in the sense of controlling space, mainly the peripheral, is much clearer, also in its unequal aspect. Luxemburg and Lenin explain it by the concept of imperialism given that control over markets is exercised directly by the central states through military power in alliance with productive and banking capital. The new forms of international relationships involved mainly in accumulation on an extended scale itself, in concentration and centralisation also entail the concept of imperialism given that they are centred on hegemony and control, not only based on commerce. But the concept of imperialism is much more evident in the case of commercial internationalisation – still present today – given its military character. The process of globalisation also embodies within it the same concept only in a more subliminal domination based on an apparently economic aspect, given that it has in front of it transnational capital that is installed within the space of the states that it seeks to control, "imposing on each country, its parties and governments a certain line of conduct" (Chesnais, 1996:34).

It is worth raising some points. On the one hand, capital, in its search for realisation beyond frontiers, has its movement in the sense of seeking to weaken them in their political aspects. This movement exercised by commercial internationalisation is involved in power relations between states. In the past, these power relations were based on military capacity and led to two huge world wars. Later, during the process of productive internationalisation of capital in the post-war, the states of the central countries did not hide from supporting dictators on the periphery that guaranteed the interests of their large capitals (Schoultz, 1999).Today, despite recent facts demonstrating that this "military face" is present more than ever, it is weakened, given that capital, by foreign direct investment made by multinational companies, has occupied different regions and modified the relations of economic power over them, changing itself into a new form of imperialism. That is why, the exercise of this power over the spaces continues unequal and the periphery continues being so. Capital puts pressure on all spaces and states, but manages to weaken only the peripheral countries (including with arms if necessary) and not the central countries. On the contrary, it is the strengthening of the state at the centre that defines its power of control over the periphery, the weakening of the peripheral state.

"The reality of the modern world-system, the capitalist economic world, is about a hierarchical, unequal and polarised system, whose political structure is one of an interstate system in which some states are manifestly stronger than others. To help the incessant process of capital accumulation, the stronger states are constantly imposing their will on the weaker states, in so far as they can do. This is called imperialism and is something inherent in the structure of the world system" (Wallerstein, 2004:138).

At any rate, commercial internationalisation is characterised by the state as centre of its articulation, the element that goes in front, whilst the globalisation of capital, typified by productive investment and by the installation of productive plants in different places, is articulated by transnational capital based in corporations (Arrighi, 1996:88). Thus the appearance of dominion is modified over the process but not the symbiotic relation between the state and capital. Capital continues relying on the power of the central state and in the co-option of the peripheral state.

2.8 Capital Centralisation

The process of accumulation itself, as much as the concentration that results from it, intrinsic outcomes of the nature of capital accumulation on an increasing scale, as much as the problems of realisation, make capital seek to go beyond the local area and move towards accumulation on a global scale. They are processes that expand capitalism according to the precepts of accumulation: they seek places that guarantee accumulation and realisation so that they may have resources and markets, and give a level of a rate of return (extracted surplus) to maintain the process of expanded accumulation. As pointed out by Samir Amin, these are "integrating" processes and creators of interdependencies, although they affect places and regions in an unequal way and, the opposite of reducing the differences of unequal development, it leverages them. They are part of the expansion of capital in the world. As pointed out in Chapter 1, accumulation and the concentration of capital are processes of expansion of individual capital as much as capital in general.

"Imperialist capital continues its forward march, exporting new capitals to conquer new spaces, submitting them to its expansion. In this sense, capital pursues in its 'constructive' vocation, it integrates more [places] than it excludes" (Amin, 2002:87). The problem is that now, as the author himself states, "Everything points to this page of 'constructive' expansion as perhaps having been turned" (ibid: 88). Everything seems to imply that the process of capital centralisation on a world scale has turned this page.

This results from the polarising nature of the process itself "putting an end to a centuries-old trend that was going in the direction of integration and convergence. Polarisation is, in the first place, internal to each country. The effects of unemployment are inseparable from those resulting from the distancing between the highest and the lowest incomes. ...In second place, there is international polarisation, brutally widening the distance between countries situated in the core of the global oligopoly and those countries of the periphery" (Chesnais, 1986:37).

Despite centralisation being a process resulting from the nature of accumulation itself and its contradictions, it is excluding by nature. It was already so, as much in its local as in its national context; now it is on a global scale. It occurred in the local space when contradictions made continuity of the process of accumulation unsustainable and superfluous capitals had to be eliminated or devalued in order that the process of accumulation might continue on new bases. This is a process that is now occurring on a global scale when these same contradictions are globalised and, at the same time, capital gains more autonomy with liberalisation and deregulation policies that they themselves, in this specific case through their nation state representatives, impose mainly on the periphery.

"This does not mean that simple concentration of the means of production and of the command over labour, which is identical with accumulation. It is concentration of capitals already formed, destruction of their individual independence, expropriation of capitalist by capitalist, transformation of many small into few large capitals. This process differs from the former in this, that it only presupposes a change in the distribution of capital already to hand, and functioning; *its field of action is therefore not limited by the absolute growth of social wealth, by the absolute limits of accumulation.* Capital grows in one place to a huge mass in a single hand, because it has in another place been lost by many. This is centralisation proper, as distinct from accumulation and concentration". (Marx I, 1887a:310 – my emphasis).

Centralisation marks, therefore, the expropriation of capital at its highest level: first, capital expropriates labour, after, in the process of centralisation, it expropriates the capitalist himself (Marx III, 1894:169). Thus, it denies capital as the property of an individual to affirm it as an autonomous entity, by the suppression of its individual autonomy; it marks, the separation between the individual and the process of accumulation; it affirms capital as a social being that has its action in the sense of accumulation on an extended scale, manifested in the action of the large company, corporation or transnational group. It is a process that strengthens and drives capital to a high degree of autonomy (see Chapter 1 in this book, Mészáros, 2002:97, and Baran & Sweezy, 1978:39) as capital that occurred in the local space and now occurs on a global scale. This is not a specific movement of centralisation, but of accumulation itself, but centralisation, in so far that it transforms many individual capitals into few, leverages this autonomy.

On the other hand, the centralisation of capital at the same time in which it exacerbates the contradictions of the process of accumulation, conversely, being the mechanism for the qualitative reordering of the productive structure by the destruction of superfluous capital, by the centralisation of many capitals into just one, it is a process that permits the individual capital that survives to be strengthened and preserve its level of profitability faced with the contradictions created by accumulation itself on a large scale (see Chapter 1). On presupposing simply a new division of the capitals that are already functioning, it guarantees the individual capitals that remain either a larger slice of the surplus value generated or the maintenance of the volume of this surplus value in the hands of a smaller quantity of individual capitals. Thus, the result of the process may be to raise the rate of profit of those that remain as much as to simply maintain it under the "absolute limits of accumulation" as Marx states. At the same time that it excludes and exacerbates the contradictions imposing limits on accumulation, it ensures its continuity and the profitability of the individual capital that remains, at least until the new wave of centralisations.

This process is manifest in the action of transnational companies, in the form of productive and administrative restructuring (often called "re-engineering") or in the form of mergers, acquisitions, joint-ventures and other types of accords[12] and contracts such as outsourcing. It may thus involve "...a network of subcontracting, in which, legally autonomous companies and those not controlled by a shareholding, do not constitute autonomous capitals from the point of view of capital valorisation". Thus they may function as companies involved in portions of valorisation process or integrated production lines. The degree of integration depends on the technical-economic relations over which no individual company has influence (Aglietta, 1979:196). These forms of centralisation aim to increase or maintain the profitability of each individual capital. It is an action that occurs in the context of the power over individual capitals whose aims are always to remove competition so as to raise the rate of profits, freeing individual capital from risks and uncertainties.

Centralisation always gains greater impetus in circumstantial crises, normally connected to problems of realisation and to the fall in the rate of profits, the results of contradictions themselves in the movement of capital. At these times, the strongest capitals survive through the expropriation of weaker ones, resulting in greater centralisation. Capital destroys a part of itself to maintain and strengthen itself as capital on a smaller basis of accumulation and realisation, resulting from the crisis.

Thus, the process of centralisation, at the same time in which it exacerbates the contradictions, feeds upon them. It leverages the contradictions because is excludes not only labour but also the capitalist himself, reducing the basis of realisation itself of the value created. On the other hand, it strengthens the capitals that overcome the crisis on the smaller basis of accumulation, creating new conditions for the development of accumulation. The process of capital centralisation acts therefore as an element of compensation for the crises of realisation, maintaining the process of accumulation as a whole, on a basis of reduced accumulation, in which a reduced number of individual capitals participate (Aglietta, 1979:196).

Crises of realisation have in fact demonstrated that they do not make the process of accumulation unfeasible, be they of under-consumption or of over-accumulation as Luxemburg thought. She also thought that this problem would mark "the final period of capitalism" (Luxemburg, 1983:364) when it becomes generalised throughout the world. The process of capital centralisation is, on the contrary, strengthened by these movements of crisis by stimulating a rearrangement of the productive structure and in the division of surplus value between capitals, strengthening the remaining individual capitals. The result is always an increase in the numbers of excluded, exacerbating the

---

12 A series of examples of inter-relationships between companies in search of maintaining profitability is given by Porter (1998: Chapter 9).

contradictions, stimulating new crises and new rounds of centralisation, but it removes the idea of the end of capitalism for this reason, given that it strengthens the surviving capitals. "...The destruction of a part of capital ... reduces the total mass of capital employed in production and provides new possibilities for valorisation for all the capitals" (Aglietta, 1979:196).

And this does not create incongruences for the process of accumulation in itself, at least whilst the hypothesis is not taken to its extreme. On the contrary, the process is capable not only of maintaining itself as to preserve or increase the rate of profit for the individual capitals that survive. This is because there is no contradiction between high rates of profit and a large contingent of the excluded as Keynes demonstrated well. Capitalism for him, may be in equilibrium below full employment, of the full occupation of the "resources". This reduces the potential for accumulation from the macroeconomic viewpoint but does not make the system unfeasible (Keynes, 1982:40) from the point of view of the microeconomic, individual capital.

At any rate, if the argument that centralisation, as a form of capital solves the problems of circumstantial crises or of under-accumulation, was taken to its limit, in an exercise of "futurology", there would only remain a large group responsible for all production (Marx I, 1887a:311) and only those that took part would have access to income, employment and goods, whilst the rest would be completely excluded and impoverished, as commented by Lenin in his preface to Bukharin's work (1984:11) and by Mandel (1982:235) commenting Lenin's statement. But, this is not a probable scenario, given the perhaps more accurate hypothesis might be the one that would much earlier have been established, the opposite of the revolution predicted by Mandel[13] and Marx,[14] the chaos described by Kurtz in his "The Collapse of Modernisation" (1992), given the volume of the excluded.

The process of centralisation also experiences an additional pressure that goes beyond its own contradictions from the process of accumulation. It is accelerated by the pressure to obtain a level of profitability imposed by the

---

13 "Lenin himself did not exclude in any way, evidently, the possibility of a greater international concentration and centralisation of capital – including those of the big imperialist powers: in fact he expressly stated that the long term historic tendency was heading 'logically' towards a single global trust. But he was convinced that much before this development reaches this point, imperialism would suffer a collapse, as much in consequence of its internal contradictions as the revolutionary struggle of the oppressed peoples" (Mandel, 1982:235).

14 " A development of productive forces which would diminish the absolute number of labourers, i.e., enable the entire nation to accomplish its total production in a shorter time span, would cause a revolution, because it would put the bulk of the population out of the running" (Marx III, 1894:180).

rationale of finance capital on productive capital. This fact imposes on the companies, processes of restructuring and re-engineering that accelerate the waves of centralisation. In the same way, it imposes or is directly responsible for accords, mergers and acquisitions aimed at increasing the profitability of companies to the level of profitability of finance capital. Banks have specific departments for the realisation of this type of business between companies, acting as brokers, even before they are sought out. Thus, in the globalisation stage where direct productive investments predominated, the element that moved the multinational was more related to the competitive growth of the company. Today, this imposition of high profitability has come to drive the companies' actions: the principle of competitiveness is surpassed by the principle of profitability (Michalet, 2002:109).

Deregulation and liberalisation policies also act in the same direction of increasing centralisation. Given that the centralisation of capital is an integral part of the process of accumulation and is much strengthened faced with these policies that are demanded or imposed on nation states by capital itself, mainly on the peripheral states. Liberalisation and deregulation are specific mechanisms that result in ending the logic of accumulation exclusively in the hands of capital. Free capital tends, in its movement of accumulation that has already created exclusion locally, to now exclude entire regions globally.

Going somewhat further, the policies of liberalisation and deregulation that often appear as mechanisms for attracting and keeping transnational capital in the (included) industrialised periphery, at the same time in which it attracts them, contradictorily it also exacerbates the exclusion given that: it allows the transnational capitals to eliminate national capitals; it reorganises the production of the companies installed in the periphery increasing unemployment; it eliminates local production replacing it with imports; it permits mergers and acquisitions between transnational companies themselves; and, it liberates them to sell freely by eliminating the barriers that previously obliged them to keep subsidiaries in the countries that interested them. Thus, it imposes on the periphery new contradictions that destructure its internal market, the opposite of what it might desire with liberalising measures. Capital itself ends up by destroying part[15] of what attracts it.

"The destruction of jobs at a much higher rate than the creation of new jobs, is not only a fatality attributed to technology itself. It results, at least in equal measure, from the almost total mobility of action that industrial capital regained, to invest and disinvest at will, 'at home' or abroad, as well as the liberalisation of international trade. The effect of these factors, in turn, is accentuated

---

15 One says "part" because local factors of production would also have to be analysed as elements attractive to capital, typical of those economies called "enclaves".

in a growing form by the change in ownership of industrial capital … the new owners (investment funds, pension funds, insurance companies) [exert] also a strong pressure to reduce costs…" (Chesnais, 1996:304–306).

Thus, it again poses the question of the place in the new reality embodied in the form of organisation of the accumulation process that centralises capital through the movement of multinational companies in search of profitability and competitiveness. The processes and contradictions previously restricted to the local space, today, are exposed on a global scale starting from the centre. Today the process of centralisation that occurs on a global scale has a dramatic impact on the periphery that is still included in the system. Individual capitals and local industrial structures are eliminated to centralise them in some clusters of accumulation elsewhere. Thus it is created, by this movement, a type of "return" of capital to its bases of accumulation. It is worth repeating Marx: "Capital is accumulated here in the hands of one, only because it escaped the hands of many others elsewhere".

"The anarchic character from which the competitive base of capitalism derives induces it to solve through the force of competition, that which leads inevitably to concentration, to centralisation … This happens as much in the national environment as in the international. But if monopoly does not totally eliminate competition, it creates new forms that oblige it to a continuous struggle to maintain hegemony. This contest assumes contradictory forms in its development. The general tendency of the process is for integration under the imposition of a hegemonic centre: but this tendency cannot be realised completely because integration develops new levels of contradiction, leading to new confrontations and, therefore, to partial disintegrations or total disintegration, that forces a new wave of centralisations, and so on" (Dos Santos, 1977:20).

2.9 The Centralisation of Space: The Exclusion of the Periphery

Two contradictory forces make up the movement of capital: one of expansion and occupation of new spaces; another of retraction, of reordering and return to the central space. Both ensure the continuity of the process of expanded accumulation. Capitalism expands itself extrapolating regional spaces because of its intrinsic need for accumulation and its own contradictions that it generates within each new space it occupies. It reproduces in this movement, on a global scale, an unequal character, occupying these regional spaces always starting from the centre. Thus it recreates the same contradictions in the world, on an expanded scale, resulting in international movements of centralisation that ensure the existence of some capitals in detriment of others on a more reduced base of global accumulation. In this process, the tendency of the free movement of capital is to return to the centre and to exclude the periphery after projecting its contradictions there which limit the continuity of its growth in this space.[16] It is the reproduction of the exclusion that previously arose in the local space, afterwards in new places occupied by capital and, now, it occurs on a global scale. The centralisation of capital results in a kind of return of capital to the centre, at the same time in which it regains its capacity for expanded accumulation.

So, the capital that was already polarised around the countries of the Triad, with the processes of centralisation, tends to strengthen itself and reorganise itself closely around these centres. "The movement of globalisation is excluding" (Chesnais, 1996:33). The visible indicators of this process are the growth of direct investment and of trade clustered around the centres formed by the countries of the Triad as clearly shown in the data in the "World Investment Report" of UNCTAD (2000).

Centralisation is what characterises the process of globalisation in the 1990s. "Cross-border mergers and acquisitions, particularly those involving large companies, vast sums of money and major restructurings, are among the most visible faces of globalisation. Not only do they dominate foreign direct investment in developed economies, they have also begun to take hold as a mode of entry ... into developing economies..." (UNCTAD 2000:159). That means that the main characteristic of the current process of the globalisation of capital is the centralisation of capitals, a process described by Marx (see Chapter 1).

In this process, one gains a sense of the logic of capital's struggle for liberalisation and deregulation as essential elements in order that it may manage to maintain its process of accumulation in this new stage of productive restructuring that implies centralisation of capitals, now on the global scale. This struggle takes its direction from the free movement of capital and by the definition of rules that benefit this process of centralisation by the states of the centre, at times imposed on the periphery. It is not possible to structure the logic of production polarised in centres of control and producer centres if capital in its commercial, productive and financial forms were not free to move themselves. It is this free mobility that ensures the possibility of centralisation

---

16   This tendency to spatial centralisation of capital when it is given the freedom to be so is not new. Lipietz notes that in 19th Century France, when transport conditions to the capital were improved to move around, France moved from a dispersed productive structure in various spaces to a more centralised structure, which "caused the ruin of many small cities by the fall in local production" (Lipietz, 1987:86).

and its efficacy as a mechanism to maintain the process of accumulation and the rates of profit of each individual capital, faced with the contradictions that its own movement creates in various spaces.

"The operations of the multinationals are characterised by increased mobility of investment, by the capacity of constantly redirecting their activities and, in concerning the countries of the Third World, by the total absence of having roots in a given country or a compromise with it. They are characteristics that explain the enormous retreats experienced in the last 20 years by countries in development..." (Chesnais, 1996:223).

Chesnais, despite not relating this movement directly to the centralisation of capital, calls it "forced disconnection ... that may result ... in disinvestments decided by the large groups..." (Chesnais, 1996:222). This author states that the current tendency is not the spatial distribution of the subsidiaries in various countries, but the concentration in centres, "combining technical modalities and organisations of Toyotism" (Chesnais, 1996:132–135; Michalet, 2002:118). This model leads to greater rationalisation, it eliminates jobs and excludes regions. Capital that had expanded itself starting from the centre, in the process of centralisation, returns to the centre (mostly its research laboratories and high technology products). It is worth remembering that capital does not need to include everybody to maintain itself functioning, as Keynes pointed out. It expands itself in the direction of the periphery of the system in so far that there are elements to be exploited in these regions and, once the contradictions are installed that make it fragile and impoverish it, their operations are only centralised in the places that still ensure them continuity of accumulation.

This process generates in the periphery an enormous competition between countries (Dicken, 1992:44 and Michalet, 2002) that developed, having as a strategy the attraction of transnational corporations over the last 50 years leaving them free to do what they want. Some peripheral countries made their economies strongly dependent on the strategy of companies and large transnational groups that incorporate this current movement of capital. In this scenario of the free productive reordering of these companies, these countries see themselves dealing with the need to construct an "ideal scenario" in a furious competition between the peripheral states to keep them within their territories (Michalet, 2002:110).

Thus, they (mostly Latin-American ones) give up their hegemony as a state, of control over their local space, believing they may be able to keep on being participants in global capitalism in a "dependent and associated" way to transnational capital, an idea that "seduced the local elites who believed that doing their homework they could play with the big boys" (Michalet, 2002:114). But, contrary to managing to achieve success, they exacerbated the internal contradictions that, opposite to what was intended, frightened capital away.

Capitalism today is limited to a zone defined by the Triad around which are clustered a handful of new industrialised peripheral countries (Michalet, 2002:125) that compete between each other to survive in such a position. That is for the time being. Michalet includes among them Brazil, but points to Argentina with a question mark, having perhaps already passed into the group of the excluded (ibid, 147), if it maintains the current tendency or type of liberalising policy. China, which is not the subject of this work, is acting strongly to enter into this process of global capital accumulation in a differentiated way in relation to the strategy adopted in Latin America. It guarantees almost total control over the transnational capital that was accepted via FDI. Only history will demonstrate if it will obtain success.

Capital autonomous and free, walking on "its own feet", has its agent in the company or transnational corporation, it implies the exacerbation of the processes of accumulation, concentration and centralisation that imposes contradictions on a global scale. If so considered, centralisation as a tendency of the movement of capital as pointed out by Marx, without any attempt to control its movement, the result may be in the increase of the number of countries totally excluded from the process of accumulation, reproducing, analogically, the tendency to exclusion that exists concretely and that is visible in each place where capital has installed itself, including in that place, the "periphery" formed by the excluded within the countries of the centre itself.

CHAPTER 3

The Inclusion of the Periphery in the Process of Global Accumulation

3.1   Introduction

The connection between economic growth and the development of a nation is an old discussion. The idea of economic growth in capitalism is directly linked to an economy that has its dynamic of accumulation based on a modern industrial structure that ensures the production of a surplus both for the consumer and for the realisation of new investment. Thus, only through industrialisation is it possible to promote the process of increased capital accumulation, growth. Development, on the other hand, is a term that to a certain extent involves the participation of various social groups that constitute a particular nation in the wealth created.

For some, development would come as an effect of the creation of this industrial apparatus, of economic growth, of the structuring of capitalism as an image of the centre in the periphery. The logic of development of Cepal – Commission for the Development of Latin America – is included in this spectrum. Thus, it advocates the creation of conditions for the construction of an industrial structure on the periphery as a way of making it modern and developed. Through the positive action of the state, in the sense of drawing up policies that might give incentives to the creation of industry within the periphery, it aimed to create the basis for the internalisation of the Keynesian dynamic flow that would allow an autonomous and independent development of the periphery.

The objective thus aimed for was the inclusion of capitalism from the developed world inside the periphery, internalising the process of capital accumulation, but it is worth emphasising, by building productive structures that bring the process of capital accumulation, its dynamic flow, to the periphery. That would only be possible according to the logic of capital by means of industrialisation. So, the idea of development is connected to the logic of capitalist development, but the way to bring economic autonomy to the periphery is by disconnecting it from traditional forms of dependency in relation to the centre. The central question which one aims to verify here is the strategy for the goal used, entailed in the ideas of Cepal, adopted for the development of capitalism in various peripheral countries, as for example, Brazil that will be analysed as a specific case in Chapter 4.

In this sense, it is worth underlining that, on the one hand is the movement of capital in the world (analysed in previous chapters) and on the other, the mechanism adopted by the periphery for its integration in this global capitalism. The current chapter seeks to analyse this movement starting from Cepal's strategy, seen as in part responsible for the way, as part of the Latin American (as periphery as it is), it is integrated in the process of world capital accumulation.

For Cepal, the process of inclusion of capitalist industry in the periphery should have the support of transnational capital as investor, given that this already had the financial and technological capacity that could accelerate the process of modernisation of Latin American countries, in so far that it could bring to the periphery a modern and competitive industry that might reduce the pressure for imports. This transnational capital, along with the participation of the nation state as organiser and producer, appears as a strong partner in the industrialising effort.

It is worth stressing that this movement of attracting transnational capital to the periphery occurs historically in perfect synchrony with the process of capital expansion in the world starting from the central countries. This is when at their places of origin the process of the productive internationalisation of capital results from the movements of accumulation, concentration and centralisation. The individual capitals of the central countries, after European post-war reconstruction, went off in search for new spaces to continue their process of accumulation on an increasing scale. The Latin American periphery put together its development strategy, widely supported by the active role of the nation state, but strongly linked to constructing a scenario to receive and incentivise transnational capital to become part of its industrialisation policy.

State action and the attraction of transnational capital were therefore, through the Cepal strategy, the ways planned to free the economies of the Latin American periphery from the perverse logic of underdevelopment entailed in the *modus operandi* of the strait-jacket of primary-exporter which imprisoned these economies, so as to free them from the constraints of a perverse flow that left them tied to the need to export primary products to be able to import manufactured products, under the yoke of the process of the international capital accumulation. The aim was to insert themselves into global capitalism in another way, bringing the dynamic flow of capital to within their productive structure so as to make the Latin American economies more autonomous and independent of the central economies. A classic article of Prebisch

(2000), one of the thinkers of Cepal, written in 1949 shows how difficult it is for countries focussed on raw-material and agricultural primary-export to develop. The mechanism advocated for the industrialisation of the periphery was the structuring of policies, through the state, to replace imports whose most simple meaning is to create industries in the periphery to produce domestically that which was previously imported from central countries while creating a dynamic independence.

The question raised here, is not related even to the formula of introducing the flow of capital to the periphery focussed on industrialisation, nor the idea of import substitution as mechanisms for structuring an industrial complex in the periphery. Industrialisation, despite being controversial, is considered a strategy for the insertion of the dynamic of capital – its flow of accumulation – in the periphery and, the import substitution, as a mechanism for this. This strategy, which is not the privilege of the Latin American economies (it was adopted in Japan) and not even exactly an invention of Cepal, given that it had already occurred before it (Cepal was created at the end of the 1940s) in a spontaneous and disconnected way. What one is seeking to emphasise here is the way how this industrialisation arises in Latin America starting with its connection to transnational capital in expansion in the world after the Second World War. As will be seen, the criticism made here is little related to the import substitution strategy and much more related to the coupling with transnational capital as its basis. On promoting development in alliance with transnational capital, Latin America laid the foundations for its submission to globalised capitalism.

The industrialisation process of Latin America very closely followed the process of global capital accumulation. In a way, the primary-exporter period has a strong correlation with the commercial internationalisation of capital, a stage in which the centre sought new markets to continue the process of accumulation on an extended scale, and found in the primary-exporter periphery a market that made possible the realisation of the production at the centre (as stated Luxemburg, 1983). Starting in the 1950s/60s, a period that marks the start of the process of the productive internationalisation of capital, capital comes no longer to seek markets to give continuity to its process of accumulation (realisation of value), but seeks new places for its expansion, ensuring the continuity of the accumulation on an increasing scale, now worldwide scale. It is in some countries in the periphery that this capital will find the space and support for its investment starting from the policies of import substitution. It is in this movement of capital in the world that the periphery – mainly some Latin American countries – manage success in their policies of import substitution and, a part of the periphery, attracts the transnational capital that was in expansion in the world, transforming its industrial structure in a radical way.

Through this process, transnational capital, by occupying the periphery's most dynamic and high technology sectors, becomes the dynamic centre of capitalist accumulation in the periphery, imposing its rationality of accumulation on the periphery. This relationship, the contrary of reducing dependency and making the periphery more autonomous, results in introducing the dynamic of the global accumulation of the centre, manifest in the action of transnational capitals, in some countries that compose it, among them, Brazil, Argentina and Mexico. It makes the periphery more dependent and subsumed into the dynamic of global capital accumulation, a dependency that ties the periphery to the logic of the investment and the strategy of transnational corporations in the world; a dependency manifested as technological, commercial and financial dependency to which the Latin America makes itself a prisoner; a dependency that appears as enormous foreign debts that place the periphery under the administrative yoke of multilateral bodies as the IMF (International Monetary Fund), the representatives of transnational capital.

In this sense, the central question is linked to the fact of the policy of import substitutions, in the way it was implemented, making the Latin American peripheral economy much more submissive and vulnerable to the movement of global capital by the reduction of its power of control over the movement of this capital. As expounded in earlier chapters, what characterises the movement of this capital in the world in the 1990s was the process of global centralisation that, by its own nature, is not part of the mechanism of the expansion of capital, but of its retraction, that is why it tends to be excluding. Faced with this scenario, the periphery, which was already vulnerable through its historic "partnership" with transnational capital, by implementing liberalising policies with the aim of giving continuity to this strategy, it comes to run the risk of exclusion or of "forced disconnection", as pointed out in Chesnais (1996) and Michalet (2002), given that who comes to decide where, when and how to allocate capital is the large transnational conglomerate, the specific representative of capital, according to its strategies decided at the head office located at the centre (North-Atlantic countries) and not at the periphery.

3.2 The Logic of Development through Import Substitution

That the development of capitalism and the insertion of the logic of the process of accumulation in any peripheral economy comes through industrialisation, there is not much to argue about. The functioning of the industrialised economy is blended with the accumulation of capital itself in its dynamic process. So, to promote economic growth or the development of capitalism in a peripheral economy comes through the creation of an industrial structure that inserts it in the logic of the capitalist dynamic. For Cepal, the creation of a dynamic capitalist flow of a relatively autonomous accumulation appears as the centre of this strategy of peripheral development.

The idea that the promotion of the development of a nation as a capitalist society occurs through industrialisation accompanies economic theory from its earliest times. It was already included in *The Wealth of Nations* of Adam Smith who demonstrates how the division of labour in his "pin factory" manages to raise the surplus value of the worker – it makes work more productive – being, for him, placed at the disposition of all society, in the free market, promoting the general enrichment and, at the same time, allowing the creation of a greater surplus in the future. Thus it was proposed in the concept of capitalist development, industrialisation centred on production in series, as the radiating centre of progress and the enrichment of the nation in so far that it is capable of generating an excess of capital that allows the expansion of accumulation.

Marx would not disagree with Smith's vision. For him the development of the productive forces, of capital, is focussed on the production of value by capitalist industry and by how the capital from it is appropriated, ensuring the continuity of the creation of wealth, the process of accumulation of capital on an increasing scale. However, the form of extraction of the social surplus value and its allocation in the process of accumulation itself is what makes capitalism extremely dynamic in its task of accumulating capital, also perceived by Smith. This leads to continuous development of the forces of production, to the development of capitalism. But, as Marx pointed out, this process cannot be confused with social development. Little does it have to do with social inclusion in the sense defined in Chapter 1, or with the reduction of poverty as Smith imagined. On the contrary, Marx shows how the system leads to the enrichment of a class, that which controls the means of production, it leads to the processes of concentration and centralisation of capital that transforms capital into the subject of the process, it leads by extension to the exclusion both of the workers and the capitalists, as well as the impoverishment of the class that only has its labour-power as a commodity in the relation of exchange that permeates social relations, and that loses the possibility of using it by unemployment. It is in this way that the system is capable of generating surplus in a growing and efficient way, it is capable of accumulating capital in an expanded form. This fact, at the same time that it impels the development of capitalism, creates its contradictions that may lead to its collapse, as Marx points out.

Being thus, social development with inclusion and economic growth are not directly connected. One may say that development, whilst generally enriching the nation, for all, is separate from the development of the productive forces, of the economic growth of the nation, of the process of capital accumulation. It is not the same thing. In simple terms, one may thus place the contradiction that arises from this in capitalism in contrast to the harmonic and "egalitarian" vision of Smith. In Marx's logic, there is not a direct relation between capitalist economic growth and development in the sense of reducing poverty and social inclusion. There exists, on the contrary, a strong tendency that there occurs a rise in impoverishment and exclusion with the development of the processes of accumulation, concentration and centralisation of capital that characterises capitalism, what one could not call development in the classic sense of Smith, but one could call capitalist development in Marx's sense. This is the tendency when capital is that which dictates the rules of its own accumulation according to its own logic, without contrary actions, according to the logic of the "market".

The non-separation of the development of the productive forces, economic growth, from the question of development in the sense of inclusion (or raising the living standards of people in general) always ends up by leading to the conclusion that it is enough (to have) economic growth, or, the development of the productive capitalist forces, in order to unleash a process in an "automatic" way of general enrichment, given that, with growth, the multiplying mechanisms of the dynamic flow would generate the inclusion of social groups in a continuously ascending form. So it would then be sufficient to promote economic growth guided by the insertion of the mechanisms that make up this capitalist flow into the peripheral economies[1] that at least the basic elements of social inclusion would be assured. It would be enough, therefore, to introduce industrial production, with all its stages of the productive chain and its departments,[2] organised by a fomenting and planning state, that economic and social development would come in response. For this to happen, therefore, it would be sufficient to bring capital to the periphery.

Leaving aside the automatist idea of Smith, Keynes would also relate economic growth directly to development in the broad sense. For this author, it is enough to incentivise the private investor (which was automatic for Smith, but not for Keynes) through the political action of the state in order that the economy takes the path of growth, generating employment and income in a dynamic flow, moving in the direction of achieving the full employment of resources, a point at which all would be included in the process, participating in economic growth and social development. The difference is in the automatism

---

[1] By this logic, called underdeveloped for still not being in fact inserted into modern, industrial capitalism.
[2] Departments of consumer goods and capital goods.

of the process and not in the form. Keynes proposes the administration of the process of accumulation by the state in order that development occurs (Keynes, 1978: 125), but it can only occur by way of economic growth, in capitalism, by the planned implementation, one could say, of the flow of capital accumulation on an extended scale.

In a way, this was the vision that prevailed among developmentalist authors like Prebisch and Furtado in their theories of development and underdevelopment of the periphery.[3] Its foundations were in creating the necessary conditions for the construction and growth of industry in the periphery that would have, as a result its insertion in the developed capitalist world. The difference between development and growth was, for them, that the first, development would include the idea of economic growth, reflecting transformations that would occur in society based on this growth, these transformations that refer to a set of changes in social mentality that ensure a developed society (Furtado, 1971: 83–84). This conception connects, on the one hand, development to the creation of a consumer market that may guarantee the realisation of growth and the formation of a dynamic internal flow and, on the other, the creation in this process of a new social mentality of a developed nation not only present in the consumer, but in a business class with an innovative role capable of giving continuity to the growth. It is as if one might create the mentality of the innovative entrepreneur of Schumpeter (1961), responsible not only for the invention of new technologies, as for maintaining the dynamic growth based on this innovation,[4] starting from investment in the "new" as occurred in the developed economies. In this context, the reduction of poverty and the social inclusion, would be the consequence of this civilising process in the periphery that has its basis in economic growth induced by the nation state.

"Industrialisation was the key" to overcome backwardness, the archaic, underdevelopment understood "as an economic, social, political and cultural situation ... perceived under the title of bourgeois revolution" (Dos Santos, 2000: 74).

The logic entailed in this conception of development comes from Keynes, an economist with strong influence over Cepal's thinking (Rodriguez, 1981: 37). Cepal would construct the theoretical apparatus for the process of industrialisation in Latin America as a way of overcoming underdevelopment based

---

3 In Furtado's case, in his first theories, taking as the basis his work "Theory and Politics of Economic Development" (1971), given that in author's later works he reviews his positions.
4 The idea that technical progress has its origins in the innovative individual entrepreneur, despite its presence in the heads of many economists and sociologists, was abandoned by Schumpeter himself in his "Capitalism, Socialism, and Democracy" on verifying that innovations occurred in large corporations by contracted specialists (Schumpeter, 1961:133).

on the ideas of this author. Keynes (1982) demonstrates that the dynamic of growth and development has its beginning in the action of the entrepreneur capable of overcoming the uncertainties about the future, making investments, a bet, waiving cash liquidity and buying productive assets with the expectation of obtaining income (profit) in the future. This action creates employment, including other social groups in the productive process (it establishes itself as a form of inclusion, participation in the process of accumulation); at the same time, it creates a consumer market that will incentivise businessmen to make new investments, raising the numbers of jobs in an ascending spiral flow of growth, social inclusion and development, raising production, employment and society's income. Investment, in so far that it employs means of production (capital and labour), generates a flow of income to the workers in the form of salaries and a flow of income to the entrepreneurs themselves in the form of profits that, together, make up the aggregate income of the community, the capacity of society to acquire the production that it created and generates new investments, maintaining the flow.

For Keynes as much as for those at Cepal, once the process has started, a virtuous flow of growth is created given its own internal dynamic. The action started by the investment, fomented and organised by the state – a fact that is stronger for Cepal given it deals with the development of underdeveloped economies – it has as a consequence almost an automatic positive reaction in economic growth. The need for state action comes from the fact that this process that starts the virtual flow is not automatic. Mostly the entrepreneur, faced with an uncertain future, does not make the necessary investment letting a crisis establish itself, or making the economy remain in a state of equilibrium with unemployment (a case closest to the situation of "underdeveloped" economies). In this sense, the action of the state, through economic policies or from its own investment may create a positive scenario to incentivise private action in the direction of investment. What Keynes is saying is that capital often breaks its flow of accumulation in crises and it is the role of the state to regulate the way out or the rearrange the economy to resume the process of accumulation. Keynes' logic permeates Cepal's strategy and is present in advocating the state's role as fomenter and manager of the economic flow, all the rest being assured by growth itself.

Thus for Cepal, the basis for the realisation of peripheral development is in fomenting industrialisation as a form of internalising this dynamic flow. The introduction of industry in the periphery would promote increased productivity in all sectors, as well as creating mechanisms, both in raising the surplus per capita, as well as the capacity for consumption by the insertion of new social groups in this flow. Of course, the objective was the development of capitalism in the periphery, having in this the foundations for poverty reduction and the modernisation of society. Thus was industrialisation proposed as the way out from underdevelopment en route to being developed countries. Development was thus seen as the growing integration of the population in modern life, reducing poverty, raising the standard of living, increasing consumption that "depends, at the final instance, on an expressive quantity of capital per worker employed in industry, in transport and in primary production, and of the capacity to manage it well" (Prebisch, 2000: 76).

Octavio Rodriquez describes Cepal's logic in the following way: "Economic development is expressed in the increase in material well-being; normally reflected by the rise in real income per habitant and conditioned by the average growth of labour productivity. It is considered that this growth depends on the adoption of methods of indirect production whose use implies the increase of capital funding per employed. The greater the density of capital, in turn, goes on being obtained in so far as it leads to the effect of accumulation that is propelled by the technical progress, needed to ensure its continuity" (Rodrigues, 1981: 36).

Development depends, therefore, on the creation of an industrial structure in the "underdeveloped" countries that internalises the cycle of capitalist accumulation in these economies. This means implanting in the peripheral economies certain conditions for the dynamic of accumulation observed historically in the logic of the capitalism of the central countries, so that this dynamic is established in the periphery, and that it creates, as a mirror of the centre (Hunt, 1989: 50), a flow of production/income/consumption that makes the process of accumulation less dependent, more autonomous, in relation to the capitalism of the centre. Or rather, although the idea might not reproduce historically the stages of the centre's capitalist development, described by Rostow (1978), the logical basis of Cepal's developmentalism was the internalisation of the dynamic of capitalism of the centre within the periphery, "leaping" over Rostow's stages seen as "natural" to the development of any nation. In this sense, in the face of the discussions of the epoch it was a revolutionary project.

In this context, one of the great innovations of Cepal's thinking was not the idea of what came to be economic development, but the way how to reach it. That was the basis for the critique of Rostow's "stages". This author, on analysing the process of development of the central economies, pointed to historic natural phases to reach it, without checking the differences that had occurred to that development and the type of connection that the periphery had in relation to the already developed economies, without observing that the periphery was not at a "stage" of the process of accumulation, but had in itself a way of specific connection (primary-exporter) in the process of global capital accumulation, factors pointed out by Cepal.

Cepal demonstrates the different characteristics between both processes of development, stressing the perpetuity of underdevelopment if the logic of insertion, prevailing up until then, is maintained, of the periphery in global capitalism. The development of capitalism on the periphery could not come naturally according to the historic "model" of the centre. Thus, Cepal breaks with Rostow's logic, dominant at the time (Furtado, 2000: 261). But, on the other hand it does not break with the idea that a certain type of development (the example of the centre) should be the benchmark to be reached by the periphery. In this sense, both rationales see the insertion of the process of capitalist accumulation on the periphery as something to be achieved.

The central point of the Cepal strategy was the need to create mechanisms that free the peripheral economies from the relative backwardness imposed by the specific form of connection to global capitalism to which they were subject, as primary-exporter economies, that characterised their dynamic and that imposed on them, like a straitjacket, a standard of development different to what had historically occurred in the developed centres, dependent on a *modus operandi* other than the needs of the periphery, dependent on the accumulation of the centre. By the primary-exporter logic that characterised the functioning of the Latin American peripheral economies, these would be fated to a development dependent on exports of low value primary products to the centre, from where the necessary resources originated to deal with the import of manufactured products. Thus, these economies had a dependent development given that their dynamic of economic growth was totally at the mercy of what happened with the markets for primary products at the centre. This would leave the periphery in a subordinate position in relation to the economies of the centre, subordinated to the process of capital accumulation at the centre, to a perverse type of international division of labour that impedes it from creating its own flow of accumulation as expounded above, this being the factor that creates unequal development between the centre and the periphery: "in the centres, the productive structure is diversified and homogenous while in the periphery it is specialised and heterogeneous" (Rodrigues, 1981:42). For Cepal, this lack of diversification of the peripheral economy structure is what constrained and impaired its autonomous development, it blocked the creation of a flow of capitalist accumulation in the periphery itself. So it would be necessary to break this form of symbiotic connection of the periphery in relation to the process of global accumulation, entailed in the primary-exporter logic.

The solution therefore would be to bring the dynamic of the process of capitalist accumulation to the periphery. This was the key to a more autonomous development, the basis for Cepal's thinking in the 1940s and 1950s. (Dos Santos, 2000:74). To create an autonomous and diversified economy was the target. As Furtado pointed out "In an economy that may have reached a certain degree of development, production entails such a structure that accumulation becomes an automatic process...". (Furtado, 1971: 140). This meant internalising the capitalist flow of accumulation in all its stages, attracting to the periphery the sectors that compose the productive chains so as to create a "homogenous structure", as occurred in the capitalist countries of the centre. For this it would be necessary the internalisation in the periphery of all the stages of the productive process so as to create endogenous development, or "towards within" (Rodrigues, 1981: 43 and Tavares, 1982: 42). This consists in the creation of productive agricultural and industrial structures related to each other in a dynamic flow of production, employment, income and consumption both between the people involved and between sectors.

"This simplified scheme contains what is essential in the economic process. From the side of production, appears the creation of the surplus; of distribution, the appropriation of this surplus by a minority group; and, from the accumulation side, the possibility of increasing productivity with the expansion of the market and the incorporation of the surplus in the productive process. If we observe this process in time, we see that the third phase meets the first again; the increase in productivity caused by the incorporation of new capital and the expansion of the market, gives place to the creation of a new surplus, which is appropriated by the minority group and will be transformed into new capital etc". (Furtado, 1971:139).

The creation of this mechanism that Furtado defines as a source of development in the peripheral economies, freeing them from the primary-exporter straitjacket, is the basis for the creation of an endogenous capitalist flow that would make the peripheral economy less dependent on the central countries by bringing the capitalist dynamic to within the peripheral space. "It was widely accepted that industrialisation was the key to economic development and this would not be the result of the indefinite concentration in expanding the primary exporting sector...". (Hunt, 1989: 46).

Of course, in capitalism, industry is the centre of this process because it is from it that the mechanisms for increasing productivity radiate to all sectors, it is this that creates the endogenous dynamic; it is the central element in the creation and dissemination of technology that raises productivity, increasing the surplus available for a new cycle of accumulation at a higher level. It is from it that the dynamic flow that characterises capitalism could be established. Thus, accumulation, growth and development are, for Cepal, intimately linked to industrialisation and to the technological progress that results from it, "through which one obtains the gradual increase in the density of capital and the increase in labour productivity and in the average standard of living" (Rodriguez, 1981: 37). "The superior stage of development is reached when the industrial nucleus is diversified, making it capable of producing part of the equipment required so that development is effected" (Furtado, 1971:187).

The strategy therefore was to create an industrial structure through a directed policy to replace the importance of primary product exports as the main (exogenous) dynamic determinant of accumulation by the "endogenous variable of investment", whose amount and composition would come to be decisive for development (Tavares, 1982:34). Thus, it would be possible to channel part of the income that was formed in the periphery itself and was destined to imports – generating a multiplier effect on income abroad – to the development of an internal market that might acquire the manufactured goods produced within the periphery, strengthening, along with production, the internal market, a fundamental element in the creation of a flow of endogenous accumulation towards the periphery, internalising the multiplier effect of income and of employment.

It is interesting to note that the idea encapsulated in this logic is one of bringing to the periphery the process of capital accumulation as it occurs in the centre, creating a more independent and autonomous nucleus of capitalist accumulation in the periphery in relation to the process of accumulation at the centre. It does not entail preoccupation with the fact that the process of accumulation of the centre itself, in its logic of accumulation, having as a tendency to extend itself over the periphery, occupying the peripheral space as a form of maintaining its accumulation on an extended scale. On the contrary, the logic of inducing industrialisation in the Latin American periphery acts, much more in the sense of taking advantage of this movement of capital, incentivising its entry into the periphery. Neither does it appear to be present in Cepal's thinking much less the logic of concentration and centralisation of capital according to which capital is reorganised in relation to the centre (see Chapter 2), in reality imposing its dynamic of accumulation on the periphery. What the Cepal proposition appears to be is still imbued with the logic of the commercial internationalisation of capital and, that is why, it is very much tied to the principle of the "import substitution" to make the periphery less dependent commercially.

This fact makes the strategy of industrialisation of Latin American enter into almost perfect alignment with the phase through which capitalism went through in its process of post-World War II expansion via direct productive investment. It ends up thus being an incentive mechanism for transnational capital to enter the periphery, to the occupation of its spaces of accumulation. In part through this synchrony, the economic policies of development carried out in the periphery within Cepal's scope, resulted in the process of capital expansion from the centre to the periphery becoming much stronger in Latin America, submitting its accumulation in a radical way to the process of global accumulation. It is worth stressing that this alignment, not evaluated by Cepal, ended up by not resulting in breaking up the relationship of subordination as might be supposed, on the contrary, it implied an alignment of interests of the periphery with the interests of the transnational corporations of the centre, even though Cepal did not wish it. It implied a new form of subordination.

Thus, with the initial aim of seeking "autonomy" though the logic of industrialisation, the Latin American countries, by promoting the substitution of imports with transnational capital, ended up by integrating itself into a structural form in the process of accumulation of the centre, inserting itself in a deliberate way in the contradictions that are constituent parts of this process of global capital accumulation. That is why the relations of dependency ended up reinforced and the contradictions of the process of global accumulation of capital exhibited themselves in a more radical way in industrialised Latin America. This occurs in a clearer and more accelerated form in Latin America because the policy of industrialisation implanted here permits the logic of the process of capital accumulation of the centre, in its new phase of productive internationalisation, to couple itself in a nearly perfect way to the import substitution policy. And the peripheral state will be a central agent in this process. The structure of the state and the strategy were born together.

It should be here highlighted that Cepal, in the same way that this book seeks to do, starts from the perception that there exists a process of accumulation in the centre interwoven in a form of relation with the periphery that makes it subordinate. The objective of Cepal was to understand the mechanisms of this subordination, how they impair development and how to break them, the same aim as is proposed by this book. Therefore, the critique that is made here of Cepal's logic is specific, it refers to the fact of it having given little importance to the logic of the processes of accumulation, concentration and centralisation that already, at that time, had taken on global characteristics. What the people at Cepal lacked was deepening their study of Marx.

3.3   State Participation

In order to promote this industrialising strategy it was necessary to create mechanisms to implant the centre's logic of accumulation in the periphery so as to develop it, given that this is not a process that occurs as a "natural" impulse especially when one is dealing with an economic periphery that has a subordinate form of insertion in global capitalism, entailed in the mechanism of being a primary-exporter of low value added products. To move away from this situation that perpetuates the periphery as underdeveloped, it would be necessary planned action on the part of the state. Not that the process of industrialisation does not happen at the periphery, at times in a spontaneous way (such as "restricted industrialisation" in Brazil – Cardoso de Mello, 1982:110), when it sees itself faced with a temporary international crisis that impaired its capacity for importing manufactured products. But, it became clear that if this were a planned process, apart from avoiding the natural imbalances of the spontaneous process, it could have a very high degree of efficiency, in the sense of inducing industrialisation by the formation of a "homogenous structure" that might permit development "towards within". This was the role of the peripheral state that would be advocated by Cepal and used in the process of development. A state with the role of orienting and organising these "spontaneous" flows, the introduction of the process of accumulation of capital at the periphery.

"...it is accepted that the free play of market forces leads to the persistent manifestation of balance of payment problems, of accumulation and under-utilisation of capital and work force, etc., given that these are inherent in the spontaneous process of industrialisation: they arise from, ultimately, from the conditions that go into producing the transformation of the peripheral productive structure during this process. Thus, according to the conception of the system centre-periphery [of Cepal], in order that with industrialisation one manages to substantially increase the levels of productivity and to optimise the allocation of resources, it is necessary to orient it through a deliberate policy of development" (Rodriguez, 1981:48).

The need is posited for a peripheral state capable of organising, planning and acting, often occupying the places where private capital had no interest, in order to implant industry in the periphery in a way to make the process more efficient in that concerning the "allocation of resources" and thus permit the introduction of the logic of capitalist accumulation within the periphery, by the construction of a diversified industrial structure, able to internalise and make its development "autonomous" in relation to the centre.

It is worth stressing that development planning through the state at the time was a well-accepted idea.[5] "Soon after the Second World War, there was a general adherence of governments, companies, politicians, technocrats, economists and other social scientists to governmental planning, as a technique

---

5   Japan used this strategy in a radical way (Allen, 1983).

for reconstructing national economies and of import-substituting industrialisation in countries of the then Third World. The Marshall Plan was part of this story, as was the IMF and the IRDB... created at the end of the 1940s and engaged actively in projects of planned economic development...". (Ianni, 1999:188). It is worth remembering that Cepal would also be created at the end of the 1940s (1948), as an arm of the United Nations to promote and create mechanisms for the development of Latin America.

The mechanism proposed and in fact used in countries that industrialised themselves in Latin America was the import substitution, planned and organised by economic policies, with the state also occupying areas in specific sectors to complete the industrial structure. The state directed policies advocating the substitution of imports were not connected to substitution, pure and simple from what was imported before, but to a planned substitution that might be capable of internalising the capitalist dynamic in peripheral economies (Tavares, 1982; Cardoso de Mello, 1982) through the creation of conditions for the attraction of investments in sectors that might establish themselves as key to this dynamic.

The principle then would be, through an institutional apparatus with strong state participation and industrial policies formulated by it, to organise and stimulate the process of import substitution, as well as the participation of the external agent (transnational capital) and planning the use of hard currency from exports to make substituting imports. The opposite of importing consumer goods, incentives should be given to internalise the production of these goods, giving priority to the import of equipment and machinery for such, as well as attracting the foreign direct investment that makes them, starting with less sophisticated products, to afterwards move towards the substitution of more sophisticated goods and of capital intensive sectors linked to the industry of capital and intermediate goods (Tavares, 1982: 43). The idea was "to repeat in an accelerated way, in different historical conditions, the experience of industrialisation of developed countries" (Tavares, 1982:35), as a way of reaching development, the mirror image of the centre. The policy of import substitution organised by the state in this way would be a weapon to resolve the problem of low productivity and the lack of technology that characterised the economic structure of the periphery, factors that did not allow the creation of a sufficient surplus for the internalisation of a flow of significant growth.

The creation of a policy of organised substitution of imports, also comes from the need to optimise the use of resources obtained still based on the primary-exporter economy, as well as to programme a series of incentives in order that sectors and large international groups of producers of imported goods might gradually, create productive structures within the frontiers of the peripheral economies. This would involve deciding what types of goods could be imported, creating on the one hand barriers to imports that might protect the nascent industries that were the focus of substitution, as well as, on the other, permitting only those strategic imports to form the industrial complex (Hunt, 1989:141). On the other hand, political action for the development via the state was fundamental for the success of the proposal in all its broad range given the constraints entailed in the logic of primary-exporter that tied Latin America to the movement of international commercial capital. According to Furtado, the solution to underdevelopment was linked to political action given that "an underdeveloped economy must not be considered in isolation from the system of the international division of labour in which it is inserted, and that, at its roots, underdevelopment is a phenomenon of domination, or rather, of a political nature" (Furtado, 1971:191).

Thus, the peripheral Latin American state ends up by occupying a central space in all the countries that achieved success in their process of industrialisation through import substitution. Apart from being organiser and mentor of economic policies, it acts mainly as producer in sectors such as infrastructure and basic intermediate goods. It thus allows the supply of raw materials like steel, chemical products, minerals, as well as energy, transport, telecommunications, at relatively low prices through state companies, creating a structure and an environment that permits private capital to be profitable. It thus becomes, responsible for the construction of a series of floors in the "building" (Tavares, 1982:46) that make up the dynamic flow thought of by Cepal for Latin America. It thus incentivises private national and transnational investment.[6]

The state acts in a way to stimulate the insertion of the periphery in global capitalism seeking, contradictorily, its independence in relation to the process of global accumulation. This action ends up modifying only the form of insertion of the periphery in global capitalism, the form of dependency in relation to the centre. At the same time in which the Programme of Import Substitution implanted by the states of the Latin American countries break with a process of dependency implicit in the logic of primary-exporter, in so far that the capital that it attracts to the periphery is transnational capital, it creates new forms of more complex dependency.

This "developmentalist" form of action of the state that permits industrialisation will only transform itself in the 1980s and 1990s, especially in

---

6 In Brazil's case "the action of the state was decisive ... because it showed it was capable of investing massively in infrastructure and basic industries...". as well as by establishing "the foundations for the association with the large foreign oligopolised company" (Cardoso de Mello, 1982:118).

Latin America, by a series of policies combined with the international strategies of reorganisation of transnational corporations, these policies that will advocate a greater freedom for capital with a view to seeking to ensure its space for accumulation in the periphery. Thus, in these years the countries that were successful in industrialising themselves in Latin America, adopted liberalising policies that have as a focus the removal of the state from the process of accumulation in the periphery. Argentina, Mexico and Brazil undertook wide-ranging privatisation processes reducing the role of the state as producer. At the same time, they implemented policies of macroeconomic adjustment to fight inflation and solve external problems, policies prescribed by the IMF that distanced the state including from its power of undertaking economic policy in the periphery. This movement of separating the state from the productive process and the resulting reduction in its capacity for intervention occurs completely in tune with the desires of the large transnational corporations that is installed in the periphery. It is the result of policies in the peripheral state's own hands, created in synchrony with the movement of transnational capital starting in the 1950s. This will be the subject of the next chapter.

3.4 The Participation of Transnational Capital

Transnational capital, alongside the state, becomes an integral part of the strategy entailed in the industrialising package, as a means of accelerating the process of peripheral development and as partner in the development of peripheral capitalism taking care of high-tech sectors. The attraction of foreign direct investment – FDI was, thus, a central element for the realisation of such development. Through this period, the Latin American countries end up by inserting themselves definitively into the process of global accumulation, but, contrary to conquering their "autonomy", they end up by increasing their dependency, subsuming themselves in a radical way to the movement of global capital. Questioning the participation of transnational capital in the process of import substitution will only arise at the end of the 1960s in a Latin America faced with the contradictions that result from this partnership.

It is worth remembering that this alliance was also in line with the logic advocated in the post-war by the central countries themselves (Schoultz, 1999; Heilbroner, 1963). The explicit idea was that the periphery would not develop through lack of productive and financial capital. This could be overcome by opening the doors so that transnational corporations might supply it, a solution at the same time for the periphery and for the expansion of transnational capital, in a game in which everyone wins. By this logic the states of the central countries were disposed even to support the dictatorships of the periphery that supported foreign investment (Schoultz, 1999:381), given that they acted through policies of development attuned to the interest of transnational capital. Therefore, the policies of import substitutions end up corresponding to the interests of large transnational corporations.

But, at the same time, industrialisation having this capital as a partner was mainly connected to Cepal's logic that saw it "as essential support to economic and industrial development of our countries" (Dos Santos, 2008: 85). The argument was that to have large transnational capital as a partner in the industrialising effort would help the "jumping of stages" in development, in the strategy of internalising the dynamic flow in the periphery, given that the technology and financial resources were already available in its hands. Bringing technology developed in the research centres of corporation's head offices would accelerate the process of freeing the periphery from the constraints of underdevelopment, it would accelerate the creation of the most diversified industry possible, raising productivity and the generation of a surplus produced in the periphery itself. This would contribute to creating as a consequence a dynamic internal market, an environment favourable to new investments, income and employment. The large transnational corporations therefore had as a central role to help in the rapid increase of productivity by internalising the dynamic sectors that they already dominated globally so as to accelerate the internalisation of the dynamic of accumulation in the periphery.

It was, therefore, proposed opening up to the entry of transnational capital in the periphery as a strategy in order to create an industrial structure independent of the central economies. As Prebisch pointed out, "nobody questions that the economic development of certain Latin American countries and their rapid assimilation of modern techniques, in everything that might be beneficial to them, depends on a high degree of foreign investment" (Prebisch, 2000: 75–77).

At the same time, apart from accelerating the process of industrialisation of the periphery through the power of jumping stages in the development of technology and construction of a modern industrial complex, direct investment from transnational capital also serves to increase the potential for imports in the substituting effort. Faced with the scarcity of strong currency that characterises peripheral economies, the entry of foreign investments through the hands of foreign capital itself allowed the resources coming from exports and other foreign loans available to increase the imports substituted, relieving the pressure of the policy of substitution on the balance of payments, increasing its substituting potential. So, also for this reason, the attraction of direct investment by the implantation of productive structures of transnational companies within the frontiers of the periphery came to be central to the industrialising effort.

On the other hand, at the same time that the logic of import substitution was benefitting from foreign direct investment, this would serve the interests of transnational capital itself. The effort of attracting this capital to the periphery as a complement to the substituting effort undertaken by the peripheral state will become the point of entry for foreign capital in a time in which this is also in its process of productive internationalisation. The movements took place symbiotically. The industrialisation of Latin America coincides with the moment in which corporations from the centre of the system are avidly in search of new spaces to continue their process of accumulation inaugurated in the post- war, after European reconstruction, also after the structuring of the economic enclaves of protection from the expansion of communism in Asia.[7] Thus, capital, in its symbiotic action with its states of origin, comes to focus on the Latin American periphery as part of its strategy in global accumulation in synchrony with the state and the peripheral elites.

"The redefinition of the international division of labour in course accelerated after the ending of post-war European recovery transforming the terms of action of international capital in relation to the peripheral dependent economies: now, the industrialisation of dependent economies entered into the international division of labour in the capitalist world as a new form of expansion of this system, increasing it from the old level of producers of raw material *versus* producers of manufactures to producers of manufactured consumer products *versus* producers of manufactures and capital goods" (Oliveira, 1977:83). So, as Oliveira seems to have perceived, the periphery ended up included in a new form of international division of labour, no less dependent.

One may say, therefore, that the process of industrialisation of the periphery was attuned to the phase of capital expansion in the world, in its process of occupation of new spaces – found in parts of the periphery – based on the need that capital, manifested in the action of each individual capital, had to continue the process of valorisation of value on an increasing scale. After the wave of investment undertaken in the central countries provided by post-war reconstruction, to maintain the value created in the process of accumulation, new spaces are needed. Thus it will be, in some countries of Latin America that this capital will find political support from social groups embodied in specific

---

7 As Shoultz states, the preoccupation of the states of the central countries (led by the USA) with the development of Latina America only takes shape rom the 1950s, when North American companies are incentivised to invest in the region. "Far from the frontiers of the Soviet Union, Latin America was no longer threatened and therefore, did not merit much attention [until then]" (Shoultz, 1999:370).

economic policies to expand their accumulation worldwide through direct productive investments.

It is worth recording that participation in the process described above was not contained in Cepal's formulations. It does not seem to have been Cepal's view to propose and advocate the process of industrialisation by import substitution through using transnational capital. At any rate, this synchrony with this capital in expansion is what ends up occurring and, if on the one hand it is what allows the industrialisation of the periphery, on the other it intensifies and creates new relations of dependence. The perhaps lack of consciousness over the impact in terms of increasing dependency and vulnerability based on the association with transnational capital for the promotion of national development, can be noticed in the discussions themselves proposed in some of Furtado's texts. This author who had been one of the mentors of Cepal's proposals that were expounded in his "Theory and Policy of Economic Development", comes to radically question the role that transnational capital ended up having in the Latin American productive structure from the 1960s, a discussion that is present in "The Myth of Development" and "The Hegemony of the United States and the Underdevelopment of Latin America", where he criticises, at times in a radical way, the submission to foreign capital that resulted in the process of Latina America's industrialisation.

3.5 Transnational Capital as Dynamic Centre

The relative success of the policy of import substitution from the mid-1950s is due to its being in step with the interests of large foreign capital in its process of accumulation in the stage of productive internationalisation "... governmental economic policy and the tendency for expansion of the transnational company combined themselves positively" (Ianni, 1986:274). It is for this reason that the most intense period of import substitution has as a basis large investments from big transnational groups, giving "the start to the denationalisation and *subsidiarising* phase of Latin American industry" (Sunkel, 1972: 22). Despite this movement of capital being generalised across the entire world, it is in Latin America that internationalisation becomes strongest. The way how import substitution programmes were structured by the Latin American states with the support of their local elites is one of the explanations. The others refer perhaps to the place that Latin America occupies in the geopolitical strategies of the central states in the post-war.

This strategy will be responsible through the creation of an industrial structure that places transnational capital in control of the most dynamic sectors in the flow of accumulation implanted in Latin America – those that radiate productivity to the whole economy or that have a strong multiplier effect – in the same way that it controls them in the centre.[8] Those sectors are in the core of value chain control. It marks the form of insertion of Latin America in the process of global accumulation. Thus, the strategy leaves space available so that the global capitalist dynamic may involve the periphery in its logic of accumulation that will in fact modify the relationship of dependency. The dynamic of the process of capital accumulation introduces the periphery into its new movement, which is one of the productive internationalisation of capital (see Chapter 2). The strategy of development of the periphery becomes the strategy of accumulation itself of large capital that starting from the occupation of the spaces that were made available to it on the periphery, imposes its logic of accumulation and its contradictions.

"Foreign capital entered above all in the so-called most dynamic sectors and, if these sectors are the engines of expansion, foreign capital in a certain way "controls" the process of this expansion; as opposed to national capital which "controls" the economy less … than it did 20 years back" (Oliveira, 1987:50).

Hence, one does not here wish to infer that the process of industrialisation in Latin American economies might be dominated and undertaken under the control of national capital as Oliveira[9] himself points out, also because this is a hypothesis that has not already happened, it is no longer part of history. But one must be aware of the fact that it is this strategic alliance between the periphery and transnational capital that will result in a Latin American productive structure that will always be hostage to the interests of foreign capital and to the central economies, given the leading position this capital comes to occupy in the peripheral productive structure, that is to say, it makes the periphery much more subordinated to the process of global capital accumulation. This will end up not resulting in the greater independence or autonomy of the periphery in relation to the centre but the opposite, it will result in its umbilical connection to the globalised reproduction of capital, as well as, to the need for huge battles if the aim were one day to break this structure.

---

8 Ianni, commenting on Brazil notes that "The analysis of governmental economic policy since 1964 reveals the predominance of an international tendency … what happened was a reintegration of the Brazilian economy as an economic subsystem in the context of global capitalism … This process was facilitated and accelerated by governmental directives that propelled the concentration and internationalisation of capital … in various sectors of the Brazilian economy" (Ianni, 1986:289).

9 "Specifically, in the Brazilian case, the 'fifty years in five' [The Target Plan of President Kubitschek, 1956–1960] could not have been managed without recourse to foreign capital – … comparisons with Japan do not take into account the huge difference between the Japanese and Brazilian business classes" (Oliveira, 1987:47).

One also does not wish here to say that it may be possible, given the way how capitalism works, a totally independent peripheral economy. Interdependency is inevitable. The question is therefore much more connected not to the idea of isolation but the idea of power, of control. The way how some Latin American countries submit themselves to global capitalism gives them little room to manoeuvre to defend their national interests in relation to the interests and strategies of transnational capital. And, the more they are submitted to this strategy of subordination (as we shall see occurring in the 1990s), the less is that possibility and the greater the fragility and subsumption to the movement of capital according to its nature. This becomes more worrying from the moment that the movement of this capital in the world comes to be a disintegrator and not an integrator, in the process of centralisation.

The question, it seems, is in the fact the process of modernisation proposed by Cepal is largely connected to the idea of the apparent dependence on international trade, and to the fact domestic growth is linked to the realisation of production abroad in the mechanism of primary-exporter, that needed to be overcome with the internalisation of production. Realisation appears as the central thread in Cepal's logic, the logic of demand. The idea of dynamic internalisation is in bringing this realisation to within the periphery. And, for such an objective, transnational capital is not only welcome but necessary. It is thus implicit in the logic of import substitution and in the logic of internalising the dynamic flow, not the possibility of totally suppressing the commercial relationship with abroad, which would not make sense, but the idea of making this relationship with the exterior an exogenous element in the process of peripheral development and not endogenous as it was in the relationship primary-exporter. Apparently it is abstracted from here the logic of who controls the process of production as well as the process of capital accumulation.

The logic implicit in this process of conquering the "autonomy" of the periphery seems to believe that, even placing transnational capital within the periphery, these countries would win their autonomy in relation to the movement of global capital. Thus, it was enough to implant a modernising policy that might create an industrial structure, via import substitution in partnership with foreign capital that this autonomy would be reached, even if having its dynamic centre dominated by foreign oligopolistic corporations.

In fact, this alliance with transnational capital results in contributing to making the contradictions present more entrenched in the nature of the process of global accumulation itself, in that the periphery, mainly Latin American, is included. From the start, it is a process that looms over the peripheral state which, contrary to managing the movement of global capital in its process of accumulation, intensifies its movement through policies of supporting it and, as a consequence, leverages in the periphery the manifestation of its contradictions. This is the opposite of other peripheral states such as the Asian ones that seek to manage its movement. In Latin America this becomes a process that is strengthened based on the idea that the role of the state is to build an attractive scenario for foreign capital. On placing this capital within the frontiers of the periphery, it radicalises the submission and vulnerability to "external factors" in relation to transnational capital and the contradictions of the process of global capitalist accumulation.

The outcome in fact results in the introduction of the peripheral Latin American economies in the process of capital globalisation and not, the introduction of capitalism as "the mirror of the centre" in the periphery with its own dynamic flow. And this results in the creation of new forms of dependency that perhaps make it more fitting to use the term subordination to the global movement of capital instead of dependency, although these forms are manifested as commercial, technological, financial and political dependency, in the sense that the participation of the periphery in international trade ends up by depending on the strategies of the transnationals established in the periphery. The modernisation of the economy depends on importing technology that, in turn, depends on the existence of hard currency resources; domestic policy becomes dependent on the decisions of multilateral bodies and other institutions and states that look after the interests of globalised capital.[10]

3.6 Materialisation of the New Dependency

This strategy of industrialisation through import substitution transformed the industrial structure of some Latin American countries radically. The state, combined with transnational capital, and with private national capital as "junior partner", implanted a relatively modern industrial structure in countries such as Brazil, Argentina and Mexico. The state, apart from acting as investor, created the policies and environment suitable for foreign investment as a basis for the process of industrialisation in tune with the global movement of capital accumulation. But, this did not mean more autonomy for the periphery.

---

10   David Korten is more radical in his analysis by stating that "a revision of the accomplishments of the three institutions of Bretton Woods brings their true functions into clearer focus. The World Bank has acted through establishing export finance for large corporations... The IMF has served as debt collector for the financial [financial] institutions ... GATT [the current WTO – World Trade Organisation] has worked to create and enforce a charter of rights for corporations against the intrusion of peoples ... and democratically-elected governments...". (Korten, 1996:211). See also Carroll (2010).

Brazil,[11] for example, experienced two large cycles of growth and the implantation of its industrial complex in the second half of the 1950s and from the end of the 1960s to the 1970s, consolidated an industrial structure by the "Tripod of Accumulation" – combining the state, transnational capital and national companies – that will only be broken up with the removal of the state in the 1980s and 1990s.[12] It created a relatively diversified industrial structure that would have, in fact, been unthinkable to achieve were it not for the implementation of policies of import substitution. A variety of sectors came to have productive installations in the country, the structure of GDP was changed in favour of industry, creating a new class of industrial workers and new markets for manufactured products (Sunkel and Paz, 1975: 130–133).

Argentina also saw substantial modernisation of its economy, but that also was translated into a strengthening of transnational capital. As Dupas points out "the leadership of Argentine development was mainly in the hands of the subsidiaries of transnational corporations. Their branches began to gain dominant positions in the car, chemical and metal-mechanical industries, attracted by a protected domestic market. In 1955, the share of foreign companies in Argentine industrial production was 20%. In 1975, it came to a third of the total, having an even greater involvement in sectors such as cars" (Dupas, 1999:141).

One may say with some certainty that in fact the "modernisation" undertaken in the periphery changed the whole set of dynamic relations of these economies. But this was not a process that acted in the direction of increasing the autonomy of these economies, nor in moving them closer to the dynamic logic of the structures of the central economies. The results were far from those sought. It managed by the policy of import substitution, aligned with the movement of capital internationalisation that occurred in the world starting from the centre, to create a diversified industrial complex. But this does not have the same meaning that was contained in the idea of introducing the dynamic flow to the periphery, so as to make it autonomous, as had occurred historically in the developed economies.

The way in which industrialisation occurred resulted in introducing the periphery into the dynamic capitalist flow of the centre, controlled by transnationals, a fact that established new relations of dependency as well as leveraging the contradictions of the process of accumulation of peripheral

---

11   This will be the subject of Chapter 4.
12   For Francisco Oliveira, this process of separating the state began in the final phase of the military dictatorship in Brazil (Oliveira, in Sader & Gentili (organisers), 1995:24–25). It is marked here in the 1990s because of processes of privatisation that were strengthened then.

capital. It made these economies much more submissive and vulnerable to the movement of global capital by reducing their capacity of control over their own processes of accumulation, given that this control, manifested in transnational capital, is external. So, new, much more complex relations of dependency are created in the centre-periphery relationship starting from the way industry was implanted in the periphery. What ended up being modified was the quality of the insertion of the periphery in the process of global accumulation.

"What characterises this new international economy is the control, by groups headquartered in the dominant subsystems, of the dissemination of new techniques, or rather, of new products and of new productive processes.... One may therefore state that in the underdeveloped economies, development tends to entail an increase in international connections, in the sense that in the great majority of cases, it is linked to the expansion of the activities of a company that has its decision-making centre outside of the subsystem in question [the peripheral economy]. As this development involves the adoption of a new standard of consumption or its dissemination, and with these new standards they bring with them a connection of an international type (import of inputs, payment of royalties, patents, etc.), one may also say the development referred to is a structural transformation of the global system that tends to strengthen the relationships of dependency" (Furtado, 1971:233).

These new contradictions to which the Latin American economies will be submitted are manifest in new, more complex forms of dependency in relation to the dynamic of the process of global accumulation that give substance to how they are subject to it from the processes of industrialisation with transnational capital. If the people from Cepal believed that it might be possible to reach a dynamic and independent autonomy, this was not the result of the process of development with import substitution backed by foreign capital. Import substitution alters the primary-exporter relationship, but creates another much more complex type of relationship that accelerates the contradictions of the process of accumulation and reflects them in the periphery by the logic of global accumulation. These contradictions are manifested in the dependency that the periphery will have on the movement of transnational capital vis-a-vis the strategy that the latter will have in the process of globalisation.

The apparent forms of this dependency are manifested as dependency on technology and finance as well as not forgetting, trade. They are dependencies that become increasingly great and real the more the peripheral economy subordinates itself to the process of global capitalist accumulation and the state is separated from the process. This makes more distant the hypothesis that the introduction of capitalism in the periphery would result automatically in development in Latin America as was imagined. The capitalism that was implanted in the periphery, under the control of large international oligopolised capital, is already born, through the contradictions that it develops, based on exclusion and is strengthened by it as Furtado and Oliveira showed, a fact that is embodied in the creation of an elite market as a dynamic element, that is strengthened in its phases of growth impacting imports when investment increases, and in a structural need to seek an export market, mainly in periods of crisis. This contradiction is evidenced in external vulnerability, manifested in enormous foreign debts that accompany these economies throughout past and recent history.

Authors such as Dos Santos (1978), Sunkel (1972), Frank (1980), Ianni (1974) and Furtado himself (1971, 1974, 1987) – being this last one, it is worth remembering, the one that constructed and placed in a theoretical model Cepal's ideas – was already pointing to a series of problems and results of the policies of import substitution of the 1950s (the "Plano de Metas" [Target Plan] in Brazil) and in the 1960s to some from other Latin American countries. They reformulated the theory of dependency faced with the restrictions that arose in the periphery (the ones that managed to have success in industrialising themselves) already by the end of the 1960s and start of the 1970s. After all, with the policies of import substitution in the way they were implemented, they managed, up to a certain point, to dissociate foreign trade from raw materials from peripheral growth, but made these economies much less autonomous. These economies, despite being more industrialised, found themselves in a situation of greater dependency than previously. The control over their internal dynamic came to depend largely on decisions taken abroad by those that controlled the large transnational companies installed in the periphery. New needs for imports, mainly of goods with embedded technology, along with the impossibility of developing technology internally and the foreign restriction that this resulted in, placed the peripheral Latin American economies in a new straitjacket.

Starting with import substitutions, the periphery transformed itself from the importer of finished manufactured products into the buyer of parts and capital goods, mainly those with high technological content, which becomes a structural problem for them. When the import of these products is impeded by protection measures for the industry installed in the periphery, it loses competitiveness and the prices rise; when imports are allowed, industry installed here is modernised but, at the same time it affects resources in hard currency, which end up in cycles of foreign restrictions evidenced in the accumulation of foreign debt.

For Theotônio dos Santos this was a structural problem that resulted from the process of import substitution that was already appearing in the 1960s. In so far that the substituting process in the segments of durable consumer goods created new import needs for intermediate goods, parts and capital goods. This importing becomes obligatory for the continuity of the process of production in certain sectors. This is why, dependency becomes structural. Before, imports of finished manufactured products could occur if there was an amount of hard currency available obtained through the export of primary products, but now [the 1960s], at the start of import substitution, the purchase abroad of "raw materials for industry, ... machines and products ... semi-manufactures ... [become] more than essential for the survival of the economy (Dos Santos, 1973:67). For the economy to grow in the periphery and modernise itself it is imperative to increase imports. Thus, this restriction becomes a structural problem for peripheral economies.

It is worth underlining that despite Dos Santos referring to the 1960s, this problem will always be present given that the question of the production of technology in the periphery will never be solved. The strategy of intensifying the process of substitution based on the premise that it would be possible to build the complete "edifice" within the periphery (Tavares, 1982:46), implanting all the key sectors simultaneously, making it less dependent on imports, will also not solve the problem as in Brazil's case. When one imagined the "edifice" completely ready at the end of the 1970s, as did Castor and Souza (1985), the economy faces difficulties and loss of competitiveness in the 1980s. This happens because Latin American peripheral capitalism had its dynamic structure in the hands of transnational capital, which makes it necessary to buy technology produced in the headquarters of transnational companies, a mechanism of constant pressure on imports that promotes the modernisation of transnational companies themselves in Latin America. And this did not result from a lack of natural technical capacity in the periphery, but from the fact that these companies had already developed this technology and its related products at the centre.

It is not part of the logic of transnational companies to develop technology in the periphery (Chesnais, 1996: Chapter 7). If one day they happened to produce it in the periphery, mainly in Latin America, it was in a marginal way. When one takes, for example, the number of patents as a measure of the creation of new technologies, one notes that "not more than 10% of patents granted [data from 1992] by the US Patent Office to international companies came from subsidiaries abroad" (Hirst and Thompson, 1998:151). It is worth stressing that these numbers involve both central and peripheral countries, making it possible to infer that patents coming from subsidiaries on the periphery must be insignificant. Therefore, transnational companies do not have a tendency to develop technology in the periphery. The majority of the strategic decision-making centres and of research and development of transnational corporations are located in developed countries (Dupas, 1999:47).

Apart from this, the strategy of the companies for the production and implanting of new technologies has little to do with the policy of development of the periphery. "... the transfer of technology and the process of learning ... are increasingly circumscribed by the global strategy of the transnational companies and are not related to the strategies of development of the countries that receive them" (UNCTAD 2003:103). This point is also reinforced by Porter who points to the fact that transnationals "cannot ... be the only engine for the creation of national advantage in advanced industries. The transnationals locate activities in the value chain of foreign countries as part of globally integrated strategies ... rarely is it of interest for a transnational to make a developing country an important centre for the production of sophisticated components or for undertaking essential R&D ...". (Porter, 1989:756).

"From the point of view of the accumulation of capital, this has profound consequences. The first and most obvious is that the countries or peripheral subnational capitalist systems may only copy the expendable, but not copy the headquarters technical-scientific unit; in a kind of eternal race against the clock. The second, less obvious, is that the accumulation that is done in terms of the expendable copy also enters into accelerated obsolescence ... This demands an effort of investment always beyond the limits of the internal forces of accumulation that reiterates the mechanisms of dependence on external finance" (Oliveira, 2003:139).

The other side of this new technological dependence resulting from the type of industrialisation that is implanted in Latin America, perhaps much more structural than it was in it its primary-exporter form, is the dependency on resources in hard currency to face up to the new needs for imports, mainly in the cycles of modernisation through which peripheral economies go through. At every new wave of investment in modernisation of the productive structure, with each cycle of economic growth, the tendency is to accumulate enormous foreign debts that end up by feeding on themselves. Argentina, Mexico and Brazil lived through these crises in the second half of the 1960s (Oliveira, 1977:87), in the second half of the 1970s (ibid., p.109), being that the latter was extended and subjugated the countries throughout the 1980s and, again at the end of the 1990s, now beyond the strategy of substitution.

So much is the need for imports in the periods of growth and industrial modernisation as is the payment of foreign debt obligations in the periods of crisis they bring with them. They need to generate trade surpluses abroad, or to obtain new loans, or even, attract new direct foreign investment, the only ways of bringing hard currency to the periphery. These elements materialise in what is called external restriction, an element that becomes recurrent in the periphery and ends up by placing it under the yoke of multilateral organisms that come to define the economic policy of the indebted periphery[13] (Clarke, 1996:301; Chossudovsky, 1999; Korten, 1996:211).

So, the peripheral economies see themselves faced with the obligation to carry out economic policies capable of generating these resources. One of the ways out, the most traditional and historical one in the periphery, is the promotion of currency devaluation to make their products more competitive abroad, a policy that, facing the needs for imports, has a strong inflationary impact by raising the costs of imported raw materials. Another way, also traditional both in the periphery and in the centre, is the promotion of recessive policies through a restrictive monetary policy – this result in an increase in domestic interest rates – and a restrictive fiscal policy, both have the aim of reducing aggregate internal demand and generating exportable surpluses. Another important impact of this type of measure affects the state[14] in so far as monetary control is undertaken through the means of issuing public debt, which greatly increases state indebtedness, also fed by high interest rates, factors that make it impossible for the state to act in the direction of economic growth and development, as it traditionally acted in the processes of import substitution.

Now, this set of policies, traditional at each balance of payments crisis experienced by the peripheral economies, are widely recommended by international bodies like the International Monetary Fund. They are clearly policies that ensure the payment of foreign commitments. They have accompanied the periphery since the crises of the 1960s and have been used as argument for liberalisation policies in the 1990s.

But, the impacts of these policies on the periphery are a little more perverse. Recessive adjustments that impose a kind of planned crisis on the economy end up by reinforcing the processes of concentration and centralisation of capital in the periphery, processes in which the stronger companies occupy the spaces of the weaker. As the foreign companies nearly always have greater financial fire-power given the support that they have from their head offices, they have a greater capacity for enduring each recessive crisis on the periphery, a time when they take advantage to occupy the spaces of the weaker companies. An example of this is demonstrated by Oliveira when, at the end of the

---

13   Stiglitz asserts that the IMF takes on the role of "colonial administrator" in the periphery (Stiglitz, 2000:70).
14   Carneiro & Modiano show that the Brazilian state increased its debt by pursuing monetary, fiscal and exchange policies to save the country from external restrictions in the 1980s (Carneiro & Modiano, 1990: Chapter 12).

1960s, "... a policy of calculated recession, whose purpose [was] to prepare the institutional basis for a process of capital concentration" (Oliveira, 1977:92 and 93) was implanted in Brazil and ended up by strengthening transnational capital. "... the privileged position in which are found foreign companies, relative to domestic ones, facilitated their survival and expansion" (Ianni, 1986:265).

On the other hand, this set of policies also aggravates the problem of income concentration. The needs of exports imposes lower costs on domestic production that, apart from being achieved by currency devaluation, are also the result of pressure on salaries which must always be low. This negatively affects any idea that still remains of the possibility of internalising the dynamic flow given that, faced with external restrictions, the realisation of the dynamic occurs externally, through exports, weakening the economic need for creating an internal market to feed the endogenous flow. Thus, contrary to any pressure for increases in the share of salaries in the national income, the perverse dynamic created damages it by the new form of dependency. The concentration of income comes to be a link in this dynamic. Any attempt to change this always faces political problems raised by those who control the process: transnational corporations together with the national elite (industrial junior partners and banks).

3.7 The Development of Submission to the Movement of Globalised Capital

"The theory of dependency sought to demonstrate that this industrialisation would not bring the hoped-for outcomes according to the developmentalist and national-democratic vision. It did not bring autonomy of decision-making because the industrialisation came to be commanded by foreign investment, in the hands of multinational corporations, whose centre of power continued [and continues] to be in the central hubs of the global economy" (Dos Santos, 2000:127). Thus, the Latin American economies, even the ones that were successful in industrialising themselves, continued to be peripheral.

The policies of import substitution placed the dependency of the peripheral economies on a new level. They made the link with the process of global capital accumulation much closer mainly due to the fact that the representatives of global capital, transnational capital, occupied leading positions, in the core of the value chain, in deciding the internal dynamic of the peripheral economies. It made the dynamic of these economies connected to the specifications and the investment decisions and sales of these new members of the periphery's industrial structure, transnational capital, by putting the advanced technology sectors under their command. It made the Latin American economy more subordinated to the movement of globalised capital.

The industrialisation of the periphery, centred on transnationals, created new relations of subordination in relation to the central countries that were manifest in foreign restrictions. These relations of subordination place the peripheral country directly under the yoke of the global process of capital accumulation, mostly, totally disconnected from the needs and national aims of the peripheral economies. When this model is rooted in the productive structure of the peripheral country, it makes itself a constant threat to whatever policy intention of any peripheral state that does not suit the interests of large transnational capital. "Even though [the peripheral states] totally reject the theories of development that are being offered them by the developed countries, even so their options in terms of strategies would be circumscribed by the predominance of foreign companies in their economies" (Evans, 1982:191).

The Latin American economies that achieved success in industrialising themselves not only ended up by not reproducing the development of the central countries, but also ended up by making it more difficult for any attempt to build a process of accumulation more suited to national development in the broader sense, as apparently they may have desired. The type of insertion of the periphery in the process of accumulation did not transform it into "developed" in the sense of the centre but only accelerated its form of insertion and submission to the process of global accumulation. It altered the relationship of dependency, but replaced it by another, much more complex type.

Development and inclusion in the movement of global capital are not the same thing. They may in fact be contradictory. Perhaps they may in part be synchronised through political action that acts in a contrary or compensatory movement in relation to the movement of capital, at least whilst capital does not reach the scale of concentration that challenges this same compensatory action of the state. But this state action becomes more difficult when the origin of decisions is outside the geographic limits of the nation state, when they are subordinate to the movement of capital in symbiosis with its state of origin. This subordination is aggravated by the fact that the transnational capital that comes to the periphery is in the sectors that are at the dynamic centre for spreading technology. It is also strengthened by the fact the specific process of substitution of imports that occurred in Latin America was the result of an international movement of capital supported by Latin American elites, administered by their nation states. So, by strengthening transnational capital at each cycle of accumulation in the periphery, the result will be at the end of the 1980s and 1990s, an enormous pressure to weaken peripheral nation states, until then the central coordinators of this process, now in charge to give more freedom of movement to capital itself, eliminating the institutional hurdles in the new phases of the process of globalised accumulation.

Thus, one can arrive at a true idea of what the Latin American economies are. In a way, for Cepal the term peripheral was associated with backwardness and underdevelopment, connected to the question of technology, low productivity and the lack of homogeneity of the productive structure in relation to the developed centre (Rodriguez, 1981:144). On the other hand, one comes to the conclusion that the solution found to overcome this dependency does not achieve success in the sense of a dynamic transformation from dependency, when based on transnational companies in alliance with the internal new elites that were born in the process. The Latin American periphery continues being the periphery after years of import substitution because it is linked to a specific form of insertion in the process of global capital accumulation from the centre that was, on the contrary, strengthened by the strategy of industrialisation by import substitution as implanted in Latin America. The periphery continues connected to the productive structure and to the hegemonic power, one form that is not defined without the other. "Peripheralisation is an economic, social, political, cultural process through which a country loses a part of its autonomy in favour of the centre" (Nagels, 1993:85).

This periphery, in its relationship with the centre, is inserted in the process of accumulation of global capital accumulation, dominated by transnationals, in the most complex way. Perhaps this may be the explanation for the fact that the peripheral economies that managed to industrialise find themselves, in the end "as much intermediaries as they were 50 or 100 years ago ... a fact that falls short of expectations as much as from the theory of modernisation [of Rostow] as that of dependency" (Arrighi, 1998:138).[15] It is worth stressing that it also differs in relation to the development of some Asian countries that made use of another type of a less or no submissive strategy to transnational capital (Fajjnzylber, 200:868).

The centre, formed by the countries that have control over the process of global capital accumulation, hosts the centres of control of the representatives of capital, the areas of marketing and technology, the centres of command of the corporations. For this reason, the form of insertion of the periphery guarantees to these countries of the centre formed historically from the stronger

---

15   It is worth stressing a point that does not appear to have been taken into consideration by Arrighi that is the fact that "near the beginning of the First World War, income per capita of Argentina ... was superior to that of France, Germany, Italy and Spain. The income per capita of the region [Latin America] exceeded that of Japan and was around three times the average of the rest of East Asia" (UNCTAD 2003:127).

states, today, the global hegemony, also strengthened by a symbiotic relation between the corporation and its centre-states (Triad ones), one guaranteeing and working to perpetuate the political and economic power of the other over the periphery. For this periphery, all that remains is to surrender itself to this movement of globalised capital giving up its autonomy and independence, playing the game of capital – that it has done many times – or attempt to manage this process of insertion so as to seek to promote, in fact, development.

Thus, the process of industrialisation of the periphery that achieved success can be seen, in fact, as a process of the expansion of capitalism starting from the centre, subjecting the periphery to its mechanism, to its logic of accumulation with the collusion and support of the state and of the peripheral elites. The periphery thus became increasingly to be controlled from the centre, by the logic of accumulation of the centre. Therefore, it becomes much more vulnerable to the mode of functioning of globalised capital when this enters a phase of global capital centralisation, when it runs the risk of being excluded from its movement, following capital's own logic.

Of course, this movement of capital is reinforced by the strategic policy from within the Latin American economies. The policies throughout the years were increasingly supporting productive internationalisation by the creation of conditions for the installation of transnational industrial plants in the most dynamic sectors of the periphery. The industrial structure was becoming increasingly vulnerable to the control and the strategies decided at the centre. The contradictions were aggravated on the periphery generating crises that resulted in weakening these economies and strengthening international control, be it productive, through the intermediation of direct foreign investment following the global strategies of the transnationals, be it political, manifested in the degree of submission to restrictive economic policies that tend to aggravate the situation and increase productive control by the recurrent internal crises that they generate. In the 1980s and 1990s they crowned the process: the periphery continues waiting for the good will of transnational capital in a new environment, one of centralisation; the liberalising policies open space for this centralisation of global capital that places the periphery under the risk of exclusion by deindustrialization

CHAPTER 4

Brazil in Capital's Globalisation

4.1 Introduction

The introduction of capitalism to Brazil was always connected to a decided state strategy. It may be said that it was partly something planned and implemented, not being in any way the result of some kind of natural force of a free "market", although its direction has always been one of engaging with the movement of capital, the specific, real arm of the "market". One may thus say that it was constructed according to the forces of accumulation of global capital, but by a deliberate option of the internal forces that embodied state action in the structuring of capitalism in Brazil, and they promoted the alliance with world capital. It was, on the one hand, the result of the "political fragility of the state bureaucracy facing the conservative interests of the dominant class … that channelled … Brazilian economic development … along the path of least resistance, creating a highly developed industrial structure, however, without self-sustaining finance and technology" (Fiori, 2001b:274). And it is these dominant groups, sometimes in a more explicit form and at others less so, that allied themselves in a deliberate way to foreign capital to advocate the development associated with it. "As a direct result of this alliance, international capital assumed and maintained a hegemonic industrial position, living alongside various segments of local capital that, despite great weakness, managed to preserve their profitability" (Fiori, 2001b:276).

The way how industrialisation and its subordination to the process of global accumulation emerged was, therefore, a deliberate process. Hence, it is intended to highlight the way the Brazilian economy entered into the process of global capital accumulation, how it was integrated into globalised capital and how this resulted in its growing vulnerability or submission to its logic of functioning, it was organised in various ways within historic political arrangements that made it a reality. It is these arrangements that explain the path chosen, the strategies outlined. In fact, "… the development or growth is a problem that involves the opposition between internal social classes…" (Oliveira, 1987:12) and, specifically in the Brazilian case, the result of this relation of internal forces is what drove the Brazilian economy to tie itself to world capital in its strategy of development in the specific form how this occurred. This being the case, the country's form of insertion in capitalism, the way how its dependent development arose, ends up by its form of connection to global capital, being at the same time, "… precisely a 'production' of the expansion of capitalism" (Oliveira, 1987:12).

This means to say that capitalist development in Brazil could have been different. But to say that is really not to say much. It is to work with hypotheses and if that had been the aim of this work, it would have had to start from comparisons with Asian countries, which will not be done because that is not the proposal. One wishes only to be attentive to the fact that capital, in its process of globalisation comes, here in Brazil, in a growing form, occupying more and more significant spaces throughout history, subordinating the country increasingly to its movement, radicalising the condition of dependency. Thus, one does not have the aim here of discussing if there could have been or not historical possibilities in the context of social and political relationships, faced with global capitalism, of realising another type of strategy for Brazilian economic development. That would be another, totally different discussion from the one proposed here. Revisiting the history of Brazilian economic development has the unique aim of emphasising, picking out relevant points that reveal which was the path taken and discuss the possible consequences of this action. The forces that are organised here historically as well as in their relation to the global movement of capital that, with all their setbacks, constructed the productive structure that there is today in Brazil, which is much more dependent than associated. That is why, one may say that it also resulted in the vulnerability and in the structural problems that the Brazilian economy faces. The central focus of this chapter is not to reconstruct the history of capitalism in Brazil, a task that would be impossible for the time, space and analytical capacity of this work, not least because this task, has been undertaken in recent years by numerous authors of renown some of whom will be quoted here. The aim is to retrieve, beginning with them, the process of Brazilian development following the central thread of development associated with foreign capital that results in the internationalisation of the Brazilian productive structure, principally from the 1950s, to demonstrate how, in this story, Brazil becomes increasingly vulnerable and subordinated, by its own will, to the movement of global capital, facing the forces that here became hegemonic, by the way how the game of internal political forces was organised. The process of productive internationalisation of the Brazilian economy is the result of an internal movement and, at the same time, of the movement of global capital, in the same way that in the 1990s, the policies of liberalisation also will be in symbiosis with the globalisation of capital characterised by the process of centralisation that took place. As stated by the Institute of Studies for Industrial Development: "… the attractiveness of the Brazilian economy to foreign capital is not recent. We may add that not always was this process accompanied by the denationalisation of

Brazilian companies, it is worth mentioning, the transfer of national ownership to foreigners. In respect of the industrial sector, it is possible also to state that the Brazilian economy has long been an open economy. It is worth highlighting that the characterisation of a "closed economy" for the Brazilian economy until the 1980s resulted from a reference to international trade and the restrictions to the flows of foreign investment in the financial system and in certain segments controlled by state companies, especially public service utilities and basic sectors (oil for example). It is well known that Brazilian industrialisation had a significant share of foreign investment. The policy of attracting foreign capital, initiated in the second half of the 1950s, was expanded ... in 1964, making the country more attractive compared to other countries in development [with one of the lowest levels of restrictions. In the 1990s that policy became more radical when] "the distinction between domestic and foreign capital was eliminated" (IEDI, 2000:16–17).

In a gradual way, Brazil submitted itself to the movement of global capital and so became increasingly vulnerable and subordinated to it. That process, apart from increasing the dependency pointed to in Chapter 3, created a growing difficulty for the action of the nation state in movements sometimes contrary to the interests of large global capital, or that responds to the national interest in the construction of a more autonomous capitalism or less vulnerable to the movement of global capital. This process of submission to the movement of capital which in a gradual way becomes stronger from the second half of the 1950s, reaches its peak, its point of greatest vulnerability and consequently, of greatest difficulty to take a more autonomous path, starting from the liberalising policies of the 1990s, that apart from reducing the space for the weakest link of the Brazilian productive structure in the "Tripod of Accumulation" formed in the 1950s, private domestic capital, practically cuts off another leg, productive capacity and the intervention of the state that gave form to the Brazilian productive structure.

The Brazilian State, as producer and planner, constructed and reformulated since the first government of Getúlio Vargas (1930–45) and, principally in his second period (1951–54), is practically dismantled in its capacity for intervention in the 1990s as a result of the programmes of privatisation as well as fiscal, economic, monetary and exchange policies that were blocked from being realised through pressure for macroeconomic "stability", a necessary scenario for the full freedom requested by the now globalised capital, this globalisation is manifested in the processes of centralisation of capitals that have taken control of direct foreign investment in the world since the mid-1980s.

It is certain that this form of Brazilian economic insertion in the process of global capital accumulation is not linear nor free from contradictions.

Noteworthy are the attempts at recovering the control of Brazilian development in the two governments of Getúlio Vargas (1930–45 and 1951–54), in the Triennial Plan (1961–64) of Furtado (Ianni, 1986:307) and in II PND (the Second National Development Plan 1974–76) of the Military Government (Lessa, 1998; Fiori, 1995:71). But what dominates history is the growing internationalisation that will culminate in the 1990s. It is full of contradictions because it was with this growing productive internationalisation and of external control that made it possible for the country to reach the economic growth and its insertion in industrial capitalism; Brazil constructed an extremely strong productive industrial structure, with international renown in various productive sectors, a situation that arrived through undertaking a strategy and not against one. Brazil did not build the productive structure that it has despite the strategy, but because of it, it became what it is because of it, even though it may be one of the most unequal and unjust countries in the world, even if this strategy results in the reduction of the power of control over the destinies of national development for its association and subordination to multinational capital by its form of submission to the process of world accumulation. But, it is this strategy that gradually reduced its power of intervention in the process and raised the degree of vulnerability of the Brazilian economy that, the reverse of more autonomy, has become more dependent and submissive to the movement of global capital.

It is important to point out that this structural subordination to external capital which happened to the Brazilian economy is one of the starting points used as a justification for the liberalisation of the 1990s, based on the idea that the solution for the development of the country would be to strengthen the links with globalised capital given that it is the engine of progress (that brings in technology and productivity to the peripheral economies). But, with the deepening of this relationship, with the increased submission to globalised capital through the establishment of liberalising policies, the result will be the destruction of an already fragile (for having multinational companies at its centre) productive and institutional apparatus created in Brazil. This makes it possible for capital, now engaged in a wide-ranging global process of capital centralisation, to freely realise its global restructuring to the detriment of the national economy, by de-structuring it.

The logic of Cepal's import substitution (presented in Chapter 3) was what shaped the form of Brazilian development. This strategy was present in each economic plan, in some more and others less, undertaken by the political configuration on each occasion. Here one wishes to stress that the strategy of substitution was the basis for the industrialisation of various countries that protected or incentivised their nascent industry to allow it to strengthen supported by government policies. Ha-Joon Chang (2001), reviewing the history, shows that several countries undertook protectionist policies through exchange rates, import barriers of various types, etc., to impede competition from the industry of other countries that might hinder the flourishing of their domestic industries. The classical example most debated is in some Asian countries, but the author stresses, in an historic analysis, the types of protection implemented to impede competition of English textiles with the Indians (Chang, 2001:22), as well as the way the United States incentivised and protected its nascent industry from the competition with English production (ibid., 2001:25–27). This fact demonstrates that the question, therefore, which leads to increase the vulnerability of the Brazilian economy (and of part of the Latin American economy) is not focussed on the substitution of imports in itself. This strategy for the introduction of a domestic industrial complex, in capitalism, is thus indisputable for what is here proposed. The central question one wishes to point to here is, on the contrary, in the construction of an industrial structure based on transnationals, in a substitution of specific imports, that within its strategy counted on foreign capital for the formation of its productive structure in the most dynamic sectors as a way of introducing capitalism. This is the crux of the problem of vulnerability. It makes the impact of the process of the global accumulation of capital more radical in this economy. It is also aggravated by loss of control over the capacity for making autonomous economic policy faced with this growing submission to the movement of global capital. Therefore, the more vulnerable to the movement of global capital now engaged in a process of centralisation of capitals, to international capitalism manifested in the movement of large corporations that are connected to other national states, the less is the autonomous capacity of the local, peripheral state that is submitted to this movement in acting as a counter-weight to the process of capital accumulation, of diminishing the impact of its own internal contradictions to this movement, characteristic of any capitalist economy. That is the most radical consequence of the strategy of development adopted, aided by transnational capital. It is much easier for the national state to be co-opted as an agent in the process of global accumulation rather than national accumulation, as it appears to happen in the 1990s.

"... if what is given internationally sometimes is imposed on the rest of the world today ... the state is called to exercise an increasingly more important role each day. Thus the importance of the dispute between the big powers to control the political apparatus of the peripheral states". (Milton Santos, 2002: 230).

Whilst during the post-war period until the 1970s the process of capital accumulation in the world context was a process of productive internationalisation in a movement of inclusion, capital materialised in large corporations, created productive structures in Brazil and in part of the periphery. As mentioned in Chapter 2, this was a movement of expansion, a kind of overflowing of frontiers manifest in the establishment of subsidiaries in the periphery. In this context, making policies to attract this capital in search of new spaces for investment was related to the promotion of industrialisation in the periphery, even though that might imply a loss of national sovereignty.

The question is that, starting from the 1980s, as shown in the UNCTAD (2000 and others) report, the movement of capital in the world is no longer one of creating new installations in the periphery in a movement of expansion, but is focussed on a huge process of world restructuring of production manifested in mergers and acquisitions, characterising a process of global centralisation of capitals, as will be shown in Chapter 5. In this context, to undertake pro-capital policies with the idea of attracting it may, on the contrary, stimulate centralisation that has no sense of inclusion, but the reverse, it has a sense of leaving the periphery in direction of the centre or elsewhere, of abandonment, of de-industrialisation of the periphery, a movement that in part is noted by the increase of imports of products that were formerly produced in the periphery. In this sense vulnerability and subordination to the movement of global capital acquires a new character, a character of disintegration and exclusion, which tends to affect those nation states subordinated to global capital in a certain way like Latin American countries.

At any rate, it is important to stress that when one here argues about the loss of capacity to make autonomous policy in the industrialised periphery to transnational capital, one does not wish to say that one cannot do it and that it only remains to implore foreign capital, so that it does not go away. Very much the contrary, a strategy of development, in this case, comes through breaking these historically rooted patterns and structures in the dependent periphery, in Brazil. What is aimed for here is therefore simply to be alert to the fact that however great the degree of submission to the global movement of capital, the greater will be the interests that will have to be challenged with a change in the direction of a development policy. But it is worth emphasising that to break with consolidated interests is part of the movement of history. "The historic and current dependency of the subspaces in relation to international demand, gives them as a characteristic a limited autonomy... While, the state remains as the only organisation capable of opposing this or that form of realisation of the external forces" (Milton Santos, 2002:230), even though it may be in a temporary way faced with the growing contradictions that are present in capitalism itself.

4.2 Vargas – The Institutional Apparatus for Development

The history of Brazilian industrialisation has its landmark at the end of the 19th Century, according to Suzigan, "the formation of industrial capital on a significant scale apparently began in the period between the beginning of the decade of the 1870s and 1890" (Suzigan, 1986:350). This industrialisation is strengthened and has its growth, at least until the 1930s, dictated by bottlenecks and setbacks arising from what was happening with the coffee economy, which was strongly connected to the movements of global economy. That is why it may be considered as an industrialisation that up to a certain point was spontaneous. The coffee economy as much created the importing capacity of the nascent industry, as it strengthened the national market by the internal income that it generated for a middle class involved in its structure of production and trade, as well as by the substitution of slave labour by free labour. "The coffee economy created... (1)... a mass of monetary capital... (2) it transforms the work force into a commodity; and... (3)... it creates an internal market" (Cardoso de Mello, 1982:99).

For Suzigan, foreign productive capital began to have some importance starting in the 1920s, when "direct foreign capital investment performed an important role in the diversification of the industrial structure..." (Suzigan, 1986:351). At any event, this foreign industry was connected principally to some sectors of intermediate and middle income consumer goods (Cardoso de Mello, 1982:163) and here it installed itself as the counterpoint to periods of difficulties in terms of import capacity. Despite this, in no way can this entry of foreign capital be comparable to that which occurred at the beginning of the second half of the 1950s. These foreign investments showed that Brazil would have been "the stage for the *avant-première* of the movement ... of internationalisation" which was to happen later; they are movements that occur before industrialisation becomes central to Brazilian development. It was a movement in which, the foreign subsidiaries were still under the "command of the hegemonic national mercantile complex" and "they accepted a position subordinated to other capital orbits that determined the command of the movement of capitalist expansion" (Lessa & Dain, 1982:219–222). At any rate, it is in the wake of this process that the symbiotic relationship was born which would strengthen itself between national and transnational capital in the 1950s. The Revolution of 1930 in Brazil marks the start of the process of detachment of the industrial economy in relation to the accumulation of the coffee economy (Tavares, 1998:128; Almeida, 1995:90). For a long time still, industrial growth will be coupled to the agricultural export sector and only in the 1970s will industrial GDP exceed that of agriculture. But, it was in the 1930s that "a basic institutional framework was constructed that allowed the Brazilian state to take the following steps in the direction of our industrial modernity" (Fiori, 1995:101), this industry that "… starting from the mid-1950s formed a new standard of accumulation under the unequivocal hegemony of industrial capital" (Lessa & Dain, 1982:225). Thus, the processes (that) occurred before the 1950s established the "internal pre-conditions that made the country one of the peripheral economies chosen by capital blocks, in a vigorous phase of competition [between individual capitals in the world], as a zone for the migration of new subsidiaries" (Lessa & Dain, 1982:225). It will only be starting from this, a movement that will only happen in the 1950s with a base previously structured, that transnational capital will come to occupy a larger space in the process of Brazilian capitalist accumulation, whilst still not dominant, given the strong presence of the state, as well as, although modest, national capital. The structuring of the institutional framework that the national state will establish and allow capitalist development in Brazil is undertaken by President Getúlio Vargas. Despite debate about the nationalist character of the Vargas government,[1] it is a fact that during his two mandates, the national state was structured, in terms of its capacity for planning and development, as well as in its action as a producer-director. The construction and strengthening of the state is what will permit the drawing up of the Targets Plan (Plano de Metas, 1956–60). In this sense, it was Getúlio Vargas who structured and instrumentalised the first "leg", the national state, of what will be called, "the Tripod of Accumulation" starting from the 1950s. It was done because of the external restrictions that hindered the import of basic industrial products If he did so on behalf of some interest in attracting without much success foreign capital, or even, by the impossibility of attracting foreign capital to industrialise the country, the fact is that it was in his government that the state increased its power of intervention as planner and producer that will be the basis, as well as empowering itself, in the period of the Targets Plan.

---

1   While Ianni (1986: 143–147) points to the more nationalist character of the Vargas government, Oliveira seeks to affirm that it is not this element that leads to the structuring of the state for development (Oliveira, 1977:78). On the other hand, Fiori notes the attempt to implant a national-developmentalist project during the New State (o Estado Novo, the first Vargas government). In Vargas' second government at the beginning of the 1950s and after President Giesel's II PND, attempts were vetoed or made difficult by the North American government (Fiori, 2001b:280). In Almeida's opinion (1995) the Vargas position was more complex, it was not about fighting foreign capital in general, but of facing up to capital committed to a type of dependency in which Brazil is inserted as a primary materials exporter … and of attracting foreign capitals that propel industrialisation (Almeida, 1995:122).

The institutional structures as well as the state-owned productive bases that allowed the advance of the industrialisation of the Targets Plan (1956–60) were largely constituted in the two periods when the country was under the administration of Getúlio Vargas. In his first mandate (1930–45), it will be created in 1942 Companhia Siderúrgica Nacional-CSN (the National Steel Company) and Companhia Vale do Rio Doce-CVRD (River Doce Valley Company – today's giant mining concern "Vale"); in 1943 Companhia Nacional de Álcalis (The National Alkalis Company); 1939 Instituto Brasileiro de Geografia e Estatística-IBGE (Brazilian Geographic and Statistical Institute); 1941 Fábrica Nacional de Motores (National Engines Factory); 1945 Superintendência da Moeda e do Crédito-SUMOC (The Money and Credit Administration). This demonstrates the importance of the developmentalist strategy of this phase. In the second Vargas period (1951–55), this national productive structure with broad state participation was expanded: between 1952 and 1953 Banco Nacional de Desenvolvimento Econômico-BNDE (The National Development Bank), Banco do Nordeste-BNB (The Bank of North East Brazil) and Petrobrás (the state oil company) in 1954 Eletrobrás (the state electricity company). "It was evident that the state was in fact creating new conditions for the expansion and differentiation of the Brazilian economic system" (Ianni, 1986:131). Hence one may say that before the Targets Plan the productive structure in basic state sectors was already partly assembled and it is this structure that accompanies and gives shape to future economic growth cycles until the 1980s.

In the context of the industrialisation strategy, Vargas also implemented SUMOC Instruction 70 in 1953[2] (which will be widely used in the Targets Plan), with the clear intention of stimulating imports of capital goods that would allow the modernisation of the Brazilian industrial complex, in an effort to accelerate the process of import substitution. This measure had no direct connection to any productive internationalisation, although it also permitted the modernisation of foreign capital already installed in the country. In the same way, it was also Getúlio Vargas who created the BNDE-CEPAL commission in 1953 to discuss projects for national development. This commission took advantage of projects that had already been discussed by the Brazil-United States Joint Commission. This commission had been abolished, according to Ianni, because of US dissatisfaction given its political orientation (perhaps a little nationalistic) adopted by Vargas (Ianni, 1986:141). At any rate, the proposals drawn up by the BNDE-CEPAL commission would be the basis for the

---

2 It creates a policy of multiple exchange rates.

formulation of the Targets Plan, defining its operative "rationality" (Oliveira, 1977:84) in the project of industrialisation. The report of this commission, which pointed out bottlenecks and strangulation points in the Brazilian economy which should be overcome, was incorporated in the Development Council (Conselho de Desenvolvimento) created in 1956, responsible for drawing up the Targets Plan (Orenstein & Sochaczewski, 1992:176). So, one may say that the Plan's characteristics followed recommendations contained in the documents concerning the needs for industrialisation.

Thus, Lessa states, that "At the beginning of the 1950s, with the change processed in the political commands, a succession of economic policy measures aimed at modifying the national economic structure were observed.... arrangements [were made] that later came to make up a substantial part of the nucleus of the instruments used in the Targets Plan..." (Lessa, 1982:20). Despite this, it was not proposed or at least made explicit any strategy of industrialisation with foreign capital by Getúlio Vargas, even in his second government.

The landmark of change which makes explicit the strategy of association with foreign capital in the productive structuring of the Brazilian economy appears with SUMOC Instruction 113, created after the exit of Vargas and before the entry of President Juscelino Kubitschek (Eugênio Gudin was treasury minister in the period when Instruction 113 was created), but widely used in the Targets Plan. This measure has the aim of accelerating and facilitating the entry of foreign capital in Brazil. Thus it may be considered a landmark in the change of the trend in economic policy between the two periods in the direction of development associated with foreign capital. What Juscelino keeps of the Vargas period is thus, mainly, the state structure and its institutional apparatus for the development process, its role as planner as well as producer in specific basic sectors. The difference, marked by the indiscriminate use that was made of Instruction 113 throughout the Targets Plan, is its character of being associated with foreign capital that will take over the strategy of development from 1956. Thus, "... it will be the Targets Plan that will widen the gap opened by the Gudin administration, in such a way and to such a point that thus pattern will end up moulding the structure of capital reproduction in the country" until the crisis of the 1970s (Oliveira, 1977:82). And, as Oliveira points out, one of the reasons for the success of this association with foreign capital goes beyond internal measures, being also related to "the redefining of the international division of labour underway after the ending of the recovery of post-war Europe [that] transformed the terms of action of international capital in relation to dependent economies: now, the industrialisation of the dependent economies entered into the international division of labour" (Oliveira, 1977:83).

4.3 National Associated Development – The Targets Plan (Plano de Metas)

The Targets Plan (Plano de Metas) of President Juscelino Kubitschek (1956–60) marks the beginning of the process of the Brazilian economy's internationalisation because it places the participation of transnational capital within the national productive structure on a new level. Foreign companies have been in Brazil since the 19th century in an unorganised way and, as seen, in a way subordinated to national accumulation. The Targets Plan represents the beginning of the occupation by transnational capital of an important part of the dynamic sectors of the Brazilian productive structure, an occupation that was strengthened in the following years. It is responsible for the definition of the national productive structure that will remain until the 1980s and by the leading place foreign capital occupies in this structure until the enlargement of its space with the withdrawal of the state in this process by the reforms of the 1990s.

"Foreign direct investment in already existing industrial plants or even entirely new ones… of a size without precedent, and the opening of new multinational subsidiaries starts to occur at a rhythm without previous parallels. As a consequence, the middle of the 1950s may be considered a milestone for both the industrialisation process as well as registering the presence of the international corporation in Brazil" (Possas, 1983:19).

The core of the plan was the development of capitalism in Brazil through the creation of a dynamic industrial structure that would internalise the flow of production-circulation in a more autonomous and independent way from the world economy and that would complete the national industrial complex. "The Plan gave absolute priority to the construction of the higher stages of the vertically integrated industrial pyramid and to the basic social capital to support this structure. It would continue the process of import substitution that had been developing in the two previous decades" (Lessa, 1982:27). Thus, the strategy "… implied accelerated growth of the productive capacity of the capital goods sector and of the consumer durable goods sector…" (Cardoso de Mello, 1982:117).

This perspective was not different from that which oriented the industrialisation process advocated by Getúlio Vargas, mainly in his second government, in which he accentuated the national state's role in this project. The differences between the strategies of industrialisation were much more connected to the role that foreign capital should take on in this new context. This change of perspective, from one of the development of national capitalism to an associated capitalism is what marked the differences of strategy. "What is essential for understanding this government [of Juscelino Kubitschek] is its economic policy [Targets Plan], and that it adopted then a political strategy of development that resulted in consolidating and expanding dependent capitalism; or associated, according to the perspective of the government of the time" (Ianni, 1986:159).

Starting from "extremely favourable treatment for the entry of capitals[3]... [and of the] expansion of the direct participation of the public sector in the formation of capital..." (Lessa, 1982:56), multinational capital ended up by occupying a central place at the side of the national state in the Brazilian productive structure starting with the Targets Plan. But, it is worth remembering, the place of the national state in development had already been defined in the Vargas period. "There was not in this period, except for rare exceptions, any preoccupation over the instrumental reformulation of redefining the role of the state. The old apparatus was mobilised and used intensively..." (Lessa, 1982:99), "instruments inherited from previous stages" (Lessa, 1982:92).

What was redefined in the most profound way was the role of foreign capital in the new configuration that will be called the "Tripod of Accumulation". In this arrangement transnational capital takes on the central role connected to the development of the sectors with higher technology, mainly in the sectors of consumer durable goods, and they end up occupying a crucial area in the dynamic of accumulation, in the inter-sectorial relationship, in the value chain, in "forward and backward linkages" (Hirschman, 1981, p. 75) of the process of production. But, more than this, it thus ends up by occupying a central place in the internalisation of technology, an element present in Cepal's strategy and, as proposed in Chapter 3, that which again poses in a radical way the question of a new dependence.

"If ...we take this concept [of industrialisation] as one of 'constitution of the specifically capitalist productive forces', that is, capable of guaranteeing the dominance of industrial capital in the process ... [of] accumulation, we have to wait until the 1950s in order to have this verified, through the decisive entry of the state and international companies. The action of the state is decisive for the establishment of a heavy capital goods industry, and from international companies for the installation of a differentiated and 'dynamic' sector of capitalist consumer goods" (Tavares, 1998:128). Getúlio Vargas had built the state structure and its capacity for planning in order that, at a second stage, international corporations might enter the process.

---

3 SUMOC Instruction 113 of 1955 was widely used to attract foreign capital at exceptionally favourable exchange rates, advantages and facilities for the remission of dividends; "the entry of company capital was realised at the free market rate, which increased ... profitability in foreign exchange" etc. (Lessa, 1982:58).

Expansion was "supported by the state and by the *new* foreign capital that was transferred [to Brazil] in the form of productive capital" (Cardoso de Mello, 1982:118 – author's emphasis). It was down to the state "to invest massively in infrastructure and the basic industries under its responsibility ... it was also down to it, moreover, an essential task: to establish *the basis of association* with the large oligopolistic foreign company, defining clearly, a scheme of accumulation and of granting it generous favours" (Cardoso de Mello, 1982:118 – author's emphasis). "The presence of the large foreign company is not explained just by the excellent investment opportunities, ... but, also, in the last resort, by the dynamic itself of oligopolistic competition in the central countries, whose point of arrival consisted, as is known, in the financial conglomeration and in the oligopolistic expansion on a world scale ... the state and the large oligopolistic company commanded, unequivocally, the process of heavy industrialisation [of 1956–60]" (Cardoso de Mello, 1982:119). For Serra also, the second half of the 1950s is what marks "the massive entry of foreign capital in the production of manufactured goods destined for the domestic market" (Serra, 1982:73).

This does not mean that the process of growth during the period might not have benefitted, and even in part strengthened, national capital. Only, it needs stressing, it is not the leader of the process and it will benefit from the stimulus that it receives from foreign capital to operate a cordon of minor companies centred around the leading foreign company, developing its associated character, as well as a "junior partner". This role appears clearly in the metal-mechanical sector, in which "the demand derived from the large foreign company stimulates the emergence, growth and modernisation of the small and medium-sized national company, forming itself into a differentiated oligopoly centred on the large foreign company, ringed with small and medium-sized companies, suppliers as well as distributors" (Cardoso de Mello, 1982:120). This is the form of participation where the national companies will have some possibility of access to technology developed by the central-company and its headquarters (the classic example is the relationship between car assemblers and their component suppliers[4]). On the other hand, the traditional national company in the sectors of non-durable consumer goods – of lower technology and where there was already national capital predominance – will also benefit through the growth of the consumer market. That is the place that national

---

4 The industry of car components experienced enormous growth mainly stimulated by the policy of promoting local production. It reached around 1,200 factories in 1960 (Lessa, 1982:47–48). Just so as not to lose a comparison that will be important, according to Anfavea (Brazil's automotive producers' association), in 1990 there were 1,500 car component factories in Brazil.

capital will occupy. Certainly, faced with the industrialising strategy of the time, it could occupy no other place. But it is worth emphasising: this demonstrates that transnational capital did in fact occupy the dynamic centre of the Brazilian economy beginning with the Targets Plan, although still, alongside a powerful national state.

The symbiosis between foreign and national state capital is what is new in this cycle of growth. On the one hand is a strategy for development, planned and drawn up in the state apparatus, which now seeks and creates new conditions for the participation of transnational capital; on the other, is the expansion process of capital in the world itself that seeks new places to ensure continuity of its accumulation. The Targets Plan enters into this gap. "Evidently, in the period from 1937 to 1954, the association [with foreign capital] is less visible and the profile of foreign domination is more attenuated than from 1956–57. That may be due [in part][5] ... to the orientation itself of the expansion of world capital "intra-centres" in the immediate post-war which was not particularly interested nor demanding a new wave of expansion on the periphery. From the point of view of the new technical and economic structures of the "differentiated oligopoly" and its international forms of competition, the periphery was not yet a market, but marginal for investing new industrial capitals" (Tavares, 1998:143). But, starting from 1956/60 this reality is changed and global capital begins a "process of widening the frontiers of expansion of capitalism, in its advanced and oligopolies phase, [that] transformed in a significant way some peripheral economies, incorporating them ... to the fringe of the industrialised world" (Coutinho & Belluzzo, 1982:21). Possas (1983) also points in this direction in relating the process of Brazilian industrialisation to a new phase of internationalisation of capital in the post-war period (Possas, 1983:21).

Even more reinforcement for the argument is supplied in points made by Ianni: "After the rapid success of the Marshall Plan, of the experiments of the Truman doctrine (liberal in the 1940s) and the end of the Korean War, North American capitalism needed to find new frontiers for expansion; or to intensify its development in areas where it was already installed" (Ianni, 1986:153). The Targets Plan coincides, therefore, with this stage of the process of expansion of capitalism "from the demands established by capitalist reproduction itself, in the world environment. Thus, when the United States consolidated its hegemony over Europe and Japan, the government and the most powerful North American companies could reformulate their economic, political

---

5 In part, because Tavares also raises the hypothesis that this movement would be due "to the fact that the forms of expansion and accumulation in the Brazilian domestic market did not require, in this phase, greater liquid entries of foreign capital" (Tavares, 1998:143).

and military relations with the ... dependent ... peoples" (Ianni, 1986:155). In this sense it seems clear that there was strong support and international interest in relation to President Kubitschek's plan, in part because the idea of planning for development was no longer considered absurd by the national or international institutions, decision-making centres, believing that planned economic growth by the state "is the least bad if compared with the deterioration of social tensions" (Ianni, 1986:158). In fact, "... in the mid-1960s, President Eisenhower publicly adopted the proposal for development of President Juscelino Kubitschek", as Schoultz points out (2000:392), on affirming "We need to consider together with other American republics practical means by which the countries in development may make progress more rapidly" (Eisenhower, in Schoultz, 2000:393).

Certainly foreign productive capital was already present in the Brazilian economy since the 1920s (Suzigan, 1986:351), but in no way reached the proportion that the Targets Plan conquered. Some data helps to demonstrate this point. In 1939, a little more than 46% of the aggregate value of the Brazilian economy came from the textile and food sectors (Baer, 2002:60), typically in the hands of private national capital. Despite companies such as Ford already having installations in Brazil in the 1920s, one can only speak of the car sector as beginning from the second half of the 1950s. Before, what one had were only structures for assembling imported cars. In the Targets Plan "it is undeniable that the creation of the automobile industry was the project that outweighed all others by its economic significance and by its political success" (Ianni, 1986:164).

Current Brazilian Central Bank data shows that foreign direct investment grew 3.5 times between 1955 and 1957, being in this period largely productive investment "in the form of equipment covered by Instruction 113" (Orenstein & Sochaczewski, 1992:173). Apart from this, the data also shows that between 1951 and 1960, a little more than 42% of this investment came from the United States, 11.4% from Germany and 14% from Switzerland. So the Targets Plan really was successful in attracting foreign productive capital to the country mainly for structuring the sectors of consumer durables. This can be seen by the change in the structure of Brazilian industry that resulted from it. In 1953 the textile and food sectors were still predominant as leaders in industry in terms of gross aggregate value (35%), a situation that changes when in 1963 this percentage fell to 25% in detriment to the growth, mainly in the transportation equipment sector that went from 2% in 1953 to a 10.5% share in gross aggregate value in 1963, a sector under transnational domination. Also prominent are the segments of electrical materials, again with a strong multinational participation, going from 3% to 6% between 1953 and 1963 as well as the sector compromising chemical products, pharmaceuticals, rubber etc., which went from 11% to 15.5% (Baer, 2002:87) in share of gross aggregate value. This demonstrates the enormous transformation of the Brazilian industrial structure and the role of direct foreign investment in this process, resulting from the Targets Plan.

Hence, it is aimed to demonstrate that based upon a deliberate policy, proposed in the Targets Plan, synchronised with the movement of global capital, Brazil entered the internationalisation phase of productive capital expounded in Chapter 2. Of course, this process would not have been possible if the country had not organised itself to attract foreign capital, an inheritance of both the Vargas government and the stitching together of a strategic policy undertaken through the Targets Plan. Despite the need for expansion through which world capital was going, faced with the end of European reconstruction that had made it seek new places to maintain or expand its rhythm of growth, it was to Brazil, among other countries in Latin America that had also created certain conditions, that this capital came. It was here that this capital found the best conditions, created by the Targets Plan through a state policy; which found a fertile field to continue its process of accumulation on an increasing scale. This would not have been possible if it were not for this packet of economic policies along with the institutional structure, which equipped the state, undertaken by Vargas, the basis for the support of transnational capital avid to occupy new spaces to give continuation to its accumulation or even, to free itself from the constraints imposed by the contradictions that capital creates in its spaces of origin and that may restrict its expansion. It was to Brazil that this capital came because here it found the best environment to continue its accumulation, an environment strategically constructed to attract it.

On the other hand, in a contradictory way, the ample industrial growth realised by the Plan would not have been possible without transnational capital, it was with this resource that the sector of consumer durables was constructed in the country in the time proposed by the Plan (Oliveira, 1977:85). Thus, what one seeks to do here is to demonstrate that the process of internationalisation of the Brazilian economic structure is not a one-way street; it is not the result of a process imposed from outside to within by capital in a process of internationalisation, but it goes out to meet this movement and joins itself to it. It is a process that results on the other hand from an internal strategy, planned with specific characteristics given that it is different, for example, from the way industrialisation occurred in some Asian countries. At any event, it is not part of the scope of this work to make comparisons, but only to show the specificity of the process of capital internationalisation in Brazil. The fact that it was this process and, in this context, that multinational capital strengthened itself in Brazilian territory. The internal dynamic of expansion may be framed in a "favourable" way within the global dynamic of the system (Tavares, 1998:141).

It would not be correct to state that the Targets Plan inverted a previous tendency by promoting a greater denationalisation of the Brazilian economic structure. International capital had already been present in the economy since the 1920s, although without carrying within itself the strength that it would acquire from the start of the Plan and without being linked yet to the movement of productive internationalisation that characterised the post-war period. Going in the same direction, was a class of large national companies that was not only favourable to an alliance with foreign capital had already been formed as Ianni argues, and was strengthening itself, as they helped to sustain politically what the Targets Plan gave. "There was no conflict between the aims of the policy and the interests of the most dynamic sectors of the entrepreneurial class" (Lessa, 1982; 30). This comes to reaffirm the point of the Targets Programme (Programa de Metas) "it would be a possible expression of the tendencies of the Brazilian economic subsystem in combination with the tendencies of the world capitalist system..." (Ianni, 1986:155). At any event, the result is the same: it significantly raised the internationalisation of the Brazilian economy and thus its subordination to world capital.

4.4 The Attempt to Recreate a National Policy and the Resumption of Associated Development – 1960–64

The period comprising 1960–64 was characterised by large internal divisions over the direction of Brazilian development, this confrontation was also inserted within and affected by the economic crisis that followed the period of growth of the Targets Plan. According to Ianni, two currents of beliefs that were already present returned to the battle. "On the one side, were ranged the political and economic conditions as well as the ideologies favourable to the formation of a national capitalist system. And, on the other were positioned the political and economic conditions, as well as the ideologies, favouring the development of associated capitalism..." (Ianni, 1986:200). For this author, this last position was the strongest and in fact, in the end (1964) prevailed.

The economic strategy of this period is marked by an attempt to realise a policy of development in the sense of resolving national problems. It may be said that the period that precedes 1964 had at its centre two movements in relation to economic policy. On the one side, facing the economic crisis that was being experienced (inflation and imbalance in the balance of payments, foreign debt the result of large economic indebtedness during the cycle of growth and the difficulty of refinancing it), this entailed a series of traditional recessive measures of an orthodox stamp for fighting inflation and foreign restrictions on the balance of payments (public spending cuts, an active monetary policy to control aggregate demand, etc.). While on the other hand, long term measures aimed to permit the resumption of economic growth on different foundations by undertaking policies of income distribution (an example was the restoration of salary levels), land reform and by the new treatment that would be given to foreign capital (Oliveira, 1977:91). In this regard, it included the aim of distributing the benefits of growth obtained in the second half of the 1950s to a greater portion of the population, as well as to strengthen the internal market to permit the indigenising of the production-consumption cycle. The distributive measures suggested did not achieve success. The short term policies, recessive ones, usually have an immediate effect, which has contributed to aggravating the economic crisis. While the longer term structural measures, despite attempts at implementation, do not manage to be implemented through lack of support from national as well as foreign groups. "This reformist project, with strong popular leanings, was blocked and defeated by the coalition of conservative power that sustained the 1964 coup and the whole military regime. The new coalition of power gave an authoritarian and anti-social slant to development 1960–1980" (Fiori, 2001:28).

In the international field, relations between Brazil and the United States deteriorated during this period, mainly as a result of the new treatment given to foreign capital. The exchange policy was changed in the sense of removing elements that previously benefited foreign capital. According to Abreu, there was a clear change in the treatment given to this capital that made these measures transparent. Import facilities were removed, multiple exchange rates eliminated and new legislation was created to remit profits. Apart from this, foreign companies were disappropriated that acted in the area of telephony and energy, also general mineral rights were suspended, aggravating even more bad feeling with transnational capital and the United States (Abreu, 1992:202). In this sense, despite discussions on the subject (Almeida, 1995:195–196), apart from the measures not being closely connected to international interests, these specific decisions also contributed even more to keeping away any international aid to the government of the period. The lack of success that the long term policies completed will have during the period considered here is thus, at least in part, related to the fact that it would injure the interests of the large transnational capital present here and which already occupied a leading position in the economic structure.

On the other hand, the long term strategy was also rejected politically by national groups that were more inclined to the strengthening of associated capitalism. They were groups linked to the primary export economy that emerged or that were strengthened in the industrial expansion during the era of the Targets Plan (Ianni, 1986:225–226); they also involved the large national bourgeoisie such as the one that grew umbilically linked to foreign capital. The relations of dependency with global capitalism was already much more intense. The new authoritarian military government that would put an end to this strategy and take power in 1964 will be, in part, the result of the strengthening of these groups in terms of their internal support, and of course, it will also count on strong external support (Shoutz, 2000:397).

Thus the military coup of 1964 would be positively viewed by these groups as well as by the United States. One may say that in this period, at least in part, a reduction was visible in the capacity for realising a policy more focussed on the interests of autonomous national development. This is due on the one hand to the gain in autonomy of international capital represented by the United States and Europe in the Brazilian economy and, as must be emphasised, on the other, by the action of its internal allies, those that benefited from the type of association with this capital established in the second half of the 1950s, and which now see the possibility of strengthening these links since the 1964 coup. These national groups will organise themselves to not allow any change in the pattern of development planned and made explicit in the period 1960–64, acting in favour of expansion and a strengthened articulation with multinational capital, of course, with wide international support. "The military coup was 'a great victory for the free world', explained Kennedy's ambassador, Lincoln Gordon, before becoming president of a large university. The coup was launched 'to preserve and not to destroy Brazilian democracy'. Effectively, it was about the 'most decisive victory for freedom in the mid-20th century', which should 'create a much better climate for private investment'" (Chomsky, 2000, 21).

At the end of the 1950s the United States had already consolidated a vision of what Latin American development needed from the implantation of a model that involved the creation of a "military, business and even union elite that might establish a strong political regime ... the coup d'état in Brazil in 1964 was the founding moment for this new model. It managed to include the national bourgeoisie. ... In replacing this national project, the military regime created in 1964 originated a modernisation founded on an alliance and integration of this bourgeoisie with multinational capital, enshrined in a kind of dependent industrial development, subordinated to the characteristics of expansion and of the organisation of international capitalism, which would submit the local centres of accumulation to the logic of expansion of the world hegemonic centre. Starting from then, through successive military coups [in Latin America], the local bourgeoisies were submitted to the condition of junior partners of international capital which led them to abandon their prospects for national independence and pretensions for their own technological development" (Dos Santos, 2000:95).

To further reinforce this point, according to Atílio Boron "Latin American dictators better guaranteed the protection of North American interests than the turbulent and instable democracies. ... certain company interests preferred to be "protected" by the regimes of force that proliferated in the area..." (Boron, 1994:34). In cases where the interests of foreign capital and the state dictatorship are the same, transnational capital is not interested in defending liberalism. Nationalisation that is opposed to foreign capital is the nationalisation that goes against its interests (Oliveira, 1977:125). Thus, it seems clear that liberalism in this period was of no interest to large transnational capital. The time was one of maintaining a stable structure through political power that ensured its safe expansion, to continue its occupation of the periphery without deviations of a nationalist type or that might follow social demands for development. The process of capital accumulation was still in its phase of productive internationalisation.

According to Tavares, the crisis that was born in 1959 and that showed itself as a break in 1964, marks a "period in which the real possibilities, even if not the hopes, of the national bourgeoisie of keeping itself associated on an equal footing with foreign capital, through the mediation of the state, became unfeasible" (Tavares, 1998:147). This does not mean that national capital, except in periods of crisis in which it is the first to perish, will not benefit from the cycle of growth starting from 1967 (Tavares, 1998:147). What is being noted by Tavares, and is worth emphasising, is the subordinate character, as a junior partner of foreign capital that national capital will assume, but that, even in this position it will benefit from that association in the new cycle of growth that will begin in 1967.

One of the important elements to be emphasised in the crisis of the 1960s that preceded the "Economic Miracle" (1967–74) is the strengthening that transnational capital has, through the means of the recessive policy, adopted during the period, undergoing processes of capital centralisation (in favour of foreign capital) in the interior of the Brazilian economy. "When demand begins to slow down markedly in the 1960s, an era of absolute concentration [centralisation] begins, in that the rate of profit and the expansion of large companies can only be maintained at the cost of small companies, at the same time that it increases the degree of denationalisation of traditional industries (Tavares, 1998:156, 172–173). This process becomes more acute from 1966, when the military government created the PAEG (Government Programme for Economic Action), a strongly contractionist plan to combat inflation that ended up accentuating the crisis and the process of capital centralisation. National companies did not have credit because of internal restrictions, a situation not experienced by foreign companies that could and were incentivised by the policy of 1966 to obtain resources from abroad. The sectors most affected by bankruptcy or being put into administration were clothing, food and construction, traditionally less oligopolies and where small and medium-sized national companies predominated (Abreu, 1992:223).

In the sectors of consumer durable goods such as metal-mechanics, this process of centralisation is achieved by the strategy of expansion of the large company, generally foreign, given the way national/transnational capital is organised in which the weakest connection is with the former. This sector is structured by a relationship of "complementarity between the large monopolistic company at the high end [foreign] and the small and medium-sized national company in the sectors of metallurgy and of metal-mechanics [including car components] that were modernised and expanded taking advantage of the demand originating with large foreign companies, ...[in a] type of differentiated oligopoly, organised horizontally and vertically, which gives way to a star-shaped industrial structure, in which the company has a ring of small and medium-sized companies, suppliers as much as distributors...". (Tavares, 1998:157).

This structure described by Tavares even in 1974 demonstrates well how oligopolies, centred in foreign groups, begin to fix themselves in the Brazilian productive structure starting from the Targets Plan; they already impose a certain form of functioning that is under the command of large transnational capital that is strengthened during the crises starting from the processes of centralisation. That is the structure of the market that is reinforced beginning in the 1970s based on economic policies that will create the "Economic Miracle". It also seems clear that without state policies for the preservation of private national capital associated with multinational capital as described above, the fate of this national capital is in the hands of companies that command the oligopoly, transnational capital.

According to Ianni, the idea in defence of some type of growth aimed at solving national problems vis a vis the historic strengthening of transnational capital in the economic structure, will only be in part returned to in II PND (the National Development Plan II – 1974–76), perhaps the last attempt at political action by the state in favour of resuming some kind of control over economic development in national hands, through an enormous package of state investments.

4.5 The Strengthening of Transnational Capital – The "Economic Miracle"

Despite the first period of military government (1964–67) not having characteristics that may be called "developmentalist" because of its recessive policies, this period does not define the standard of later pro-growth economics that was unleashed starting from 1967 with extensive and important state participation as well as that of foreign capital. The military government "Came to affirm, modernise and give the state a wider role in society and the economy, through a restricted pact of domination between civil and military elites, with the applause of the middle classes frightened by the previous period of turbulence [1960–64]. In this pact institutional changes imposed in an authoritarian way ensured favourable conditions for the resumption of a new era of capitalist development in Brazil" (Tavares and Assis, 1986:11). In this process the national state will be strengthened, but most of all, transnational capital, through the arrangement that will benefit it linked to the recovery of the world economy and of international liquidity, elements that will lead to new investments in the periphery. At any event, one may say that the period of the "Miracle" (1968–73), despite having the state as a counterweight, increases the internationalisation of the productive structure by the strengthening of large multinational capital based on economic policies adopted and of ensuring foreign resources that take into account its closer relationship with international finance capital. Also, one cannot forget, the international support the military government received after the 1964 coup.

"On analysing the countries of Latin America, we can say that one of the key factors that determined its possibilities for expansion was precisely, the degree of integration of their economies with international capitalism" and its relationship with the national state, mainly in the case of Brazil. This meant that in Brazil "... the weight of the participation of dynamic sectors controlled by the state and international capital were increasing ..."[6] (Tavares, 1982:176–177). For Paul Singer, "there is no doubt that Brazilian economic development, after 1964, was deliberately oriented in the sense of taking opportunities that the new global strategy of multinationals offered the country ... [which served as].... an industrial entrepot for several multinationals, for example, they

---

6 The Miracle has at its centre the participation of the state and multinational capital. But, when compared one verifies that throughout the expansive cycle the state loses its relative share. Using current prices as a comparison, between 1970 and 1973 the share of public administration and the largest state companies in the formation of Gross Fixed Capital (investment) fell from 43.7% in 1970 to 39.4% in 1973 (Lago, 1992:241).

penetrated with greater ease into the markets of the Latin American countries...". (Singer, 1985:92). Thus, one may say that deliberate integration is present in national state policies to the global movement of capital, which is still expanding in the sense of occupying spaces in the periphery in the process of productive internationalisation. It is what results in the economic growth of the period, strengthening multinational capital. It is therefore as before, a double movement.

The "Economic Miracle", the second great cycle of Brazilian economic growth, had the basis for its success in the following aspects: the reformulation of the financial system undertaken in 1966 which increased the possibility of indebtedness for the middle and upper classes; the structure of concentrating income distribution which facilitated the consumption of these classes; the action of state productive investment in infrastructure and basic industry; the creation of facilities for taking resources from abroad; and the changes in the international credit market making available long term resources with low interest rates. The combination of the internal factors with the liquidity and the resumption of growth in the international economy set the tone for the new cycle of growth.

It was for these reasons a period marked by economic growth led by the consumer durable goods industry, a sector in which transnational companies predominated. On the one hand these companies saw the demand for their products grow due to the concentration of income and the reform of the financial system that made credit available to the consumer of durable goods, mainly the upper middle classes; and, the on the other, these companies had ample facilities in seeking foreign resources for modernisation and the expansion of their productive bases, already largely installed in Brazil. The resumption of investment on the part of the state, mainly through state companies, as well as investment in the construction sector (facilitated also by the reform of the financial system in 1966), starting from 1967–68, gave a definitive boost to economic growth in the period. Thus, the investments of transnational companies complemented by state investments drove the cycle. National private companies linked by dint of the productive chain to the large foreign groups grew in their wake, whilst those located in more traditional sectors remained on the margin of the process, having their growth derived from the increase in employment and the mass of salaries[7] as a result of the growth cycle itself. In

---

7 Salaries per se were controlled and even squeezed during the whole period as part of the strategy of growth to lower costs for companies. They were also during the whole period at the centre of a policy of inflationary control. The growth of demand was focussed in the policy of credit for the upper middle classes and in the policies of export incentives.

the period 1967–1970, whilst the sector of consumer durable goods saw a 22% growth in production and the sector of basic industries 14%, segments linked to the consumption of consumer non-durables grew by just 10%.

"The production of consumer durable goods and the recovery of the housing market had multiplying effects on the whole economic situation, even while maintaining low salaries" (Tavares and Assis, 1986:27). Thus, "One of the main factors sparking the phase of recovery was the dynamism of demand for consumer durable goods … The growth in demand for durables was already 13.4% in 1966–67 … reflecting: i) a greater concentration of personal income that in the context of semi-stagnation [1964–66], allowed the preservation and increase in purchasing power of the medium-high groups; (ii) the rise in the margins of family debt, facilitated by the development of financial intermediation in the purchase of consumer goods [the reforms of the financial system undertaken by PAEG]" (Serra, 1982:89). One may also add to this the availability of foreign resources.

The policy of distributing income in favour of the middle and upper classes after 1964 with the relative lowering of the salaries of the lower classes, became one of the structural hallmarks of the flow of production-consumption in the Brazilian economy. The growth, which resulted in privileging consumer goods for those with the highest income, occurs not with the distribution of income but with its opposite, being an element propelling the new cycle centred on the production of consumer durable goods and of capital correlated with this sector. "It is a quite well known fact that the development of the patterns of income distribution that accompanied the recent development of economies such as the Brazilian … guaranteed growing margins of demand – from the middle and higher urban social groups … – for the productive activities of conspicuous goods which directly or indirectly are linked to the dynamic sectors, allowing a profitable expansion of the same" (Tavares, 1982:186). Thus, it becomes rooted in the Brazilian economy a perverse dynamic in favour of a certain productive structure that comes to define its logic of growth. The policy of income distribution in favour of the better-off benefitted the most dynamic sectors that are linked largely to transnational capital installed in Brazil and that is why they drove the growth cycle in question. While the sectors that supplied consumer non-durables to the population with least income, the traditional sectors, normally those that private national capital is most engaged in, only has its growth in the wake of higher employment. That is why, in the growth period of the Miracle, the sector of consumer non-durables will grow last and in a less dynamic way.

The opening up of the economy and the incentive to contract foreign funding is another factor that merits emphasis in the growth cycle. Measures incentivising foreign debt taken before the Miracle, vis a vis the restriction on domestic credit, stimulated the search for foreign loans, accessible mainly to the subsidiaries of the large transnational groups installed here, and Brazilian state companies. This trend was already established at the beginning of the growth cycle. In 1966 foreign-owned companies were responsible for 44% of the volume of funds contracted abroad, alongside state-owned companies that took 46%. Companies with private national capital took just 6.5% of the total of funding (Abreu, 1992:223). At the end of the cycle, foreign companies will still be the big receivers of foreign funds. In 1972 around 64% of those in receipt of private finance abroad were transnational companies (Cruz, 1982:78).

Thus, the availability of global liquidity,[8] low rates of foreign interest in contrast to internal restrictions,[9] stimulated the contracting of funds abroad, a fact that marks the period of growth. This set of factors is what will kick off the period of vast foreign indebtedness of the Brazilian economy. "What there was ... was a huge convergence of a situation of great international liquidity with an expansive internal cycle in which the demand for credit in domestic currency exercised by the private sector grew at high rates and where the institutional characteristics of the domestic financial system which resulted in the growing part of this demand was met ... by operations that involved foreign resources" (Cruz, 1982:65).

This means that domestic financial policy and the facility for taking foreign loans, faced with the availability of global liquidity, were factors that favoured foreign capital in the growth cycle to the detriment of national capital given the ease of the former in accessing these resources. Foreign debt was the way used by large transnational capital in the process of modernisation and expansion of its activities in the Brazilian economy on finding greater facilities and finance for importing the necessary equipment. It is worth highlighting that the entry of these resources which came in the form of loans was not necessarily connected to needs related to financing the balance of payments.

As a consequence of the economic policies adopted, the deliberate re-engagement with world financial markets, as well as the change in the international scenario in the sense of global economic growth, the transnational companies in search of new opportunities, but mainly preoccupied with

---

8 "The significant influx of foreign financial resources to the Brazilian economy was caused ultimately by the transformations that occurred in the market of euro-money currencies and they were translated into, above all, in an extraordinary availability of credits at increasingly long terms and in increasingly narrow spreads ..." (Cruz, 1983:65).

9 The reforms of the financial system undertaken in 1966 aimed to create a system of financing for investment, but they did not achieve success, which restricted the growth of internal credit and left this responsibility exclusively on BNDE.

modernising their subsidiaries and ensuring their space in the market, increased their investments in Brazil. This resulted in levels of direct foreign investment tripling during the period of the "Miracle". The United States maintained its historic position as largest investor, with a 38% share in the period 1961–70 and 36% in the period 1971–79. But Europe raised its share: while between 1951 and 1960 European countries were responsible for 31% of FDI in Brazil, between 1961 and 1970, this share rose to nearly 51% of the total, under the leadership of West Germany and Switzerland, which totalled 23% (Brazilian Central Bank).

Taking into account the innumerable advantages in receiving hard currency funds from abroad, it is important to stress that the FDI which predominates during the growth cycle differs from the period of the Targets Plan not only because of this but also because the main productive sectors dominated by foreign capital already had a strong presence in the Brazilian industrial structure since the 1950s. That is why foreign investments do not predominate in the installation of new sectors or new productive plants in Brazil. Thus, in the period in question, the funds entered much more in the form of loans in foreign currency. At any rate, it is worth highlighting that they are still earmarked for the expansion of their subsidiaries' productive capacity, as well as for the modernisation of the productive structure installed here by the importing of technology incorporated in imported capital goods. Thus, the principal factor is still related to production and to the occupation of markets.

Despite the prominent role that transnational capital has in the cycle of growth in question, one must remember the importance of state investment that divided with the former the dynamic leadership in growth, despite a slight reduction in its share in gross fixed capital formation in the period.[10] Public investments were concentrated mainly in electricity, oil and petrochemicals, railways, telecommunications, and steelmaking, in that order (Lago, 1992:241). This demonstrates the importance of public investment in the growth cycle, maintaining its strategic position in the "Tripod" as supplier of infrastructure and basic inputs to private industry. Thus, despite debates (Carvalho, 1982) about the loss of national sovereignty after the "Miracle" cycle of development, one still cannot say that the Brazilian economy had lost control over its process of accumulation, whilst it might be more vulnerable than in previous periods.

It reinforces this position the fact that the period still involves a strategy of planning for the promotion of national economic growth although in no way aiming for any policy in the sense of social inclusion.[11] It still has as a strategic

---

10   Which fell from 43.7% in 1970 to 39.4% in 1973 (see the previous note on the subject).
11   Indeed, one of the characteristics of the Miracle is the economic growth with the expansion of the least favoured social classes, the widening of the differential in income

foundation the "Tripod of Accumulation" with ample state participation. There was within government a preoccupation with the degree of internationalisation that the Brazilian economy was reaching (Ianni, 1986:295). As Ianni points out, the policy of interdependence itself of the military government generated preoccupation with the accelerated internationalisation of the Brazilian economy. The government had as its declared aim the "consolidation ... of an economic system balanced between the government, private sector, with the presence of state companies, private national companies and foreign private companies in proportions that assures, in a continuous form, the economic and political feasibility of the system" ("Targets and Foundations for Government Action", Jornal do Brasil, January 1970 apud. Ianni, 1986:256). Of course, as one has attempted to show, national private capital, mainly that not linked to the more dynamic sectors controlled by foreign capital, was side-lined in the process.

One should not let escape a new element emerging from the 1966 financial reforms that was strengthened during the period of growth. The financial reform created and strengthened[12] a new class of national elite bankers, distinct from the grand bourgeoisie, both agrarian and productive, that would follow its own interests and join itself to the national elite. This is a class that was strengthened, not as the financiers of economic growth, but in the tracks of the growth of public debt, feeding itself mainly from interest and the monetary indexing that is levied on it, as well as its relationship with foreign debt. This focus here is important not for what one wishes to demonstrate – the growth of transnational capital control over the Brazilian productive structure – but it will be one of the factors that will give leverage the fiscal crisis of the 1980s, as well as being part of the political force of internal pressure for the destructuring of the state productive apparatus in the 1990s. This new class will be allied to large international finance capital in its advance over the public state fund.

Brazil arrives at the end of the growth cycle with the following scenario. "(1) Of the 1,000 largest companies in the country in sale volumes approximately two thirds are industrial; between them multinational companies [MC] were equivalent to 12% of the total number, 50% of sales value and 43% of capital stock; (2) within industry, the MCs concentrated the most dynamic sectors. In 1970, among the leading companies, the MCs dominated the production

---

between the richest and the poorest. In a way, it shows the difference that becomes clear in the periphery: economic growth is not connected to development.

12 "The banking conglomeration advocated by Delfim Netto permitted the concentration of national finance capital ... constituting a new portion of the dominant block" (Tavares & Assis, 1985:39).

of consumer durable goods (85% of sales) and had a majority share in the production of capital goods (57% of sales). Even in the other two sub-sectors (consumer non-durables and intermediate goods) its share was significant (43% and 37% respectively); (3) The MCs operate with a scale of production, capital intensity, degree of oligopoly, technological complexity and productivity higher than that of national companies ..." (Serra, 1982:70).

"The analysis of government policy since 1964 reveals the predominance of the internationalist tendency ... in the sense of impelling and consolidating an associated economic sub-system (or better, dependent) ... the economic directives and objectives adopted ... implied in the reshaping of Brazilian economic relations with the global economy ... a process that was facilitated and accelerated by government directives ... that impelled the concentration [centralisation] and the internationalisation of capital ... In consequence ... the multinational companies acquired even greater relative and absolute importance, in the overall economy of the country..." . Thus, in the pendular movement between national capitalism and the interdependent associated capitalist system, the second project won. (Ianni, 1986: 288–289).

At any event, despite increasing the dependent and associated character of the Brazilian economy, the period of the military government does not crown this process of subordination to globalised capital. The military government still has, an ideological force, a "developmentalism" that promotes the growth of the country, even as associated, even though this might imply exclusively growth ("growth of the cake") and not development in the sense of social inclusion. The logic of this growth still protects, defends and maintains the national integrated productive state and administratively the process of Brazilian accumulation, reinforcing the power and structure of state companies. As Oliveira points out, what happened post-1964 and was present during the whole period of the Miracle was the "welding of interests between the state and foreign capital" with the "systematic application of the policy that served these two specific interests that led, at bottom, to reproduce on an expanded scale both the role as well as the power of each of these specific agents" (Oliveira, 1977:125).

Given the degree of internationalisation reached, before II PND (The Second National Development Plan) and long before the dismantling of the national state in the 1990s, Paul Singer already in 1994 did not believe very much in any possibility of another type of more autonomous development in relation to big transnational capital: he stated that "within the institutional framework formed since 1964, the Brazilian economy cannot stop developing in accord with the global strategy of the multinationals. It is enough to examine the size of the foreign debt already taken on and the role given to foreign subsidiaries in the development of crucial sectors to be able to conclude that nothing short of very broad institutional changes can divert our economy from growing integration in the new international division of labour" (Singer, 1985:95).

It is worth pointing out that this movement of global capital described by Singer was still one of "integration to the new international division of labour" and the preoccupation focussed on the possibilities for national control over it. The question of control was maintained, but it became much more complex with the increase in the dynamic importance of transnational capital in the Brazilian economy, mainly when global capitalism stopped being an integrator under the dominant process of centralisation of capitals beginning in the 1980s.

It is also interesting to note that at the end of the 1970s, the discussion intensified over the degree of importance of transnational companies in the Brazilian productive structure and the power of control over them. In part, this debate is in "Multinationals: the Limits of Sovereignty" (Carvalho org., 1982), edited by the Getúlio Vargas Foundation. In one of the articles, dated 1975, Mário Henrique Simonsen[13] states that multinational companies, "if left to the free play of market forces, tend to be transformed into simple assembly industries, importing from headquarters the greater part of the components and inputs" (Simonsen, 1982:68). That is why he supports state intervention and its action in strategic sectors. The problem is aggravated if these companies are not even the "maquiladoras" (lit. make-up artists – as coined referring to Mexican border assembly production of US components) they want to be.

The II PND seems to concentrate these preoccupations of control over the economy even during the military government. It will perhaps be the last effort related to a strategy implanted by the military government which believes in the possibility of national economic growth with the broad cooperation of multinational capital and with incentives steered by a strong and autonomous state. It will thus try to strengthen the state leg of the "Tripod" with the aim of "completing the process of import substitution" begun in the 1950s.

4.6 Brazil as a Power – II PND

II PND (the Second National Development Plan) was "without doubt the most important and concentrated effort of the state since the Targets Plan in the sense of promoting structural modifications in the economy" (Serra, 1982:101). The plan (II PND) had as its objective to solve the bottlenecks in the Brazilian economy related, on the one hand, to external dependency through a strategy of import substitution in the sectors of capital goods and intermediary goods,

---

13   He was Minister of Planning in 1979 in the military government of General Figueiredo.

and, on the other, the needs for basic inputs and infrastructure (energy, transport, telecommunications). The aim was to "complete" the Brazilian industrial complex as a means of reaching the desired autonomy in relation to international cycles.

Besides this, and for what is intended here, as Lessa points out (1998), there was a preoccupation with the strengthening of production undertaken by national companies as well as for "channelling" foreign companies "inside the national development strategy" (Speech of March 1974 of Reis Velloso,[14] apud. Lessa, 1998:31). Faced with the importance that foreign companies had acquired during the growth promoted by the "Miracle", the plan advocated the need to support national companies more in order to have a better "balance of the tripod". As explicitly mentioned in the speech of Reis Velloso, "In the broadest panorama of the country's entrepreneurial structure, it is fitting to stress that, the recent development [of the Miracle] of the national economy, has resulted in a spectacular increase, in efficiency and size of the large state companies and the increasing share of foreign private companies, at the same time as relative stagnation of the national private company. It is thus urgent to take care in strengthening this latter entrepreneurial sector so that it comes to occupy the place in the balance that it should" (Speech of March 1974, Reis Velloso, apud. Lessa, 1998:29–30).

Despite the objective aimed for, what ended up becoming more important in II PND was state investment, "the main sustenance" of the plan, given that private investment did not appear as its mentors expected (Serra, 1982:107). "Even if II PND does not say so, this conception placed the big state company centre stage in Brazilian industrialisation" (Lessa, 1998:105) this would thus be responsible for investments as much in the main sectors where they had already acted such as infrastructure (energy, transport, telecommunications), as well as in the promotion of new sectors linked to basic industries such as the petrochemical sector. Despite the greater weight of investment that fell upon the state companies, in several segments that were at the heart of the plan, the government made use of a strategy of shared participation between the state company, private national capital and foreign capital, a mechanism under the command of state planning "starting from an array of projects directly formulated and implemented by state companies" (Lessa, 1998:106). This arose mainly as a way of attracting technology via foreign capital, but positioned it as a partner to a national enterprise. The classic example of this mechanism was the implantation of the petrochemical sector.

---

14   Minister of Planning in the Giesel government.

The resources to make investment feasible came from foreign sources (Lessa, 1998:46), as in fact occurred until the outbreak of the international crisis cut these resources and placed Brazil in a crisis that would last throughout the 1980s. In fact, the external debt in this period had a double function. Apart from financing the new growth cycle, it permitted the closing of the accounts of the balance of payments, faced with the need for foreign resources that the Brazilian economy came to have after 1973. "Indebtedness is justified ... as an alternative to financing the balance of payments while it promotes a structural change with growth" (Castro, 1985:104). This will result in the aggravation of foreign restrictions that will be at the centre of the crisis in the first half of the 1980s.

For what is proposed here, one must underline the fact that II PND was, perhaps, the last attempt in government circles to implement a national project faced with the years of internationalisation that the Brazilian economy had gone through, reinforced by the strengthening of the foreign company during the "Miracle". According to Fiori (1995:63 and after) the II PND marks an attempt also to implant some backbone into the substitution of imports, a broad national development project focussed on the state, comparing this period to the same strategy which Vargas promoted – a project of the "Nation as a power" (Nação-Potência) (Fiori, 1995:61–62). Thus, if this plan (II PND) moves closer to the Targets Plan as Serra pointed out, this arose only in respect to government intervention and not in the sense of the idea of "national" development with the reinforcement of the national companies, as it appears in II PND. One may perhaps say that it was the last attempt at returning to relatively independent national economic growth, broadly led by the state and state companies, faced with the degree of structural internationalisation that the Brazilian productive base already had at this time, that was not only greater because of the enormous state productive power constructed since Vargas and expanded during the period in question. Carlos Lessa (1998) emphasises this national preoccupation of the plan.

The II PND thus marks an attempt to create a national project that might reduce submission to transnational capital, perhaps taking advantage of the main opening that still remained for a national project – the strong state-owned productive structure. The project was the result of the capacity that the Brazilian state still had in creating a significant packet of investments in basic industries and in infrastructure, with broad support from funds contracted abroad. The idea was that "the state could deal with foreign capital already internalised and with the new capital now summoned, subordinating it to national objectives. The state may move at the level of international relations taking advantage of its current configuration" (Lessa, 1998:38). It thus had the aim of trying to "channel" transnational capital towards the national interest (Lessa, 1998:253). The proposal was to use foreign capital to promote domestic development. One may consider it as an attempt to demonstrate national autonomy in the direction of growth during the process of global capital accumulation. Perhaps it may have been the fruit of the perception that control over development of the country could slip through its fingers if it were not for a strong and gigantic effort of the state to regain the sense of national economic growth. This is a wide-ranging discussion. The fact is that the II PND made possible the realisation of large projects implanted by financially healthy state companies, that because of this healthy, managed to receive large volumes of funds from international private bankers.

Furthermore the programme included the idea that technological development should also be a state role through state companies and public research bodies and with wide cooperation from transnational companies. "The large state companies should be given a leading role in national technological development – because the shortcomings are as obvious, as they are, of the private business class in general" (apud. Lessa, 1998:36). It also entailed the idea that the establishment of the "large national company in competitive opposition with the foreign company would be unattainable if scientific and technological production were not internalised. Without this quality the task of consolidation will fail" (Lessa, 1998:36). It was obvious, at least based on Lessa's analysis, what were the problems posed for the continuity of Brazilian development faced with the degree of internationalisation reached in the control of the most dynamic sectors of the Brazilian economy by foreign capital. The technological question leaps before the eyes given that it will be an ongoing problem, mainly in industrialised economies with transnational capital, given that they normally develop their technology in laboratories at their headquarters located in centre economies.

But this attempt to change the paradigm of national development and of creating a new standard of industrialisation did not take off (Lessa, 1998:150). On the one hand, as Lessa demonstrates, for there not having occurred the internal liaison of private actors around a big national project given the impossibility of creating a political-economic space for a strategy led by the state: both national private capital as well as foreign capital took little part as investors. On the other hand, but no less importantly, because of the changes that were happening in the process of global capitalist accumulation that were manifest in the upsurge of the international crisis begun in 1973, but which was only definitively established from the second oil price shock in 1979. This crisis is what marked the beginning of the change in the process of global accumulation until then governed by the productive internationalisation of capital, by the productive occupation of spaces in the periphery that had, in a way, been articulated in synchrony with Brazilian development in the 1950s, 60s and 70s.

The impossibility of articulating a pact by the state in accord with national private capital is pointed out by Lessa (1998). The state does not manage to break the historically constructed forms that defined its participation in the Tripod of Accumulation, as well as not managing to break the liaison that was constructed between large private national capital and that of the multinational. "The practice of authoritarianism, the ideological burden of positivism, the euphoria and the sensation of omnipotence originating from the Miracle, led the regime to support the state company as an instrument of power. It did not perceive that its authoritarianism was consented to by large pacts; it did not perceive that the state company is one of the instruments of sovereign pacts; it did not perceive that it itself, the state, is an instrument of greater movement of the economy. Neither the state nor state companies had the autonomy envisaged by II PND" (Lessa, 1998:154).

Thus, according to Lessa, it seems II PND did not take into account the important connections between the national company and the transnational one, thinking of an ideal national company (Lessa, 1998:288), without strong links of dependency constructed over the years. At any rate, for him, the existence of a productive structure, up to a certain point solidified, was one of the elements that made the II PND's developmentalist strategy more difficult, from the point of view of internal liaison. Furthermore, he also states that there prevailed in the strategy a vision to some extent ingenuous, over the roles foreign capital installed here would take on, for example, the internalisation of technological production or even making exports independent of head office policy (Lessa, 1998:254). The state did not manage to impose its new developmentalist paradigm and, it is worth stressing, even in a political structure in which the dictatorship prevailed, which demonstrates the degree of complexity of national-international relations that developed and were rooted in the Brazilian productive structure, increasingly commanded by transnational capital.

At the end of the 1970s there was an escalation in the international crisis. Brazil not only lost its sources of finance but also an increase in international interest rates along with problems with the trade balance, placed the country in a serious situation of external restrictions. This international crisis that is prolonged into the 1980s marks the process of transformation in the way global capital acts. The first signal of this transformation appears in the creation of the Trilateral commission[15] that started the new liberalism and the end of toleration for "developmentalist" policies that previously benefitted but now began to hinder the "free mobility of capital", the end of tolerance to strategies articulated by the state, that were much in evidence in the rationale of II PND and the programme of import substitution. This marks a change in strategy for large transnational capital that was already established in the periphery, which now, did not any more have as part of its movement the process of productive internationalisation that characterised the 1950s and 1960s as well as the 1970s. In this new situation, the state as intervenor in defence of the national interest, even in a partial form, comes to be an obstacle to the new movement of capital now one of global restructuring in the sense of centralisation (see Chapters 1 and 2), in which it seeks to redefine its areas of action. State-ownership that opposes foreign capital is that which goes against its interests (Oliveira, 1977:125), and the state as an obstacle is the one with "developmentalist" practices, located in the periphery where this capital is structurally rooted.

Jimmy Carter's Trilateral Commission in the 1970s marked the end of support for intervention through dictators in Latin America. In Brazil's case, the military dictatorship had, at first, as seen, strengthened transnational capital, giving it more space in the Brazilian productive structure in detriment to national capital. But II PND, perhaps because of an outburst of "nationalism", tried to strengthen national capital via the expansion of state power in the productive structure, as a "counterpoint" to the excess of power and control that multinational capital had managed to have in the economy. So, one may say that the military dictatorship had lost its usefulness to large transnational capital, a fact that appears clearly in the Brazilian case. The aim of the Commission "tried to produce an active separation between the western democracies and dictatorial governments based on the military ... These regimes had accomplished their repressive role and now tended to develop nationalist pretensions unacceptable to a world economy in [the process] of globalisation" (Dos Santos, 2000:100).

The Trilateral Commission that had as its associates the largest business groups in the world, thus marks the start of the "globalising" ideology that would prevail in the world throughout the 1980s and 1990s. Zbigniew Brzezinski, one of the main mentors of the Commission had already stated "The nation-state, as a fundamental unit in the organised life of man, has stopped being the main creative force: international banks and multinational corporations plan and

---

15 Created by U.S. President Jimmy Carter, the commission was thus called because it brought together a tripartite structure between the United States, Western Europe and Japan (Assmann, Dos Santos & Chomsky, 1979:20).

act in terms that have many advantages over the political concepts of the nation-state" (Brzezinski, apud. Hineklammert, 1979:85).

This new international policy is inserted and marks, therefore, the entry of the world in a new phase of capital globalisation. Thus what will happen will be a rearrangement of the productive system of capitals, now globalised. This is marked by a considerable growth in mergers and acquisitions in a process of global capital centralisation in order to continue the process of global accumulation. For this, capital starts to request freedom of movement that is apparent in the liberalising logic that, in the Brazilian case, came to be inhibited by the dictatorial "developmentalist" state; it marks a new era in the process of global accumulation, the movement of global centralisation of capital led by large transnational corporations. That is why changes occur in the global political strategy undertaken by the central economies, as seen in the Trilateral Commission's thinking. This strategy is transformed in a policy of liberalisation that "persisted in the 1980s under the aegis of the conservative governments of Ronald Reagan and Margaret Thatcher, with the support of Helmut Kohl in Germany and various neoliberal political experiences based on the Washington Consensus in 1989. In this consensus the International Monetary Fund and World Bank united with other international agencies to impose a 'structural adjustment' on the dependent countries ..." (Dos Santos, 2000:100). Thus, the objective was to eliminate nationalist and protectionist resistance that was included in the economic growth strategies of military governments and that created obstacles to the globalisation of capital (Dos Santos, 2000:102). In Brazil, the implantation of this new model would still need to eliminate the strong national leg of the Tripod of Accumulation: the state, which happened throughout the 1980s and 1990s as we shall see.

4.7 Scrapping the National State – The 1980s

As expounded above, the Brazilian state established itself as the strongest leg in the "Tripod of Accumulation" on the national side, facing the growing power of foreign capital in the process of capitalist development in Brazil. The Brazilian state, which then had in its structure a productive industrial complex at the base of its production chain, begins, contradictorily, its de-structuring in the II PND itself, which was based on foreign loans. This situation which was aggravated starting from the growth of the foreign debt and policies of external adjustment, this will weigh heavily on the public sector as a whole, as much on state productive companies as in relation to the growth of the public debt. It will benefit a new class that was strengthened during the Miracle and that made up the national financial system, the national banking system, becoming the intermediary of international finance capital, and who will become the bearer of public debt.

The situation of external restriction through which Brazil passes from the end of the 1970s and throughout the 1980s, is the result of the deepening international economic crisis that resulted in the reduction of investments in Brazil as well as in the availability of resources abroad to finance the balance of payments. A large part of the growth in Brazil's foreign debt, starting from the closing of the foreign loans market (1979–80), will be the result of the rise of international rates of interest that were levied on it. External indebtedness, the oil crises (1972 and 1979) and the rising international interest rates generated a crisis in the balance of payments that was resolved with maxi-devaluations of the national currency to increase exports. This pushed inflation rates to high levels. Monetary restrictive policy was taken by rising internal interest rates, on one hand fuelling public debt, on the other contributing to attract foreign hard currency in order to finance the balance of payments, the payment of the service of external debt.

The inflationary crisis of the 1980s caused by the maxi-devaluations further strengthened one of the most important institutional advocates of restrictive policies of IMF: the national private banking and financial system. The orthodox strategy of fighting inflation by issuing government bonds to absorb liquidity and raise domestic interest rates created a banking and financial structure whose profitability was not based on credit, but on government securities and their high interest rates. Because of that in the early 1990s, the federal debt reached 50% of total financial assets (Belluzzo and Almeida, 2002:192). The financial system "… thus exercised…a huge power over monetary and interest-rate policy…". "Public debt then became the foundations of the banks' income, as intermediaries of 'financial money' (which replaced their function as 'financial intermediaries') and absorbers of the inflation tax" (Belluzzo and Almeida, 2002:154).

The process of growth of public debt and state deficits – which also was aggravated in the second half of the 1970s and prolonged through the 1980s – is the result of policies that had as their aim, the generation of funds given the foreign restrictions that were already present throughout II PND, and the needs of paying the foreign debt. They were restrictive policies widely supported[16] or imposed by the International Monetary Fund – IMF. In 1985 the

---

16 In the first half of the 1980s, the Brazilian government apparently baulked at making a deal with the Fund for questions of domestic politics, but in practice applied its prescriptions (Carneiro & Modiano, 1992:323–344).

impact that the foreign adjustment had on the internal debt was visible. "The current financial difficulties [1985] of the public sector are, in large part, the consequence of the external indebtedness taken on by the government and of the reduction in the supply of foreign financial resources from abroad to the country ..." (Lundberg & Castro, 1987:94).

This process not only weakened the state, removing from it its power to act, but also resulted in establishing a mechanism for scrapping the state productive apparatus constructed over the years. This scrapping would open the doors so that in the 1990s there were no significant restrictions to the process of removing the state from the economy which occurred with the privatisation of state companies and would make it extremely difficult to resume its historic activity in favour of national economic growth. In this sense, the foreign debt crisis brought within itself a mechanism for moulding Brazil to the designs and interests that were established abroad and, to a certain extent, monitored and guaranteed by the IMF imposing restrictive policies. "The [Latin American] debt crisis was a formidable lever to reinforce the bonds of submission..." (Boron, 1994:36). The country comes to subject its national economic policy to the specific international interests evident in a series of "Letters of Intentions" imposed by this institution. "... the peripheral countries had to submit invariably to the IMF's discipline... a discipline that imposes norms of political, economic and institutional reforms..." (Fiori, 1995:186). Thus, in the wake of this process, the adjustment policies imposed, are what establishes the crisis of the 1980s and the nation state will be scrapped.

The II PND was wrong-footed by the international slow down marked by the oil shocks (1973 and 1979) that resulted in Brazil's problems closing the balance of payments and for paying the servicing of the foreign debt. Throughout the second half of the 1970s, foreign indebtedness of state companies was growing with the aim of both realising the projects of II PND as well as bringing in hard currencies from abroad to meet the needs of the balance of payments, a process that led to the so-called nationalising of the Brazilian foreign debt: the state, through its companies, becomes the main borrower of external resources. "... the progressive nationalisation of the Brazilian foreign debt is imposed as a result of a phenomenon that already began to be seen in the mid-1970s and it became more intense at the end of the decade: the growing need for foreign resources – first in function of the imbalance of the goods and services account and, after from the financial requirements expressed in the cumulative movement of the debt" (Cruz, 1983:92).

The growth in international interest rates from the end of the 1970s will make the financial situation of state companies more serious, a factor that will also add to the policy of constant currency devaluations, making it necessary for funding in national currency for those companies to pay foreign commitments even greater. Furthermore, to increase the hardness of the blow on the financial capacity of the state companies is the fact of having their tariffs constantly readjusted below the rates of inflation (see Belluzzo and Almeida, 2002, pp. 128–135), as a policy to fight price increases given that public prices impact on products that are in the domestic productive chain (steel, energy etc.). Lastly, given this situation which really placed the state companies in a serious financial situation, recessive domestic policies, mostly imposed by the IMF, forbade state companies from receiving any kind of credit (at home or abroad), a policy active mainly through the 1980s. This fact that impaired the state companies from making any investment (Cruz, 1983:92–93), leading them to a gradual deterioration in the services and products they were responsible for in the domestic productive chain.

The result of this was, at the end of the 1980s, a set of state companies, once efficient protagonists in national development, that had functioned, on the one hand as catalysts for foreign investment and, on the other, as a national counterpoint to it (up to a certain point, preserving the national interest), this set of companies was almost scrapped (financially and technically). Thus, it made it easier to understand how in the 1990s, they would be the focus of liberalisation and would be privatised, as well as the state removed from the productive process for being considered "inefficient". It is not without reason, given that the companies were by this scrapping process, impaired from supplying basic productive inputs to the private sector, as well as quality public services for people, owing to the lack of investment in modernisation. The defence of privatisation fitted almost perfectly the interests of national finance capital and the international holders of a large part of public debt. That is why, one of the legs of the Tripod of Accumulation that characterised Brazilian development would fall apart in the 1990s, leaving behind just one: transnational capital, as Fiori affirms (1997:177).

On the other hand, the process of adjustment imposed by the foreign debt crisis in the second half of the 1970s and throughout the 1980s, leaves other important scars. Apart from the scrapping of state companies, there was the scrapping of the Brazilian state apparatus – supplier of health, education, sanitation etc. – by the growth of the domestic and foreign debts. This process will tie the Brazilian state to the constant demands, mainly centred on the IMF and on national financial and international capitals, for the generation of fiscal surpluses that, in a persistent form, will make its capacity for action in undertaking social policies unfeasible. In the 1990s, this dictatorship of the fiscal surplus fed ideologically by the contrived inefficiency that resulted from the process of scrapping its capacity to supply quality products and services, would also lead to the campaign for the privatisation of public services in general as well as public pensions. Apart from this, it will make unfeasible the state's capacity to make fiscal policy. "The evidence... seems sufficient to dispel any doubts that might arise about the fact that it was on the public sector that the onus fell for the adjustment that the Brazilian economy went through ... as a result of foreign indebtedness" (Werneck, 1987:123).

The connection between the external adjustment and the growth of domestic public debt stems basically from the mechanism of the nationalisation of foreign debt in the 1980s. On the one hand, the policy of maxi-devaluation of the exchange rate forced the federal government to accept the payment of foreign debt of private companies in national currency, taking the external commitment in dollars. It thus exchanges private external debt for public debt, otherwise private companies would have serious financial problems. (Lundberg & Castro, 1987:94). On the other hand, given that these trade surpluses obtained by the private sector were growing and had to be monetised at a time in which the government could not relinquish the recessive policy that guaranteed the surplus itself, it had to constantly compensate this process of monetisation with a public debt issue to maintain the tight level of domestic liquidity. These processes raised the public debt substantially and this growth is also made worse by high rates of interest (through low liquidity and the need for recession) that are charged on this debt. Add to these problems the debts of the state companies themselves, mainly in foreign currency that also feed the public debt.

It is also worth stressing that throughout the 1980s the public debt had the additional role of guaranteeing a certain level of profitability to idle corporate resources and to the financial markets. In the periods of high inflation and of recessive policies that raised the rates of interest, public debt securities became a privileged asset both in the sense of security for the value of private wealth as in the wider sense of providing profitability "without passing through the hardships of production", as Marx said (Marx II, 1887b:32), for those that have resources available. In the crisis it was the Brazilian state that guaranteed the private fictitious profitability in indexed currency (public debt), that obviously expanded its financial fragility. "We put on record that, parallel [to the banks], the large non-financial companies presented corresponding super-profits in their annual accounts, an evidence... [of] the exaggeration represented by the fictitious profitability taken to the extreme against a single debtor – the public sector..." (Belluzzo & Gomes de Almeida, 2002:268).

This means to say that at the end of the 1980s, one of the main legs of the Tripod of Accumulation, the state, until then responsible for a little more than 30% of Brazilian GDP, loses not only its investment capacity, but also ends up being the target for a strong campaign for the privatisation of its productive companies and of the public services based on its, for years, contrived "incompetence" in supplying products and services. Thus a favourable environment is constructed for separating the state from the role that it had in the Brazilian economy in the construction of development, with all its contradictions that one has sought to point out up to here.

Thus, the Brazilian state arrives in the 1990s as the central focus of neoliberal propaganda that came out advocating its suppression as the source of the national crisis, when in truth, it was the central link of the external adjustment in the 1980s, of the policies to pay the foreign debt, as well as to sustain private income throughout this period. But the story will be set to one side as it becomes transparent in the affirmation of Gustavo Franco, one of the intellectual advocates of the end of the "developmentalist" state, and of the liberalisation in the 1990s as a member of the government, who states, "as an observer above suspicion would note, in the 1980s, the positive state-development identity was diluted and the state came to be seen almost as an obstacle to progress. It is not only the neoliberal ideology that gains temporary hegemony. More than this, it is the material failure of the state both in wealthy countries as well as poor ones that lead to an effort of reform that may not be modelled ideologically. The state has to solve concrete problems, with the concrete means at its disposal" (Franco, 1998:143), a sentence that is taken largely from a text of then president, Fernando Henrique Cardoso (1995).

It is interesting to retrieve a statement by Celso Furtado at the end of the 1960s, faced with the fact that the industrial structure was already delegated to large transnational conglomerates and the way how the domestic business class was associated with it. Furtado said, "weakening the state as the centre of decisions independent of international conglomerates, does not mean in Latin America to strengthen private initiative, it does (in fact) mean to renounce the formation of a national economic system, that is, a system articulated in function of the collectivity of the national interest" (Furtado, 1978:55).

To this statement could be added that, in an economy like Brazil's, to leave its movement in the hands of the market is in reality placing it "in the lap" of transnational capital, that defines and has its movement defined today in the globalisation process of capital dominated by centralisation. So, as Francisco Oliveira says, "The mystifying option and mystified by the market may, in Brazil's specific conditions, mean not only de-industrialisation, but social barbarity" (Oliveira, 1998:187). The movement of the "free market" is the movement of autonomous capital. Despite this, this is unfortunately what will happen in the 1990s, radicalising a mechanism of accumulation that has been rooted in the Brazilian productive structure since the 1950s.

4.8 The 1990s – Growing Subordination to Globalised Capital

It is interesting to emphasise that, as in previous periods, the policies adopted by Brazil in the 1990s had a double origin. On the one hand they were the result of an action drawn up and decided by government, transformed in practice by policies that gave total liberty to the movement of productive and financial capitals, sewn together with the wide support by domestic social groups, the Brazilian elites. On the other hand, they were the result of a type of international "ideology of globalisation" manifest in policy recommendations conceived in the central countries for the periphery that ensured the interests of transnational capital. From one side it appears, as in fact it is, an imposition of the global process of accumulation; from the other, it is structured around a deliberate strategy of the national elites, forged through the crisis of the 1980s. Up to a certain point, once again what one has is an association of the interests of local social groups with the interests of large transnational capital.

That is why, despite submitting itself to the globalisation of capital materialised in the movement of large transnational capital, one cannot say that the measures of liberalisation and submission to the movement of this capital have thus been imposed on Brazil in a wider sense. In history it is always possible to draw different routes, but the fact is that the liberalising strategy, in tune with the desires of capital, was taken up by the national elites that dominated the state apparatus, transforming it in a "national strategy". The period thus marks, the subjection of the Brazilian economy to the movement of capital now in a new phase of its process of globalisation that was requesting freedom of movement for its world restructuring marked by the centralisation of capital. On engaging itself in this movement, the Brazilian economy became more vulnerable to the process of globalised accumulation.

In the 1990s "... the conservative political elites and the main Brazilian business leaders enthusiastically adhered to the proposals and the policies that the North American economist John Williamson in 1989 called the 'Washington Consensus' ... The three elected governments during the decade [in Brazil] were supported by a coalition of forces of the centre right that brought together practically all the sectors of the bourgeoisie and the regional power oligarchs that had supported the developmentalist governments...". It was this that made it possible to take "forward a radical trans-nationalisation of the Brazilian economy..." (Fiori, 2001b:283), although one must not also forget that it was only possible by the "... international economic and political conditions that facilitated the formation, the transitory economic success and the electoral victory [of these] forces of the centre right..." (ibid. p. 286).

So, submitting itself to the movement of globalised capital was a deliberate strategy of the 1990s, as, in a way and in other contexts, had been the strategies of industrialisation associated with international capital in the Targets Plan and the Economic Miracle. The contexts differed greatly for various reasons, but it is worth underlining two points: Before, the leadership was in the hands of the so-called "developmentalist state" and now this apparatus is almost totally dismantled; in the cycles of previous growth the process of global accumulation was in a phase in which the periphery was integrated with it (see Chapter 2), a movement embodied in the transfer of productive plants to the periphery. Now what characterises the movement of capital in the world is productive re-ordering with substantial direct investments in mergers and acquisitions, in a process much more characterised by the global centralisation of capital, in which the strongest capitals shrink their productive structure by the centralisation of plants spread across the world into just one, as they eliminate the weakest capitals (see Item 6 in Chapter 1).

That is why, the question of Brazilian development ends up becoming much more complex once the pact of keeping the social groups together that were in the structure called the "Tripod of Accumulation", little by little dissolved at the expense of strengthening foreign capital and practically stopped existing since the policies of liberalisation: the state, the central national agent, was removed from the game and part of private national capital, even the one that made its living from its relationship in the productive chain as a junior partner of foreign capital, lost space to imports or ended up by selling its company to global corporations. Thus, what was left was just transnational capital that has its strategy of action defined outside, by its head office located in North-Atlantic countries, mostly US and EU (Carroll, 2010). In these terms the vulnerability and the dependency of the Brazilian economy are replaced, now subjected or more subordinated to the global movement of capital. "In practice the neoliberals promoted the radical trans-nationalisation of the productive structure and of the centres of decision of the Brazilian economy, a politico-economic strategy that radically fragilised the state and the Brazilian economy…" (Fiori, 2001b: 285).

What marks the economic policy of the 1990s is the extensive process of liberalisation that owes as the basic principle of its formulation the "Washington Consensus", "a consensus between the IMF, World Bank and United States Treasury Department in relation to the 'right' policies for countries in development…" (Stiglitz, 2002:43). Among these principles are stressed the freedom of trade flows with the reduction or extinction of customs barriers, tariffs and of exchange rate manipulation policies; freedom for the entry and exit of financial flows; privatisation of state companies; and the changing role of the state, traditionally with an active developmentalist role – be it for economic policies, be it as a direct investor – for a regulatory state, as agent responsible only for creating and maintaining the environment necessary for attracting direct foreign investment – given as really responsible for the new cycle of growth that should occur – without interfering in this movement. "The formulators of the policy in Latin America... adopted the "Washington Consensus" with enthusiasm (Rodrik, 2002:44).

Thus, part of the "package" was minimum intervention through traditional economic policies such as fiscal, monetary and exchange policy. Now the function of these should no longer be linked to development and the reduction of unemployment, but focussed on the aim of maintaining macroeconomic stability for the private investor, who of course, is international. This way, the rate of exchange must be the most stable possible in order to ensure that the resources deposited in the country do not lose value on exiting, the basis for the freedom of financial flows. Fiscal policy should be neutral in the sense of maintaining the fiscal balance (of spending in relation to government income) so as to leave private savings free in the market to be used by businessmen in their investments so as not to interfere in real markets (of goods and services) through public investments that, according to this vision, ends up in distorting prices given that they do not follow the "natural logic of the market conducted by supply and demand". And, finally to maintain a neutral monetary policy, preferably underwritten by an independent central bank, so that it controls the rates of inflation through interest rates. It is not the idea here to discuss the reason or the theoretical logic of each of these measures, but just to highlight that they are part of a line of economic thinking mostly coined from the orthodox or neoliberal that follow a basic principle: guarantee the conditions of stability, an environment in which the economic agents (the families, that appear as producers and consumers), placed in the free market functioning by their movements of supply and demand, they guarantee the best allocation of productive resources and, therefore, the efficient, balanced and equitable economic growth.

The argument behind the adoption of this logic is that all the problems of the Brazilian economy were the result of distortions created by government interference in free markets impairing its automatic readjustment in the periods of the "Developmental state" (Franco, 1998). From this standpoint, to leave free markets believing in their self-adjustment becomes the first and fundamental condition so that economic growth happens leaving free space for the private agent. In this scenario, both the domestic as well as mainly the international investor, would make their investments with "the maximum allocative efficiency", placing the Brazilian economy on the path to economic growth and natural development.

One should let it be clear that this strategy examined above was not drawn up in only the national environment, but is part of international conceptions based on new-classical economic theories that had been left on one side after the crises of the 1930s and WW II when Keynesianism grew in the world. The IMF itself had been created under a Keynesian perspective, according to Stiglitz (2002). These "neoliberal" ideas are revived throughout the crisis of the 1980s (both in the world and in Brazil) and, as here one wishes to stress, they serve very well a new phase in world capitalism, when it is the freedom of capital movement that guarantees and allows global productive restructuring in a wide-ranging process of capital centralisation. The explicit logic of these conceptions has its foundation in total liberty for capital that, in other words, one could call the "free market".

In reality, in line with what one wishes to note here, letting the market act freely is not to leave the decision to the economic movements of a set of "economic agents"[17] made up of "families" formed by numerous producers and numerous consumers that individually decided the best "allocation of scarce resources". But the very opposite, to leave the decisions to the market is to leave them to large capital corporations that today dominates this market globally, through large oligopolies, and that act in symbiosis with their states of origin, deciding the functioning of the economy and of the markets, and imposing a form of social organisation through this association capital-state. That is why, one may assert that submitting one to these market rules is to submit oneself to the rules of capital, now globalised and engaged in a global process of centralisation. The market is made up of a fistful of large transnational corporations supported in political power by their states of origin and other institutions like IMF, World Bank, The Trilateral Commission, World Economic Forum, etc. Therefore to act in line with the rules imposed by this market is to submit oneself to an explicit form of social organisation of production. This submission becomes more complex in the periphery given that those who incorporate the command of this form of specific organisation (the centres of decision of large transnational capital and states of the central countries) are outside the periphery. Therefore, to submit oneself, in the periphery, to the rules of the market is to submit to the movement of global capital. It is this that economic policies in the 1990s do, starting from the packet of liberalisation to build the attractive and desired scenario for this large foreign capital.

---

17   The terms in quotation marks here are traditional ones and found in any traditional introduction to economics that adopts "methodological individualism" (seer Blaug, 1984) as a method of economic analysis, that is why they are not accompanied by their respective sources.

Neoliberal power was consolidated during 1990s by the dismantling of the national State (or of what it still retained of "developmentalist" and "national"), eliminating its technical personnel and replacing them with a bureaucratic technocracy led by economists and economic engineers with PhDs. from the United States.[18] The strategy of submission to the designs of the market as a form of promoting economic development in Brazil appears in a very clear form in the ideas of some authors. Gustavo Franco (1998), for example, who was head of the Banco Central (Brazil's Central Bank), translates and justifies these "neoliberal" concepts as the best strategy for economic growth in Brazil, of course, with the attraction of transnational capital on stating it is "... the process of opening up, through its effects on the technological dynamism of the country, that will define the basic profile of the new cycle of growth ... a positive inclusion of the country in the process of internationalisation of production as a basic determinant of accelerated growth in productivity, therefore, [it is] the mechanism that will allow us to break the 'theory of the cake' and build a model of growth that manages to reduce the social inequalities without inflationary impacts" (Franco, 1998:122).

In this way, is the logic out forward entailed in adopting liberalising policies as a form of promoting development. Its basis is in the "insertion ... of the country in the process of internationalisation". The form of insertion proposed and realised in the 1990s was the creation of a scenario, according to the "Washington Consensus" itself, attractive to foreign capital, believing in a new wave of "internationalisation of production", realised by transnational companies, as Franco argues, given that for him they "stopped having nationality, or lost the notion of a centred "mother company by being related globally", they became "transnationals", he states (Franco, 1998:123), therefore they would have no reason to engage in national development autonomously anywhere.

Thus, from his point of view, in this new "globalised" world the companies would have lost their traditional relationship with their central office becoming autonomous in the world. And, as their "weight in Brazil is enormous", they are the real agents of development in the future. "Import restrictions ... together with macroeconomic instability ... [are the causes of the] extraordinary loss of importance of Brazil as the receiver of direct foreign investment" that only enters in Brazil after the policies of the 1990s, he concludes (Franco, 1998:124–125).

Within this logic, it is clear that the state, through its traditional developmentalist form of intervention "... comes to be seen almost as an obstacle to

---

18   Gustavo Franco (Harvard), Pedro Malan (Berkeley), Edmar Bacha (Yale), Pércio Arida (MIT), Lara Resende (MIT).

progress" (Cardoso, 1995:152), as pointed out by Fernando Henrique Cardoso, President of Brazil at the time – also quoted in Franco (1998:143) – and that is why it must be separated, thus losing any direct function in economic development given that "investment happens because the private sector has confidence in the sustainability of a basic macroeconomic framework. It is no longer the consequence of a 'national project', composed of mega-investments, hatched in offices. The state is no longer the foremost agent in the process..." (Franco, 1998:143). This idea is completed with the affirmation of Cardoso that says, "It is not only the neoliberal ideology that gains a temporary hegemony. More than this, it is the material failure of the state, both in rich countries as well as poor ones that lead it to an effort of reform that cannot be modelled ideologically" (Cardoso, 1995:152). He states that the role of the state changed, that now it only has the function of maintaining stability to allow large capital to move freely in a free "global" market. Therefore, according to this position, the Brazilian state must change its role. Thus, the doors are open for the real de-structuring of the Brazilian state, already scrapped as seen previously, in a programme of privatisations that will end up by removing from it the power to make developmentalist policies that it once had.

These principles are based on a vision that the new phenomenon of "globalisation" eliminates the differences between developed and peripheral countries in choosing the place where foreign capital operates given that it would have, in his view, lost its relationship with the centre. This would now place the economies of the world on an equal footing. As Cardoso states "...the phenomena of globalisation does not choose the identity of those affected. Thus, both the developed as much as countries in development win and lose with globalisation" (Cardoso, 1995:152). Thus is how the logic of liberalisation is presented. It would therefore be sufficient, to realise the policies to attract large capital in their "transnational" and "without country-base", that lives footloose in the world in search of opportunities, to the Brazilian economy, that would give it the conditions for its integration in the developed world and to break down the condition of being in the periphery.

Here the idea is explicit that the only way out from under-development, at this time, would be total adherence to the movement of capital mistakenly imagined as without a centre and disconnected from strategies drawn up at their head offices and their states of origin. This thinking is clear when Cardoso states that today "with the growing interdependence of the world economy, the rules of the international game are altered ... in the end, the game is one of reciprocity, it is necessary to have something to offer... ". So Cardoso himself points the way: "the reforms are well known: economic stabilisation in a scenario of balanced public accounts, privatisation and trade liberalisation, the creation of adequate infrastructure and of an agile and modern financial system, the availability of quality management, the redirecting of the state to its priority fields of action in providing basic services, in particular education and health" (Cardoso, 1995:155). Perhaps it might not even be necessary to show the similarities to the Washington Consensus indicated above. This conception of a global world, without a country, is very far from the reality of globalisation in the 1990s, which is, on the contrary, "the result of political and economic decisions taken increasingly in a more concentrated way by some oligopolies and banks and various national governments" (Fiori, 1995:238).

It is interesting to note that the big criticism entailed in this model of development presented is related to the role of the state and the idea of the free market, both umbilically connected. As was seen, the Brazilian state occupied an historic place in the process of Brazilian development that, at the same time in which it created mechanisms for attracting capital, functioned, even within increasingly narrow limits, as a counter-weight mechanism for the national interest faced with the power of foreign capital. The big change accomplished in this new model is in how it sees the role of the state and how its sees the role performed by transnational capital. The latter modifies its movement that was previously one of expansion, occupying new spaces, and that now seeks to free itself from policies that in the past benefitted it, but, in its new phase of accumulation, the centralisation of capital, it hampers it.

At any rate, it is worth stressing that Cardoso's positions entailed in this new model do not seem antagonistic in relation to his past when one takes as a basis the fact that he was the theorist of "combined development associated" with foreign capital. "In few words, although contradictions exist, Fernando Cardoso Henrique and his PSDB [political party] are not "strangers in the nest" of the big corporations" (Oliveira, 1998:177). As Cardoso himself points out, there is no break in his way of thinking in the full sense of associated development. On the other hand, when one imagines then what he might have changed in his thinking it would be in his ideas regarding the role of the state, he himself unpacks that illusion on stating his having criticised "widely, the statism and what I called", he says, "the state bourgeoisie", or rather, the economic bureaucracy, the heirs of political authoritarianism and favourite son of the official monopolies [state companies]" (Cardoso, 1995:149). With this statement, there remains no doubt as to the logic of the path of reform that dismantles the state and places the Brazilian economy definitively in the arms of transnational capital, defining the position of Brazil in the world scenario as "junior partner of western capital ... obeying only the interest of greater freedom of capital movement and from the geo-economic and political ramifications of its continued internationalisation" (Fiori, 1995:237). It is important just to mention that this "internationalisation" is no longer the same as that of the 1950s and 1970s.

Despite the impact of the economic policies adopted on the national political structure, which will be commented on later, these have a devastating effect on the domestic and foreign debts of the Brazilian economy. The combination of trade liberalisation with a stable and overvalued exchange rate – whose aim was macroeconomic stability with a shock of competitiveness and inflationary control – leads immediately to a loss of Brazilian economic competitiveness that is transformed into enormous trade deficits that need to be covered with the attraction of hard currency by the capital account. That is why, domestic interest rates are raised – which, with a stable currency, becomes the most lucrative business for speculative foreign capital – with immediate impact on the public debt (where this capital is invested) and on the external debt (by the increased entry of foreign funds). The result is the growth of the gross foreign debt which rises from US$96.5 billion in 1990 to something around $220 billion in 2001, whilst the domestic debt went from 36% of GDP in 1990 to nearly 50% in 2000.[19]

Apart from this, the foreign debt also grows as a result of the increasing share of foreign capital in the Brazilian economy, flowing in mainly through mergers and acquisitions. In the wake of commercial relations between the parent company and the subsidiary led to an increase of imports of parts and finished goods.[20] Foreign companies also come to be the most important receivers of foreign funds given financial liberalisation. According to the Institute for Studies on Industrial Development (IEDI, 2000), "… the foreign company came to account for 61% of the deficit in Brazilian current transactions in 2000 (31.8% in 1995) and for 66.9% of the increase in the country's foreign debt between 1995 and 2000. It is important to stress these factors because they place the Brazilian economy once again at the service of the trade and fiscal surpluses at any price – as occurred in the 1980s – using traditional recessive policies that generate unemployment, low salaries and create domestic crises. These policies serve to accelerate the process of weakening domestic private companies (as well as the state) facilitating the centralisation of capitals in favour of transnational capital in a phase of global restructuring.

---

19 Just for information, in nominal values the public debt went from around R$ 150 billion in 1995 to R$ 780 billion in 2002 and R$ 913 billion in 2003 (58% do PIB).

20 Between 1995 and 2000 imports within firms (between head offices and subsidiaries) of multinational companies grew 91%. In the secondary sector, 56% of the total of imports is realised within firms. (Lacerda, 2004:109–110). Add to this the largest importing of vehicles, for example, was realised by the vehicle assemblers themselves with factories in Brazil (Comin, 1998:139).

In this sense, the weakening of domestic private capital occurs in large part through the contradictions in the measures proposed that combine liberalisation with macroeconomic stabilisation. On the one hand, the liberalising project points to the opening up of the Brazilian economy to imports as the catalyst for a "shock of competitiveness" (as Franco pointed out), obliging the domestic company to modernise itself rapidly. Despite this, on the other hand, policies of increased interest rates as a counterpoint to the needs for foreign resources to overcome the trade deficit that arises because of the liberalisation itself, makes it difficult, when it does not impair the making of investments in the modernisation of domestic private companies. Furthermore, the policy of liberalisation, on allowing foreign capital to import freely, also placed additional difficulties in the way of those domestic companies that had been born and strengthened as suppliers to these foreign companies, given that they find themselves now exposed to a strategy of global production defined by the central head offices of these companies, that could simply leave them aside in choosing a global supplier elsewhere. The growth in the volume of imports as well as unemployment throughout the period demonstrates the fragility of domestic capital. A large part of these domestic companies do not manage to survive. In the best of cases they were acquired by transnational corporations and in the worst case, simply stop existing, seeing their products being substituted by imports.

The results of the policy appear in the words of those involved in the process at the time such as José Roberto Mendonça de Barros, Secretary for Economic Policy at the Treasury Ministry and Lídia Goldenstein, advisor to the presidency at BNDES (the State Development Bank). They saw the process as positive[21] and stated that "the interlinking of this set of processes has stimulated what ... we call the third wave of international investment and a break with the Tripod (domestic family company, foreign company and state company) that, since the 1950s and up to the start of the 1990s, had been the basis for Brazilian capitalism. "The state company is being privatised, the traditional national/family company is obliged to modernise itself, under sentence of succumbing to the violence of transformations and the international company has been changing its traditional form of insertion in the country ... coming to direct its investment to the most different segments of the economy" (Barros

---

21   It is interesting to note that both authors belonged at the time to the government and wrote this text with the aim of showing that structural transformation through which the Brazilian economy was going through was beneficial and would generate economic growth in the future, even with the strengthening of transnational capital that they saw as positive.

and Goldenstein, 1997:28). In other words, transnational capital ended up occupying other spaces left by the state's exit and the failure of national capital that does not manage to make the leap from the perverse situation in which it finds itself inserted.[22] As the authors themselves confirmed "the restrictive monetary policy, intrinsic to any stabilisation plan, resulted in making the change for national companies difficult" (Barros & Goldenstein, 1997:28).

The scale of Brazil's economic strategy faced with the new logic of the process of world capital accumulation in the 1990s may be captured by the change in characteristics of the foreign direct investments – FDI, when compared to the growth cycles of the Targets Plan and of the Miracle. As already indicated, in the first cycle of growth, FDI in new productive plants, while during the second cycle, finance in foreign currency predominates for the modernisation of companies installed here. In the 1990s FDI is concentrated in "… cross-frontier mergers and acquisitions [that] are today the principle instrument of penetration in new markets and of consolidation of the global market share of transnational companies" (IEDI 2000:8). Thus, they follow the logic of the process of restructuring the global space for accumulation through the centralisation of capitals, also captured by the volume of FDI in the world in mergers and acquisitions (UNCTAD 2000).

"The Brazilian success in attracting foreign investments is not reflected in growth because the larger part of these investments was not allocated to the construction of new productive capacity … but to the acquisition of already existing assets (the transfer of ownership)" (Arbix & Laplane, 2002:86). In the years between 1993 and 1998, Arbix and Laplane showed that nearly 70% of direct investment that was ear-marked for Brazil came for mergers and acquisitions (Arbix and Laplane, 2002:86). IEDI data also points in the same direction as far as the predominance of FDI is concerned for the same goal: in 1991, of the US$730 million in FDI, 13.7% was destined for mergers and acquisitions. In 1994 this percentage jumps to 24.3% and reaches 74% in 1998 (IEDI, 2000:9).

FDI in mergers and acquisitions results in a greater loss of national control over the economy, given that transnational corporations, as one tried to show in Chapter 2, are transnationals within central countries (US and EU), they have their head office centred in some countries (North-Atlantic mostly), they are connected to some states, and possess global strategies that cannot be confused with national strategies of development. This being the case, in the end,

---

22   In order to demonstrate the diversification, IEDI data shows that the foreign investment in mergers and acquisitions of private national companies are concentrated in the sectors of pharmaceuticals, hygiene and cleaning products, electro-electronics, chemicals, food, car parts and retail sales (IEDI, 2000:11).

the Brazilian economy became much more vulnerable and subordinated to the movement of global capital, weakened in its power of action by the state, given its de-structuring.

"The reinsertion of the Brazilian economy in the international flows of investment destined for countries in development, starting from the 1990s, implied a growth in the degree of denationalisation of the majority of most sectors, while the share [in turnover] from companies with foreign capital among the 500 largest companies in operation in the country represented an average of around 30% throughout the 1980s, this share was growing until the mid-1990s, reaching 45.8% in 2001" (Lacerda, 2004:83). The greater loss of share is from state companies, whose share fell from an average of 33% to 20% (Lacerda, 2004:84). Lacerda also used as an indicator for the process of internationalisation of the Brazilian economy, the stock of social share of capital possessed by non-residents that, according to him, went from US$41.7 billion in 1995 to US$103 billion in 2000. Also according to Reinaldo Gonçalves (2003), it is estimated that more than half of Brazilian production or assets are in the hands of foreign companies who control 40% of industry and 30% of agribusiness at the beginning of the 2000s. On the commercial side, the author estimates that two thirds of the supply of products from the electro-electronic industry were imports (Gonçalves, 2003, in the magazine Teoria e Debate, Issue 52 January/February 2003).

Hence, what one wishes to show here is that the process of internationalisation of the Brazilian productive structure reaches a still higher degree in the 1990s. Multinational capital that had already been structuring itself in the occupation of the most dynamic sectors of the economy in the 1990s, manages to install itself in the spaces left by the state's exit, starting with the process of privatisation and by private national capital that does not manage to survive faced with the new rules of the policy opening up the economy. Other productive areas are simply suppressed from the Brazilian economy, being substituted by imports.

In this way the Brazilian economy became much more internationalised and much more vulnerable to the movement of global capital, which means a lower capacity for resistance to pressures, destabilising factors or external shocks. It also makes it more difficult to use the instruments of policy available and imposes costs to any external confrontation that it might desire (Gonçalves, 1999:36). Going a little further, one may say that the Brazilian economy becomes much more vulnerable to the movement of global capital. Starting from the degree of internationalisation reached, the economy finds itself much more subject to the policies and strategies of this capital and sees its capacity reduced to realising economic policies according to its development interests.

At the extreme, one could arrive at a point in which its survival in this globalised productive structure would be submitted, in due proportion, to its attractiveness to foreign investment, that would leave it totally at the disposal of the designs and interests of globalised capital defined externally, according to global corporation strategies. Thus, this may also, according to its interests, invest in other places, to simply abandon the country where it was, as has happened with Mexico, where some of the "maquiladoras" moved to China.[23]

In order to survive and maintain itself in the process of accumulation, the economy that is under the command of globalised capital like the Latin American ones, has to constantly submit itself to competition between peripheral countries (Michalet, 2002:110, 153) to attract or maintain the direct investment of this capital upon the risk of being excluded, a fact that makes its policy of development totally subordinated to this movement and not to its own national strategy. In this context, the internal contradictions become radicalised given the policies of economic growth (for foreign capital) are not the same that aim for national development. To attract investment and keep oneself included it was necessary to follow the precepts of the Washington Consensus (Michalet, 2002:110, 154), but when one follows them, one moves away from the idea of development in the wider sense by the intrinsic contradictions to the submission to the movement of capital that this action represents. This contradiction is clear in Brazil as will be pin-pointed below.

Despite the care, in the Brazilian case, one cannot deny that de-industrialisation occurred through the 1990s, it was visible in the reduction of industrial employment and in the increase in imports. According to Belluzzo, "the 1990s were characterised by de-industrialisation, understood as the reduction in domestic value added on the gross value of production and with the elimination of jobs (more than 1.5 million during the decade) in manufacturing industry" and in the "loss of position in the ranking of aggregate manufacturing value whose share in Brazil fell from 2.9 to 2.7 (Belluzzo, 2003 – "Trade and Development, Folha de São Paulo – Money Supplement, 28/09/2003).

This process of de-industrialisation may be seen in Latin America in UNCTAD data. In the 1990s, the majority of Latin American countries had a significant fall in the share of the manufacturing sector in gross domestic product (UNCTAD 2003b:95). However, the fall of this production might be normal

---

23 Mexico, much influenced, as other countries, by the cycle of business with the USA, has been suffering a loss of competitiveness by the appearance of competitors with lower production costs like China (Cepal, 2003:28). Between 2000 and 2001 more than 200,000 jobs were lost in the "maquiladoras" fruit of the competition with China. Around 60% of the maquiladoras closed and moved to Asia (UNCTAD 2003:54).

in the economic and social development of any country through the growth of the service sector, with concurrent growth in the population's income and the middle classes, according to the report it occurs in a surprisingly accelerated manner in Latin America. "Latin America appears to have experienced a premature de-industrialisation. The region as a whole saw a sharp fall in the share of manufacturing industry in the total product during the 1980s and 1990s in the context of a low rate of economic growth, even though the share in employment of the manufacturing sector had begun to fall in the 1990s after remaining relatively stable in the 1980s. The reversal is particularly pronounced in the countries of the southern cone" (UNCTAD 2003b:95).

The UNCTAD report calls attention to the rapidity with which this transformation of Latin America has been occurring, a long time before these countries reached a GDP per capita at a certain level as occurred in the central countries. This change in the structure of GDP in the centre occurred when GDP per capita was already quite high, a fact that the report calls attention to. Looking at the data, one perceives that the share of the manufacturing sector in the southern cone of Latin America fell much faster than the central countries in recent years, going from 27.7% of GDP to 17.7% (UNCTAD 2003b:96). Comparing it with what occurred at the centre, one sees that while in Brazil the share of the manufacturing sector fell 10 percentage points between 1980 and 1999 (from 33% to 23% of GDP), in the USA, this fall was just 4 points (from 22% to 18%) and in the countries with medium-high income, by just 3 points (from 24% to 21%).

The same is valid for the whole of Latin America and, most interestingly, the report itself relates this process of de-industrialisation in Brazil to the liberalising policies of the 1990s. "The majority of the countries of Latin America ... had significant declines in the participation of the manufacturing sector in GDP. This was most pronounced in Argentina and Chile following the introduction of economic reforms (liberalising ones) in the 1970s and 1980s in Chile, and in the 1980s and 1990s in Argentina. In Brazil and also in Mexico, the sharp fall in the share of manufacturing in the 1990s coincides with the intensification of market based reforms". The report also adds that in the cases of Brazil, Mexico and Argentina, this change in the share of the manufacturing sector did not come associated with any economic growth (UNCTAD 2003b:96).

Of course this process of de-industrialisation in Brazil is an indicator of a tendency, but also it is not substantiated as a process of exclusion in the way referred to above and commented in Chapter 2. This is because, despite the policy of the 1990s, the Brazilian industrial structure, even though now less national, still maintained itself strong and relatively diversified, although much more dependent and far from developing a dynamic endogenous flow.

This does not mean that keeping the referred to strategy of subordination to globalised capital in its phase of centralisation in the world, this stops being a tendency to becoming a fact.

Throughout the 1990s, Brazil was still sought as a base for the installation of new multinational enterprises in their process of global restructuring, despite, as was said, this not being the rule. The automobile sector was what stood out in this process as an investor in installing new companies as well as expanding the groups who were long established here[24] (Comin, 1998). This specific movement is raised here to demonstrate the contradiction of the process referred to above in the Brazilian case. Even so, the vehicles produced in Brazil will use many more imported parts with a negative impact on the national companies that will close. On the one hand, investments in the car sector occurred at the time in which the liberal-globalising logic was at its peak. The car industry, in its global strategy defined centrally,[25] chose Brazil as a base for its car production – in a process of centralisation – to sell beyond Brazil, in South America (Gonçalves, 1999:113), which was not the rule in other sectors.[26] It took this decision in large part because of the liberalising policies that guaranteed the free flow of capital and goods (inputs and products), that is why, it became one of the largest importers of parts and other materials, imposing a radical readjustment in the car parts sector,[27] historically dominated by domestic companies. The fact is that the liberalising policies themselves that attracted this investment made, as expounded above, national economic growth unfeasible. The result is that these car companies suffered losses in productive

---

24 In part stopping producing in Argentina.
25 This fact is commented on by the report which states that "The continuity of growth beyond frontiers depends on the will of the head office. At Fiat, for example, the fall in exports of the Brazilian subsidiary arose after the Italian company decided to produce the Palio in other countries. It weighs also in this uncertain scenario the decision of the head office not to extend to the factories in Brazil the investments for production of new generations of models, reducing the chances of Brazil competing in more demanding markets" (Jornal Valor econômico, 19/jan/2004).
26 As seen above, the electro-electronics sector continued as an importer.
27 The sector of auto parts was traditionally occupied by national companies that were created in the context of the policies of import substitution that imposed percentages of domestic inputs in cars. With the policies of liberalisation the number of companies in the sector was reduced from 1,500 in 1990 to 800 in 1997. According to IEDI (2000) it was one of the sectors that internationalised most by mergers and acquisitions. Data from Sindipeças (the association of component-makers) pointed to a reduction in the share of companies with national capital control, in terms of number of companies. In 1996, 75.1% were companies with national control and 4.1% of only majority national control; as a contrast, in 1993, this distribution was 86% of national capital, with 12.7 % of majority capital (BNDES, 1997).

structures with an enormous excess of capacity.[28] The mechanism itself which attracted and generated de-industrialisation, unemployment and impoverishment that affected even the middle-class car buyers. That is why, the companies ended up being obliged, given that this was not the aim of establishing themselves here, to seek other markets outside Mercosur (Cepal, 2002:46). This demonstrates that, as indicated in Chapter 1, that capital walking on its own feet, at the same time in which it creates, it destroys the conditions for continued accumulation.

Hence, one wishes to state that the strategy of submission to the movement of globalised capital, which in the 1990s was clearly a process of global centralisation, on destroying the national power of interference in this movement by the state, leaves the peripheral economy much more vulnerable to the decisions of transnational capital that, at its limits, by the contradictions that it creates, may even abandon it, as it already gave signals of doing so in the 1990s. The centralisation of capital is a movement that carries within itself its excluding tendency.

"To sum up, what is Free Trade under the present conditions of society? Freedom of Capital. When you have torn down the few national barriers which still restrict the free development of capital, you will merely have given it complete freedom of action. Gentlemen! Do not be deluded by the abstract word Freedom! Whose freedom? Not the freedom of one individual in relation to another, but freedom of Capital to crush the worker". (Marx, "Speech on the question of Free Trade" in Marx-Engels collected works volume 6: p. 463).

The result of the neoliberal policies of the 1990s besides the enforcement of transnational capital in the Brazilian economic structure was to preserve and increase the power of the national private financial system, that is, of the rentiers, on managing public quasi-money, government bonds. The financial institutions did appropriate for themselves, via interest rates, 7% of GDP annually in the early 2000s. These banks have as their allies the new rentiers, the former productive entrepreneurs and non-financial companies that gain financial profits through the public debt. The banks would become the greatest power within the hegemonic bloc, side by side with big transnational capital. Also, the weakening of industry, agribusiness and mining was also increased by neoliberal policies. Its importance grew as result of strong Chinese demand. These groups form the new power bloc.

---

28 Chrysler closed its only unit in the state of Paraná some months after its inauguration; other factories reduced production and gave up on the last wave of modernisation (production of new global models) because of the crisis in Latin America, its target market.

4.9 The Lula Government Facing the Power Structure: Conciliation or Confrontation?

Despite the failure of the neoliberal project, which was clearly visible in the early 2000s, as seen in high unemployment, an exploding public debt, deficit in the trade balance and relative de-industrialisation, the players of the hegemonic power had already carried out the radical structural change of the Brazilian economy in 1990s. Thirteen years of neoliberalism had put the country in a structural straitjacket. It became much harder to implement counteractive measures, even when the elections of President Lula were apparently unfavourable to the established power. The newly elected government coerced or forced by circumstances, and perhaps even before the election, composed with – not against – the power bloc. Of course, we will never know if things could have been different; political articulation has become the central ability in any action to counter the interests that are deeply rooted in the structure of economic power.

The disruption of the State and its technical cadres – which had once made possible at least a semblance of planning – by the neoliberal 1990s era was extremely vigorous. Privatisation eliminated the State's ability to intervene productively in the economy – among companies of some importance, only Petrobras remained, and today is under attack. The uncontrolled and unrestricted adhesion to big oligopolistic transnational capital – which became mostly an importer of machinery, parts and components,[29] and also took over the strategic service sectors as well, including telecommunications and electricity – raised its power to respond with prices hikes to any glimmer of currency devaluation, as well as its power to react to wage pressures through any kind of distributive policies. The rentiers of the large private banks,[30] the elite of former entrepreneurs and the large national or transnational companies with cash to spare hold the power to easily rebel against any attempt to lower the interest rates or the public debt that provide them with income and ensure their financial profits[31] – as indeed occurred in 2012–13. The large agribusinesses and mining companies, strengthened by international speculative

---

29 In Brazil, 24% of industrial inputs were imported in 2013, with special emphasis on electronic components, auto parts, nonferrous metals, resins and synthetic fibres.
30 In 2000, the five largest banks held 50% of the system's financial assets and the ten largest 62%. In 2013, the top five rose to 67.7% and the top ten to 77.8%, demonstrating how concentrated banking is in Brazil.
31 In 2013, financial institutions held 30.2% and corporate funds 21.7% of marketed public debt. Foreign investors held 17%.

commodity prices (which ensured the Brazilian trade surplus[32] until at least 2013 – offsetting the increase in imports of industrial parts and components), began to defend the old law of comparative advantages, while pumping their surplus financial funds in the rentier market. They also, obviously, do not want any fall in interest rates.

The strategy of the new government (2003–2010) was not to confront, but rather to conciliate with the power blocs, assuring them it would not interfere in the relevant variables of exchange and interest rates. At the same time, it sought to implement policies to resume economic growth (as of 2005), distribute income and reduce poverty, penetrating the existing gaps in the power structure: a delicate operation, to be sure, but a successful one in terms of social goals and of placing the country once again on the path to growth (at least until 2010).

To appease the rentier elite, the government appointed a banker to head the Central Bank, a former BankBoston executive, trusted by the national and international financial markets. He kept virtually the entire technical staff of the neoliberal era macroeconomic team, at least until 2005, when the Central Bank began focusing on a policy of "inflation targets" that practically guaranteed high interest rates.[33] To appease both big international productive capital and domestic capital, increasingly mere importers of capital goods, parts and components, the Central Bank continued with its policy of currency appreciation,[34] which would prevent the recovery of the domestic industry. The assurance of trade liberalisation, together with currency appreciation, also served as a price control mechanism for the oligopolies while minimising inflationary pressures.[35] Exporters of agricultural and mineral commodities could easily bear the overvalued exchange rates because of the high global speculative prices. Thus, it was possible to accommodate interests, at least temporarily.

On the other hand, the government also carried out a comprehensive policy of income distribution through social programmes, as well as a deliberate

---

32 In 2013, staples accounted for 55% of exports. Together, ADM (formerly Archer Daniels Midland), Bunge and Cargill negotiate approximately 60% of soybean exports and crush 60% of the grains for the domestic market.

33 The actual average basic interest rate between 2002 and 2006 (first mandate of the new government), although lower than in the 1990s, remains around 11% p.a. Since 2007, real (off inflation) average basic interest rate fell from 7.5% p.a. to 5.3% p.a. in 2011.

34 The exchange rate appreciates in real terms nearly 25% between 2002 and 2013, or 2.7% per year.

35 Between 2002 and 2013, inflation rates remained within the specified range for the first time since the adoption of the policy of "inflation targets" in 1999.

policy of raising the minimum wage (see Cardoso Jr. and Gimenez, 2011, Chapter 6). The expansion of credit also contributed to increasing consumption. Economic growth resulting from the entire package of measures increased the average real income of society and to reduced unemployment significantly (from 12.4% in 2003 to 5.4% in 2013). Economic growth (GDP) peaked at 7.5% in 2010 over 2009, with a real upper average of 4% per year since 2003. With the resulting rise in tax revenues, the net public debt fell from 60% of GDP in 2000 to 35% in 2013. Inflation rates remained stable at around 6% per year. The government managed to maintain primary fiscal surplus above 3% of GDP.

This performance was limited by the pact (the level of rates of exchange and interest) with the power bloc. This limitation was, perhaps, best manifest in the performance of the industrial sector (production and employment). It was the one that least benefited from the growth cycle, not to mention that it had become an importer of parts and components to be "assembled" in Brazil since the wave of neoliberal policies of 1990s: its revenues rose despite lower production as 20 years of overvalued exchange rates had their effect. While the imports index grew fivefold (100 to 500), the index of industrial production increased 24% (from 100 to 124) between 2002 and 2013 (IBGE). The increase on industrial imports did not affect the trade balance only because of high international commodity prices which beginning to fall only in 2013, showed the fragility of being, after 50 years of industrialisation, commodity-dependent again. Fifty-five percent of Brazilian exports are commodities (9% oil and oil products, 14% minerals and 32% foodstuff, especially soybeans). In the 1980s 60% of exports were industrial products.

A new growth cycle was thus sustained, but without changing the economic foundations on which the power structure rested, in particular the redistribution of wealth in favour of rentiers and foreign speculative capital and the preservation of the profitability of an import dependent industrial sector through high exchange rates. The development project, although constantly criticised by economists representing financial institutions (even those who benefited from it), was carried forward, as long as it did not interfere with the high interest rates earned on government bonds and the overvalued exchange rate. The criticism of the growing share of public long-term credit in the financial market as inflationary increased. Even as growth of 7.5% in 2010 pointing to something like 10% as tendency on the first month under Dilma Rousseff's (the new president) government, the economists of the private banking sector, already unhappy with the previous policies of growth, intensified their criticism by accusing it of "explosive inflation" which they attributed to "unnaturally" low unemployment, "above productivity" wage increases and growth "above potential GDP" all thanks to the government's "populist policies".

A heavy blow was struck by corruption charges (called "mensalão") that put many leaders of the Labour Party in jail. The result, without going into the specifics of the corruption allegations themselves, was that political relations between the government and Congress broke down and opened up opportunities for the Power Bloc to resume direct control of policy by making it difficult for the government to govern.

This ensured that the Rousseff government was not a continuation of the Lula government, especially with regard to economic growth and income distribution policies. The consequences of high interest rates and years of overvalued exchange rates now matured and historically low industrial growth combined with the global economic slowdown and the fall in commodity prices in 2012-3 exposed the fragility of the external accounts. The political crisis brought on by charges of corruption, completed the picture. The power blocs had encircled the new government and this made its policy erratic.

Under such political pressure, the Rousseff government announced the increase in interest rates ensuring the policy of "inflation targeting" in 2011, in the beginning of her first semester in power. She also announced a cut in public spending to ensure the "credibility" of fiscal policy, mainly as it affected the "Growth Action Program" (focused on infrastructure projects) initiated by the previous government. These measures surprised its supporters and demonstrated the government's political subordination to the interests of rentiers. The economy plunged from a growth rate of 7.5% in 2010 to 2.7% in 2011 and it continued to fall in the following years. The Government appeared to believe that, having placated the power bloc, it could still put the economy on a growth path. It replaced the head of the Central Bank and initiated a policy to lower the interest rates on government bonds in order to force the private banks to give credit for investments at lower rates. It also devalued the currency (the dollar rose from R$ 1.50 to R$ 2.00) and announced tax cuts to productive enterprises. Naively, it believed that this would be enough for private investors to respond and change the dynamic axis of the economy, and for financial markets to calm down in the face of a guaranteed fiscal surplus. It also imagined that the private banks truly wanted, as they announced, to take on the role of public banks in long-term credit.

These measures on interest and exchange rates rattled the elites and they nearly succeeded in toppling the government and did succeed in forcing it to retreat. Low interest rates and devaluation hurt rentiers and productive national and foreign capital (which had become an importer, as we have seen) and they fought back. Newspapers wrote incessantly about inflation rising explosively now that the government had abandoned the policy of "inflation targets" by manipulating interest rates. As a result, the government once again raised interest rates and curbed currency devaluation. The economy plunged into low-growth mode, investments remained flat and cuts in public spending worsened the situation.

Thus, a catastrophic scenario was conjured up to pave the way back for neoliberal policies. The increase during the Lula government of long-term credit from BNDES, Caixa Econômica Federal and Banco do Brasil was criticised by private banks who wished to appropriate its resources which exceeded 51% of total loans. Aiming, perhaps, at its eventual privatisation, pressure was also exerted on Petrobras, the Brazilian oil company that had discovered huge oil reserves in 2000 and become a strategic element in any forthcoming industrial policy. One should remember that this huge state company was not privatised in the 1990s and is now in the dreams of world oil transnational companies to control it.

The country almost went into technical recession in 2014 and dropped completely in 2015 into negative growth after new elections had put Rousseff into office again. The government found itself totally cornered. It had believed that it could continue placating the power bloc (with cuts in public spending) and at the same time to pursue an alternative policy that directly hurt rentiers and importers. Its biggest mistakes may have been to believe that after the cut in public spending, entrepreneurs would invest and to leave its flank unprotected. The strategy was frustrated because it believed that economic growth would resume without massive government action. In 2016 a coup d'état moved Rousseff out of power and the new government imposed a destructive fiscal policy that resulted in a decrease of 7.3% of GDP in two years, with unemployment rising from 5% to 13% and the most destructive plan of social policies. Brazil was back into the neoliberalism of the 1990s, but now in a much deeper way.

The strategy of appeasing the power blocs trusting in some sort of associated developmentalism showed its frailty. Productive transnational capital, together with international financial capital, with private national banks as their brokers, showed their political strength. Brazil today (at the end of 2017) finds itself tied to a condition of renewed dependence on commodity exports, undergoing now (as before) a process of de-industrialisation and gradually losing the ability to become a global industrial player.

The lessons that can be extracted from these experiences are that the alliance to the power blocks, centrally the rentiers, has completely failed. The Labour Party (in power between 2003–2015) in this strategic alliance, perhaps full of good intentions in implementing economic growth, social policies and income distribution, ended up by destroying itself.

Today, Brazil's relationship with the global economy is increasingly as an exporter of primary products, as it had been before the industrialisation process in the 1950s. The difference is that it is now dependent on a new industrial power, China, as an exporter of commodities with low added value and an importer of manufactured goods. The domestic power bloc, rooted in a structure of appropriating wealth, especially financial wealth from the State (in the form of public debt), prevents any movement opposed to its current form of subordination to global capitalism. It was within this global logic of capital in association with the Brazilian elites that have constituted the power blocs that have been strengthened historically mainly under the aegis of neoliberalism. Attempts to subvert the logic imposed without a more radical shock to the power structure are proving ineffective.

CHAPTER 5

The Possibility of a Forced Disconnection

5.1   Accumulation, Subordination and Disconnection

Capital in its process of globalisation occupies spaces in the world and transports its logic of accumulation involving the processes of concentration and centralisation, processes previously restricted to the local space, to the world-space. In the same movement, it also transforms contradictions that previously were restricted to the local space, to the world. It is through this movement, in conjunction with strategic internal actions undertaken in Latin American countries that this periphery will be included in the process of global accumulation through its industrialisation which includes transnational capital within its most dynamic sectors.

If at a certain historic moment this capital movement was one of expansion – from the local to the regional, and to the world – occupying important spaces in the periphery, in another, limited to the 1980s and 1990s, the process of global capital centralisation took place, a movement that is not of inclusion of the periphery in the process of capital accumulation, but of exclusion. What marks the centralisation of capital is a process of capital reorganisation (that had already happened in each local space of accumulation) around certain centres, in which individual capitals are excluded from accumulation, as well as certain places. In this movement, the previously included periphery runs the risk of exclusion by de-industrialisation in a process of relative detachment from the centre instead of moving closer.

Capitalism is born and is structured on a global scale (as a process of internationalisation), an historical characteristic of its movement. But the form of occupying the world's spaces, historically, does not happen in the same way, through the same movements of capital. The characteristics of the first waves of this capital movement towards the global, or globalisation, starting from established capitalism, the occupation of geographic spaces that came to occur beginning from those countries that were the first to industrialise, advancing over other spaces, other countries in the world, were, from the start, dominated by trade relations. This so-called commercial internationalisation, which counted on the support, at times military from the states of the centre, was the result of the need to widen the potential for the realisation of the value created in the industrial centres, the realisation of commodities as value, in other places. This process not only guarantees the accumulation itself in the centre as it leverages it, at the same time in which it gives it the possibility of escaping the contradictions that the process of capital accumulation itself created in each place, in each country-centre.

But the process that impelled this movement of capital towards the global, globalisation is the result of the process of capital concentration in the centre, characterised by the increase in surplus value that each individual capital has to put into movement to guarantee its existence as such. The competition between individual capitals and the increase in productivity are catalytic elements of this process given that they constantly increase the mass of value seeking valorisation. This makes the space of the centre, the place each individual capital has its main headquarters, too small for the value that it has to put into movement. Faced with this situation, the more excess capital is destroyed at the centre (a process of centralisation), the more is begun a new type of globalisation, both are movements that ensure the conversion of the mass of surplus value created in new capital, which allows this surplus to be reinvested. Thus, the centralisation of capital leads each individual capital to extrapolate its local space to establish itself in other places in the world. In this process, it installs productive plants in the periphery – opening subsidiaries, making agreements with local companies that had been created previously by the export of machinery and equipment, and still as the result of the process of realisation of capital goods. It takes its brand, its technology created in the central head office, to other spaces. It thus occupies part of the appropriate periphery for it through the installation of subsidiary companies.

Productive occupation by the means of foreign capital that occurs in the periphery, related to the movement of individual capitals, is no longer directly linked to the need to realise the value created in the centre, but the production of value itself in the periphery. This movement results in the installation of an industrial structure in several peripheral countries, a process driven by individual capitals that become transnational capitals and come to occupy other spaces. In this movement these capitals occupy the peripheral spaces through the establishment of a transnational structure, controlled by the centre and from it, setting up subsidiaries in these new spaces. This process, despite often being able to be destructive to the traditional local economy, is still an integrator in the sense that it is a movement of occupation and "annexation" of new spaces to the global accumulation of capital. It contributes to industrialising part of the periphery that is of interest to the now globalised capital. It is no longer the result of the need for realisation (although it might be a process that continues to be present). It goes beyond this. It is the result of the intrinsic need to maintain value in the process of valorisation on an increasing scale.

This is the result of the process of accumulation on an extended scale strengthened by the concentration of capital in the hands of individual capitalists that have, obligatorily to put it in movement, in a process of valorisation, as well as by the centralisation of capitals that occurred at the centre as a result of the contradictions in each place of accumulation which made each individual capital stronger. This process of expansion towards the periphery is the condition and the guarantee for the existence of capital as such, always modifying its way of acting. It is an obligatory movement, given the growing masses of value that have to be replaced in valorisation, a real necessity that takes place through the hands of each individual capital in search of new spaces to guarantee its existence as capital so as not to perish. Competition and increasing productivity are the accelerating mechanisms of this process.

If on one side the processes of accumulation and concentration of capital lead capital to its expansion, integrating the periphery within its movement, when the process of capital centralisation takes place – previously restricted to each place – to a global scale, they are not integrating characteristics that are present. On the contrary, this movement tends to be excluding as it has already been in each local space. Starting from the moment in which capital occupied in its expansion all the appropriate spaces for the continuity of its movement in a process of capital globalisation, the process of centralisation takes on a global character, in the same way that it had made global the processes of accumulation and concentration. In so far that individual capitals, in their process of accumulation and concentration, occupied the spaces available and profitable in the world, those spaces with markets and resources available to ensure the accumulation and there install its contradictions, it begins the process of centralisation of capitals on a global scale. Of course, it does not have the same form as occurred in local spaces, where it had, up to a certain point, different geographic limits, but mainly, various political limits, given that it was a process that occurred within the nation-state that, up to a certain point, had some control over the movement of capital.

The centralisation of capital is the natural result of the processes of accumulation and concentration in restricted spaces that now occurs worldwide. It means that an individual capital has to take the space of another to continue its valorisation, to maintain itself as capital in action, which happens by the destruction of other capitals. It is a process of expropriation of the capitalist by capital. It occurs locally when the inherent contradictions are established by the movement of capital accumulation on an increasing scale and that is reflected in the crisis of under-consumption and over-accumulation. Faced with the constant expansion of the mass of value in valorisation, the space for accumulation becomes restricted, as much for the realisation of value created in the hands of each individual capital, but mainly, for the continuation of accumulation on an expanded scale. From this, the result is the centralisation of capital in each place and in each new space that it occupies. Weaker individual capitals are suppressed in this process in a rearrangement and strengthening of the stronger capitals that survive, a movement that is manifested specifically in the formation of monopolies and oligopolies, previously restricted to local spaces, but beginning with globalisation, they start to occur in the world-space. Thus, centralisation and internationalisation are mechanisms that promote the continuity of accumulation on an expanded scale, but on a more restricted capital base.

The question that one here seeks to underline is that these processes: accumulation, concentration and centralisation, had always occurred in the local space, but, in so far as capital internationalises itself and occupies the global space, it ends up occurring globally. As one sought to demonstrate throughout this book, the industrialisation of the periphery is the result of the expansion of capital and, more recently, its de-industrialisation appears to be the result of the process of centralisation of capital that has been installed on a world scale.

The movements of capital accumulation, concentration and centralisation in the world become clear when, apart from looking at them from the centre's perspective, it is looked at from the periphery's perspective, mainly from the Latin American perspective and more specifically, taking a simple example, it is looked at from Brazil's viewpoint. It was not every country in the periphery that was integrated in the movement of capital described above. Only those countries that had undertaken a certain type of policy to attract this capital which went out in search of space, and managed to attract it and internalise it in its productive structure, it is that which coupled itself to the movement of accumulation of capital from the centre. In Latin America, the Cepal strategy of industrialisation by substituting imports was at the centre of this policy for attracting transnational capital that resulted in its occupying the industrial structure of some countries, their most dynamic, productive and most technologically advanced sectors.

The case of Brazil stands out even more in this sense. Its industrialisation through the attraction of this transnational capital, based on a strategy of import substitution was only possible through the action of its domestic policy, given that it did not establish itself as a peripheral country that attracted capital because it had abundant and cheap resources available. The establishment of foreign capital in Brazil was related to a strategy drawn up internally – embodied in extensive plans for national development – in symbiosis with the movement of internationalisation of global capital. The process of industrialisation in Brazil in relation to the movements of capital in the world described is the result, therefore, of a double movement, of a synchrony between the process of world accumulation and of the strategy of introducing global capitalism in the country.

This symbiosis makes it difficult to separate that which is the result of the movement of capital in the world, as a movement with a certain degree of autonomy, as a force of capital in its expanded accumulation and what is the result of the deliberate action of the periphery itself as observed in Brazil's case. They become two amalgamated movements that are mixed together at the same time in which they interact. When looked at more closely, at times one movement responds to the other, at other times, there is a meeting, but, as is sought to demonstrate in the case of Latin America and of Brazil, it has a direction and logic. Brazil went through these processes described above as a primary-exporter, later, in its spontaneous or limited industrialisation, to afterwards become a place of attraction for transnational capitals from the centre, or, a place for productive investment realised by the companies of the centre. In the 1990s, it suffers the impact of the process of the global centralisation of capital.

Looking at the industrialisation of Latin American countries, from the point of view of the movement of global capital or from the viewpoint of a political option of the periphery, the outcome is the same. The countries that managed to industrialise themselves, they did so, in part, by the action of the state through deliberate policies and, in part, by the action of capital in its process of globalisation, mainly in its phase of productive internationalisation, participating in the movement of the capital, of the movement of the process of global accumulation, characterised by processes of accumulation and concentration. It is this alignment between, on the one hand, the movement of the periphery and, on the other, of capital in its process of globalisation, that will result in the vulnerability and political and economic weakening of this periphery, faced with the global process of accumulation. This weakening becomes clear when the process of capital centralisation takes place on a global scale.

But, the central question goes beyond the synchrony between the strategy of the periphery and the movement of global capital. It is a fact that – even though at times it might not have been an intentional synchrony, in the case of the Cepal strategy which did not wish to increase the relation of dependency – that synchrony was responsible through the promotion of industrialisation in the periphery, with all its contradictions; it removed itself from a type of subordinated relationship that marked the primary-exporter logic and permitted the building of a diversified and modern industrial complex, a productive and up to a certain point competitive one, the conditions needed to make it a capitalist economy in a specific sense because it was subordinated and dependent.

So, the question that perhaps might be pertinent is if in other times this harmony of interests was so constructive in a certain sense – from the strict point of view of the inclusion of global capitalism in the periphery, the creation of an industrial structure, although dominated by transnationals –, in the 1990s this strategy, now faced with global capital in a process of centralisation, carried out also by a president trained in Cepal's logic, has the tendency to lead to the deconstruction of what had been realised, the de-industrialisation and impoverishment of part of the included periphery in the global process of accumulation, or, at least, to its distancing in relation to the centre.

For this question two answers are pertinent. The first of them is that the problem that led to these outcomes could have been an excess of liberalism from the 1980s and 1990s. Capital always wanted freedom of movement, but the peripheral nation state only managed success in industrialising because it did not give a certain type of freedom to capital, creating, by direct intervention in the productive structure, the scenario to attract it, and now, on adopting the new scenario desired by capital materialised in liberalisation, would have let the built industrial structure slip through its fingers. The other possible reply is that previously, capital accepted and supported certain interventionist strategies, given that they benefitted from it in their interest in the process of occupying new spaces for their accumulation in their movement of productive internationalisation and, now, with each capital already occupying these new conquered spaces, a time of reordering has begun, or reorganisation of functioning capitals, on a world scale, and this movement is embodied in mergers and acquisitions, in a broad process of centralisation of capitals and that is why capital seeks total freedom, with the separation of the peripheral nation states, not accepting that type of intervention that in the past which had benefited it. For what is proposed here is, neither of the answers is incorrect. Both are true given that the current movement of capital in relation to the periphery has a double explanation: on one side is capital in a process of global centralisation: on the other, is a periphery undertaking policies of liberalisation.

Capital, embodied in the actions of various individual capitals, despite desiring freedom, always accepts a relative "lack of freedom" or interventionism given that this is in its favour, in favour of its process of accumulation on an increasing scale. Thus, the hypothesis adopted here is that the moment that this intervention in its freedom impairs the movement of the process of accumulation, desired by capital, movements of concentration and centralisation, this interventionism is radically placed in discussion. In the case of the process of capital globalisation, a certain type of state intervention was, in certain times of accumulation and concentration, useful to the movement of capital en route to the occupation of new spaces. The contradiction between liberalisation and intervention, despite always being present, does not stand out. Now, at the time of centralisation, when the struggle is between individual capitals to know which of them will survive in a space that is becoming restricted on a world scale, political actions that previously protected come to hinder the movement. Political action must, therefore, be modified to allow the restructuring of individual capitals, according to its individual relations of economic and political power, of head office strategies in the centre, as well as their central states and global institutions. Transnational capital wishes it to be so.

In this sense, the action of any state in protecting its space that is not the place of origin of individual capital, protected by the state that defends its interests and gives it protection, comes to hinder its free movement when the process of global centralisation takes place. In this case, the action of the peripheral states that once attracted this capital for their developmentalist policies comes to be counterproductive in the process of restructuring through which capital is going through, global centralisation linked to global capital restructuring. Therefore, what seems to mark this change in relation to the acceptable role of each nation state is the process of centralisation on a world scale, as a mechanism that tries to force all the states outside the game, but each individual capital is protected under the power of its centre-state, in an apparently contradictory movement. The aim is to remove the power of other states, and for this, capital uses the power of the state of origin. Who lose out in the struggle are clearly the weaker states, the peripheral ones, mainly those that are at the mercy of the movement of transnational individual capitals that dominate their productive industrial structure. This is the process that appears to characterise the search for total liberty undertaken by globalised capital, embodied in a specific political and concerted action called "the Washington Consensus", as well as in the financial power game of the countries of the centre, this is also distributed in a hierarchical form that in a way defines which groups (and central states) will have more resources to win in this global productive restructuring, a process of centralisation of capitals and centralisation of power.

This seems to be the characteristic of the process of global capital centralisation that took place in the 1980s and 1990s. When the Latin American periphery – with Brazil at the forefront – , in a deliberate action, joined this movement of capital (and of the states of the centre) as a strategy to keep itself "integrated" – even in a highly dependent and subordinated way, a historically constructed dependency –, the opposite of attracting productive capital to within its frontiers, the opposite of maintaining its form of insertion in capitalism by trying to create a "diversified and modern" industrial complex, a disintegrating and de-industrialising process enters. This is the result of the restructuring that capital goes through in the world, eliminating the weaker capitals, destroying superfluous functioning capital, in a broad process of centralisation that strengthens it as capital, that strengthens each individual capital that is left over, normally centred on some large transnational company, and that also seems to strengthen the power of the state of origin, but results in a greater subordination of the periphery to the centre, in its de-industrialisation, in increased unemployment, increased poverty and exclusion, in a much more acute separation between the countries of the centre and the periphery.

Centralisation is not a linear process. As already pointed out, it is a process that characterises the movement of capital in its accumulation process and had already occurred locally. The problem is its de-structuring outcomes and the deep-rooted contradictions entailed in de-industrialisation, impoverishment and exclusion seem to structurally modify the process of accumulation. It destroys more jobs than it creates as Chesnais (1996:307) pointed out. The centralisation of capitals is the result of a qualitative rearrangement of various individual capitals that reorganise the process of accumulation, strengthening it for the resumption of the expanded accumulation of capital in a scenario of greater exclusion and impoverishment. It is a process that previously was much more visible locally and, in a certain way, was counter-balanced by national state social policies. Now, apart from continuing to occur in local areas, it stands out globally because the productive structure of transnational corporations has become global. The theories of monopoly and of oligopoly for many years pointed to this phenomenon in each space of accumulation. What seems to be different is its predominant characteristic today of action on a world scale that is not marked exclusively by the destruction of local capitals, but by the destruction of capitals in the world embodied in the wave of mergers and acquisitions that occurred around the world in the 1980s and 1990s, involving the transnational companies themselves. The destruction of local capitals, that continues occurring, is still a characteristic of productive internationalisation, a movement marked by the substitution of national production by that of transnational groups, in the area (periphery). Already in the process of centralisation the action of the transnational capital itself predominates in restructuring what it does not replace, but tends to eliminate and centralise its productive structure in specific places, according to its global strategy of action.

The freedom that large corporations has lobbied for in recent years was the liberty to undertake its restructuring on a global scale, that is why it goes beyond the traditional desire for free trade, or to establish itself where it thinks best and remit profits freely; it is not the liberty to produce goods in the centre and to have guaranteed markets in the periphery that characterised the internationalisation of trade. The liberty that capital desires is the freedom firstly, to manage to restructure its production in a centralised form faced with the new needs of accumulation and, for this, it needs an enormous flow of free resources available for mergers, acquisitions, or, simply, for transfers of productive structures from one place to another (with the closure of units) and, in second place, to be able to create a value chain, administered and commanded from the centre, efficient and lean (extremely productive) in a system widely called *global sourcing*. It is the freedom for a broad restructuring of capital on a global scale that involves and goes beyond freedom of trade, of productive installations and even of finance.

If this is the direction that global capital accumulation took from the 1980s, this is the reason for studying it that is proposed here. That is why, starting from the moment, already real and historic, that some Latin American countries and Brazil, submitted themselves to this movement of capital, it not only weakened them in their power to act with the minimum of autonomy that still remained at the end of the 1980s, but they submitted themselves to a capital movement that is now a disintegrator of productive structures, it is excluding, and that radicalises the contradictions themselves that the process of capital accumulation creates in its expansion and centralisation. Thus, if capital comes to the periphery, if it comes to Brazil as a result of joint action with the national state that created the conditions for its occupation of the periphery, in so far that now the contradictions are rooted in a "new" movement of capital, the conditions that previously attracted this transnational capital dissolve it (for example, market size), in so far that people, workers or old businessmen, are excluded from the process and lose their capacity to participate minimally in the flow of accumulation, that which one day attracted foreign capital, on being destroyed, brings onto the scene the possibility that the process of valorisation of value of this peripheral space may stop being part of the global accumulation, and drive the periphery to a process of "forced disconnection" as pointed to by Chesnais. Brazil, adopted here as an example, seems to run the risk of a "forced disconnection" despite the strength of its economy, with the way how capital is rooted here and the strategic position it occupies in Latin America, although it is in a region that has been getting much weaker in recent years through the strategy of embracing capital in this new era. In this competition unleashed between the peripheral countries that industrialised to keep themselves in the reckoning, to try not to lose the foreign companies established in them, Brazil among them, these countries have, contradictorily, destroyed their greatest attraction: the size of their market, what most motivated the companies to invest in Brazil (Gonçalves, 2000:111–112).

Brazil is not an enclave economy that has a special natural resource that serves to keep the interest of some multinational company, neither is it the country that has the most specialised and cheapest labour in the world. What Brazil has as an attraction has been the size of its market and, contradictorily, the degree of rootedness that large transnational companies have here. This productive foreign structure is so strong that perhaps it will take many years to be de-structured.[1] But this does not mean that this de-industrialisation may not happen, after the 1990s, it gave signals of being in fast gear by the liberal policies adopted internally that gave ample freedom to capital. The proofs of de-industrialisation are worrying, and the attempt to stop this movement was blocked by the interests of transnational capital and their national elite's partners. After oil reserves discovered by Petrobras, the situation got worse because of the interests of transnational oil companies in occupy Petrobras space.

5.2 The Question of Centralisation

Marx did not develop the idea of global capital centralisation, despite pointing to the global character of accumulation and centralisation as a direct consequence of accumulation on an expanded scale. The possibility of what may be happening in a process of global centralisation of capital emerged in this work starting from the studies of globalisation by Chesnais and Michelet, the main authors in Chapter 2, as well as the data on direct investments in mergers and acquisitions in the world, issued by UNCTAD. It is by these references that one confirms global centralisation of capital as a reality present in the 1980s and 1990s, exhibiting its contradictions and limits in the 2000s. This imposes a new scenario of accumulation on the peripheries included in the process of global accumulation. Global centralisation is not therefore an abstraction, but on the contrary, it appears as an empirical reality embodied in the movements of mergers and acquisitions (M&A) undertaken by large transnational groups in the world. The impact of this movement on the periphery appears as a tendency towards de-industrialisation and productive de-structuring, mainly in Latin America, a movement that is shown in an acute form in unemployment and an increase in importing products that previously were produced in Latin

---

1   Nevertheless what occurred with the assemblers may be model: they are suffering losses and some of the last to install themselves in Brazil have closed. Chrysler closed in Paraná State, and as the president of the Peugeot Group states "all the assemblers in Brazil are losing money. The recent ones arriving have the biggest problems…" (Gazeta Mercantil, 9 March 2004 p. A1).

American countries and, mainly, in the distancing of the centre in relation to the periphery.

The aim then is to understand this movement and its relation with the periphery. It was by this route that one sought to trace a relationship between the logic of capital accumulation on an increased scale and its tendency towards centralisation expounded by Marx, complemented by Aglietta and Boccara in their analyses of capitalist flows and the crises that leverage the movements of centralisation, ideas taken from Marx himself, of the processes of global accumulation, concentration and centralisation. Marx had pointed to the tendency that capital has to internationalise itself, a movement that appears always focussed on trade, as well as, to a lesser extent, in productive internationalisation that always occurred, but was not predominant in his era. For this, it is enough to see that the predominance of external investment in 19th century Brazil was linked to infrastructure, mostly seeking to facilitate trade: at the end of the 19th century and the beginning of the 20th century, it appeared connected to the export of machinery and equipment from the centre to Brazil. Only at the start of the 1950s did it become predominantly productive internationalisation, when transnational capital from the centre expanded itself, creating productive structures in the periphery, in the first phase of globalisation. Now the processes of global centralisation, not that they might be something new, very much the contrary, they always occurred, but seem to have become the predominant form of capital's action in the 1980s and 1990s, promoting a restructuring of the global capitalist economy without precedents.[2]

Centralisation of capitals as a tendency of accumulation was already present in Marx, a process of transformation of the productive structure in the sense of reducing the number of individual capitals that follow in the process of capital accumulation, a movement that is, on the one hand, related to the rationale of expanded accumulation itself and, on the other, the crises that unleash the waves of centralisation themselves, in a movement that destroys part of the individual capitals. These were movements that Marx saw occurring in his time, but that had not yet a predominantly global scale. But today, included in the 2000s reports of UNCTAD itself, one can find empirical evidence that this process of centralisation on a global scale predominates and was central, at least during the 1980s and 1990s, in a broad global restructuring of capital. The

---

2 Cláudio Katz (June & November 2002) on analysing the visions of different authors, also one does not see many points in common with other moments of internationalisation or globalisation of capital. After all capital modifies itself historically and seems not to repeat the same story cyclically.

process of accumulation, when it reaches the global scale, comes through the formation of global oligopolies and monopolies that always occurred in the local[3] context. It is worth remembering that it was the large companies in each area of accumulation that sallied forth to seek new spaces and established themselves throughout the world. The global centralisation that is pointed to here is the result of the restructuring of these capitals now on a global scale. "In the context of the global economy, the general form of capitalism developed itself even more, a type of synthesis and matrix of the singular and the particular, all reciprocally referred, but determined by the general" (Ianni, 1999:176).

Each movement of centralisation qualitatively changes the productive structure (Aglietta, 1979), placing it on a new level of accumulation. At each wave of centralisation therefore new characteristics take control of the accumulation process, given that capital appears to become stronger and more autonomous. Centralisation is a "phenomenon that extends and expands the capacity for the intervention of capital in the social space" (Mello, 199:172). It enlarges the degree of power of capital in general that is more concentrated in facing the state, facing society, it modifies the form of organisation of competition between capitals, and it increases the quantity of the excluded from the process of accumulation, and promotes the taking root of contradictions that would appear in the 2000s. Thus, according to this hypothesis, at each wave of centralisation one will encounter a qualitatively different capitalism. This means to say that capitalism is modifying itself at each wave of centralisation on a world scale, as it was modified locally, a change that is in part responsible for the globalisation of capital itself. Centralisation now on a world scale must impose new qualitative transformations in the process of accumulation. One does not have the aim here of undertaking an exercise of projection or forecast, but only to point to changes and new contradictions that will emerge, now on a world scale, as a result of centralisation, mainly in the sense of the new form of inclusion of the periphery in this movement.

Just to demonstrate the idea of change caused by centralisation in capitalism one could consider the hypothesis itself suggested by Marx (Marx I, 1887a:311). For him, at the limit of the qualitative changes in the process of accumulation due to centralisation, one could arrive at a capitalism of just one company, or individual capitals under single control (which would not necessarily indicate geographic centralisation). The hypothesis serves to demonstrate

---

[3] Several studies on the formation and functioning of industrial oligopolies and monopolies in the local context have already been done. Perhaps the best known is the study by Silos Labini (1980) "Oligopoly and Technical Progresso" in which he analyses how industrial production is organised in several types of oligopoly.

how capitalism changes itself at each wave of centralisation, but is still very far from a concrete reality. Firstly because there is no empirical evidence and capital, even being singular, still continues in its process of accumulation depending on the variety of individual capitals competing in an anarchic and at times destructive way, increasing contradictions at other levels. In second place, because this hypothesis could be related to what here, making use of what Milton Santos, calls the verticality movement. Seemingly, it is in the "horizontality" it appears that people have the tendency to create other alternative forms of production, perhaps at the margins of the movement of large capital if they do not manage to insert themselves in its movement, to survive, despite what he himself states "the competitiveness [law of the market that involves all] ends up destroying the old solidarities, often horizontal, and by imposing a vertical solidarity, whose epicentre is the hegemonic company, locally obedient to the most powerful global interests and, in this way, indifferent to what is around it" (Santos, 2000:85). In this way it can swallow individuals and individual states. The fact is that capital is modified historically and recreates the contradictions in new scenarios. The process of global centralisation in recent years demonstrates these changes and the 2008 crises its contradictions.

5.3 The Centralisation of the 1980s and 1990s

The process of global centralisation marked by the 1980s and 1990s that is inserted in what Chesnais calls capital mundialization.[4] For this author the globalisation of capital has a first period characterised as a long phase of uninterrupted capital accumulation that would have begun in 1914, and in the second period that "involves the policies of liberalisation, privatisation, deregulation and the dismantling of social and democratic conquests, that have been applied since the 1980s…" (Chesnais, 1996:34). It is worth remembering that this expansion of capitalism to which Chesnais refers may be subdivided into a period from 1914–915 and, another post-war phase, "the Golden Age", between 1945 and 73. This subdivision which follows Hobsbawn (1995) is important given that this phase of expansion, recounted by Chesnais, only reaches the Latin American periphery in the 1950s.

In the post-war period, the so-called "golden age" of capitalism, the globalisation of capital that emerged came via foreign direct investment – FDI which meant the expansion of productive capacity of the transnational companies

---

4 Several authors work with periodisation (Chapter 2). We take up here just the discussion relevant to arrive at centralisation.

towards the periphery. In Latin America, it was this movement that predominated until the end of the 1960s. From then, one can say that FDI has the same characteristic (it is productive investment), but it is related much more to the modernisation and expansion of productive capacity – in the case of Brazil, investment in new sectors no longer predominated –, it was focussed mainly on direct investment in the form of loans in foreign currency. But, the big change appears in the 1980s and 1990s, when what happens to characterise the movement of FDI is no longer the expansion of productive capacity, but investments in the acquisition of existing capital. It thus becomes concentrated in mergers and acquisitions (UNCTAD 2000:15). "FDI is not synonymous with the creation of new capacity. It is the power of transfrontier acquisitions/mergers in which large groups seek to gain portions of the market. The selective integration of production sites and of outsourcing relations, situated in various countries, increases their capacity to make economies of scale and of breadth" (Chesnais, 1996:36). This large transnational capital undertakes this process by the occupation of the space of another individual capital that was either suppressed by the strongest, or by some crisis, characterising the centralisation of capitals.

Looking at the UNCTAD data, it seems there remains no doubt that what characterised the globalisation of capital in the 1990s, "Its most visible face" is the volume of mergers and acquisitions (M&A) that define the form of direct foreign investment-FDI (UNCTAD 2000:159), therefore, it marks the predominance of the process of the global centralisation of capital. Between 1987 and 2001, whilst the total volume of FDI in the world grew 11 times (18.7% per annum), the volume of M&A grew 15 times (21.5%). The greatest concentration of these operations occurred in the world from 1995. On average, between 1987 and 2001, a little more than 67% of FDI realised in the world was in M&A. In this sense, seemingly, what marked the 1990s was a broad process of capital centralisation on a world scale.

It is interesting to note that the greater part of M&A undertaken related to operations between developed countries, in percentages that every year went beyond 80% of the global total. This fact seems to demonstrate that what occurred in the world through the 1990s was a rearrangement of the productive structure on a world scale that was related to the periphery only in a marginal way, despite the enormous impact on its productive structure. More than this, in 1999, 26% (against 21% in 1997) of total FDI in the world was ear-marked for the USA and the other 39% distributed between some European countries. Brazil, Argentina and Mexico totalled just 5.9% in 1999, the peak of FDI in these countries (against nearly 9% in 1997). This tendency marking the movement of FDI in the world demonstrates clearly the operations of centralisation that were much more oriented to the centre of the system, between countries of the centre; it was between them that capital realised the greater part of its FDI, characterising a process of centralisation between large companies at the centre itself. As operations occurred in the global environment between transnational groups of the centre and they have subsidiaries in the periphery, it was a process that had a major impact on the industrialised periphery, but these were never at its dynamic nucleus. It was the global strategies of the large transnational corporations, shaped from the centre that de-structured the peripheral economies.

The centralisation of capitals, as could not be otherwise, was realised under the leadership of large transnational corporations and involved strategies of restructuring and of control over spaces and countries; control not only on the part of the companies themselves, but on the part of the central states themselves, as Ianni (1999), Benjamin (2001) and Tavares (1997) point out. Thus, it is characterised by a process of dispute for power and control between the large transnational capitals and, perhaps mainly between the states of the centre. The domination exercised by large these corporations over FDI in the world may be seen in the data. According to UNCTAD, the 50 largest companies in the central countries accounted for 50% of FDI in their countries, being that since the end of the 1980s until 2000 mergers and acquisitions dominate these direct investments by these large companies. Between 1998 and 1999 around 60% of the business done reached individual amounts above $1 billion (UNCTAD 2000:71), or rather, were undertaken between mega-companies.

There were also operations that involved strategies of global control and the elimination of over-capacity in the most dynamic and high technology sectors, over those sectors that ensure power over entire productive chains. The M&A operations in the world were realised, mainly in the sectors of cars, pharmaceuticals, telecommunications and energy (including oil), mainly by the acquisition of control over important parcels of the capital. Just to have an idea, between 1987 and 1998, in terms of the total value of M&As, the percentage of operations that aimed at horizontalisation (acquisition of companies that produce similar or competing products), in every year was above 50%, in six of those years it was above 60% and in 1999, it was over 70%; only a small part consisted of M&As of verticalisation (control of raw materials or final product), with the rest not defined or involving verticalisation and horizontalisation at the same time (UNCTAD 2000:231). In the capital-intensive and technology-intensive companies, where concentration was greater, mergers and acquisitions in a horizontal direction prevailed and whose main aim was "to continue to be competitive by the elimination of excess capacity" (UNCTAD 2000:126–129).

The obvious result is a smaller number of individual capitals, eliminating superfluous capitals (excess capacity) and controlling market and productive processes on a now global scale. Therefore, the M&As implied a smaller number of individual capitals controlling entire markets of products, mainly in the most dynamic sectors that lead us to infer that they acquired greater control and power over other sectors in the value chain (that depend on the most dynamic) without the acquisition of property. This means that these operations in the world really were linked to the formation of global oligopolies and monopolies in certain sectors, excluding individual capitals that previously occupied this space, increasing the degree of concentration and control over markets. For instance, while in 1996 the five largest car assemblers were responsible for 49% of the production of vehicles, in 1999, they came to control 54%. When one considers that General Motors acquired part of Fiat, this percentage rose to 60% in 1999.

The global centralisation of capital was leveraged by the policies of liberalisation made under pressure[5] by global capital itself through its central states, carried out in various countries that dismantled trade barriers and facilitated the restructuring of transnational corporations. Liberalisation thus functioned as a catalysing element for global centralisation. It allowed global productive restructuring to be undertaken in the context of the transnational corporations themselves, a mechanism that "makes leaner" the global productive structure and each individual capital globally more efficient and productive. With liberalisation, large transnational corporations could create internationally integrated production structures through the acquisition and reallocation of assets in various places in the world (UNCTAD 2003:27). They closed productive structures in one place to focus production in areas where the costs are lower and ensure, in a more efficient form, the strategy of global supply ("*global sourcing*" or "*international outsourcing*").

In the periphery, the policies of liberalisation deregulation and, mainly privatisation, with the separation of the state, permitted the action of the centralisation of capital in an even more radical way than occurred at the centre. The policies of privatisation were central to this process. Hence, it is enough to observe which were the sectors most involved. "In Latin America and the Caribbean, transport, storage, communications, oil, energy, gas and water were those that received the largest volume of FDI in mergers and acquisitions" (UNCTAD 2000:131). And, among the peripheral countries that actively took part in this process, Brazil was at the forefront in FDI directed towards privatisation, the report continues. Of the 50 largest privatisations involving

---

5   The Washington Consensus is the central benchmark of the pressure referred to here.

foreign buyers 23 took place in the periphery[6] (ibid.131), which often places these countries in front of the developed countries in this type of FDI in terms of value. "Brazil and Argentina are the largest winners, receiving US$32 billion and US$26 billion during the period [1987–1999]" (UNCTAD 2000:1311). Thus, the way the periphery participated in the process of global centralisation occurred largely through separating the state from its productive structure.

Given that it was a process undertaken on the basis of liberalising policies, the power of the process of centralisation is related as a counterweight to the weakening of the national state, especially in the Latin American periphery where this was already weak. As will be noted below, the states of the central countries weakened themselves in their role of undertaking compensatory domestic policies to the movement of capital, but they strengthened themselves as allied agents of their transnational capital in their strategy of control over processes of production in the world. "The mobility of capital, along with the process of liberalisation and deregulation, came off best in the socio-political framework of the national state, in which they were able to undertake, in the past, the famous effects of compensation ... before the fight against unemployment could benefit from measures of customs protection and include legislative measures of relatively restrictive effects for companies, limiting their international mobility. Nowadays nothing works like this" (Chesnais, 1996:306).

Going somewhat further, one may say that despite the concrete data on the processes of M&A related above, the centralisation of capital is a phenomenon that goes beyond the relations of property over capital, as pointed out by Aglietta and Chesnais. It is a deeper process than the data implies. As already commented, the centralisation of capital in the sense that has come to be used here is related to control over the value that is put in movement in the process of accumulation and, therefore, involves control over the value chain that does not need to be related to legal ownership. One of the main forms of domination over the process without the control of property is the so-called outsourcing of production. Some of the large transnationals really produce absolutely nothing. In outsourced production, the company that has control over the process as a whole does not appear as the owner of real productive structure. Normally, the corporation that controls the process is responsible for the development of the product, for the technology and for the marketing strategy, also carrying out at times sales of the product to the market or making use of a specialist distributor. Thus, often, the outsourced company only "buys" the raw materials from the central company, produces the goods and resells them to the central company itself. This is the system of production control

---

6 In fact they use the term "countries in development".

in which the large transnational corporation does not appear as the owner of the property. "For many small companies, the only path to survival (if it were offered them) is 'joining a company-network' of the Benetton type, or rather, its transformation into an outsourcer" (Chesnais, 1996:307).

In this sense, the forms of centralised control of production go beyond the centralisation of property and, therefore, the process of capital centralisation that becomes transparent through mergers and acquisitions would be only the visible part of the centralisation. The large capitalist companies are today at the centre of a vast network of companies, that are related to them, totally dependent from the heart of the system for their survival (Nolan, 2003:317). According to Dupas, these global productive structures have concentrated at the top of the chain of global production a small number of leader companies involving also part of their global suppliers. The processes most used, continues the author, for this concentration are mergers, acquisitions, joint-ventures, and technology agreements; it is on the basis of these chains, subordinated to leader companies, that franchises are found, outsourced companies, subcontractors and other forms of partnership that are incorporated in the logic of accumulation of the leaders (Dupas, 1999:67). Dicken sketches various ways how the spatial division of large transnational corporations arise (Dicken, 1992:211). In this sense, the smaller companies do not have any or very little control over the process of accumulation in which they are inserted.[7] These companies are among the most vulnerable in the process of de-industrialisation. They may stop existing or reappear according to the strategy of accumulation of each individual capital that has control of the process. The problem is that each wave of centralisations the suppression of these companies seems to tend to be greater than the appearance of new ones.

5.4 Centralisation between Countries

The concentration of capitals is not just a phenomenon that occurs between companies, but also involves countries.[8] Centralisation on a world scale is, as previously stated, a process of return to the centre, a process in which the

---

7 This is a production mechanism that is reproduced in the same way within countries. Brazil's northeast region has several factories that function in an outsourcing scheme, legally independent, but they produce a commodity whose brand they do not own.
8 Michael Porter considers countries as if they were global companies. As a specialist in company administration, his first book is called *"Competitive Advantage"* dealing with companies, but his most famous book in Brazil is called "The Competitive Advantage of Nations". He practically transposes the same logic of the first to the second.

productive structure is centralised in relation to the periphery. Of course, it is much more related to power and control than to the productive structure per se (or to where this structure is located), despite the two of them being mixed together. Peter Nolan in a study lists the main global oligopolies, he demonstrates the degree of centralisation of capital in the high income economies in relation to the middle and low income ones in the periphery. He notes that the group of central economies has (data from 1997 and 1998) 16% of the world population and 80% of the product; that in these countries are located 97% of the 500 largest companies in the world (two of the largest world companies in the 3% remaining are Brazilian). William Carroll shows almost the same reality in his book of 2010 (the only difference is the rise of China as another space but one should highlight, under Chinese control). They also concentrate 99% of the 300 largest companies in spending on research and development (R&D). In this context, the author also adds that the most prominent is the USA, it is worth remembering, the leader in receiving direct foreign investment during the 1990s. Of these 300 largest companies in spending in R&D, 135 are located in the USA; "In 1998 Morgan Stanley Dean Witter (MSDW) identified 238 companies as world leaders, of these, 134 are North American and 18 Japanese. On the list of the Financial Times (FT) of the 500 largest companies in the world by capitalisation, North America had 254 companies in 1998." (Nolan, 2003:315–316)

This data from 1997 shows well that what characterises the process of global centralisation that began in the 1980s that paused for breath from 1994/5. It shows the predominance of direct foreign investment between the countries of the centre, excluding a large part of the periphery from this movement and including only some peripheral countries, in a marginal way, in which the presence of transnational capital was important and that, apart from auctioning state assets, applied strong liberal policies that allowed the restructuring of transnational capital within their frontiers. Furthermore, it also seems that this is a process that goes beyond the battle for survival of the large transnational groups. Seemingly, it appears to entail a dispute in the context of the central countries for control of the global productive structure, a dispute between its states. Therefore, it does not seem to be just a process of economic centralisation, but also involves the centralisation of political power. The domination of North America together with Europe in the global movement of FDI shows this. As Nolan states, this US domination is prominent in this era of explosive centralisation through mergers and acquisitions because the centres of control of the strongest and most capitalised companies are located in the USA and Europe, as well as having the greatest financial power to acquire other companies (Nolan, 2003:316; Carroll, 2010). Thus, seemingly, this process of centralisation is related to hegemonic power and the fight for this power (Benjamin, 2001:80–81). It is now a North Atlantic power.

Apart from this, Tavares (1997) raises another hypothesis about this movement. From the point of view of the states at the centre she says that these also would have another interest in advocating policies of liberalisation that leverage global centralisation. According to her, during several decades, linked to a strategy of control over the global space, the central states supported the transnational capitals in their search to occupy new countries, agreeing with what had been noted here. Often, she continues, this movement means that these corporations leave the centre to produce in the periphery, generating unemployment and de-industrialisation in the centre. Now, the new strategies seem to show that these states would be making an effort to bring them back to the centre, and that is why they advocate the favouring of liberalising trade policies in other spaces (Tavares, 1997:46) and, at times, of returning to protectionist policies in their national spaces. Despite verifying this movement is not part of what one seeks to analyse here, it seems a relevant hypothesis. The states of the centre's own strategies would be contributing to this return of capital to the centre of transnational capital, and the consequent de-industrialisation of the periphery.

5.5 Centralisation and Financial Flows

The question of finance is crucial in this game for power and control that characterises the global centralisation of capitals. That is why the liberalisation of financial flows is a central demand. Power over financial resources may decide who comes out victorious in the process of centralisation. Capacity to bring together financial resources is crucial, be it for a transnational corporation, be it for its host state that has the role of providing it with a currency with international buying power. Credit and the availability of finance are the most powerful levers for the centralisation of capitals, Marx states.

Financial power decides who controls this process and who has the greatest chances of surviving it. The pressure for liberalisation of financial flows when centralisation takes on a global character becomes the crucial factor in the restructuring of economic and political power. That is why authors such as Chesnais (1996 & 1999) and Tavares (1997), among others, will give so much importance to finance capital and the hegemony of the dollar in the 1990s. Finance capital is the catalyst for the movements of global centralisation in the 1990s. It is the power of the currency at the centre that defines who has resources to acquire the capital of others and who is going to have control over the new productive arrangement of capital in a possible new cycle of accumulation. "Financial globalisation accelerated the expansion, for the countries of the Triad, through the advantages of new and varied instruments that the financial institutions ... placed at the disposal of the groups for their international operations of mergers and acquisitions..." (Chesnais, 1996:281).

This was already pointed out by Aglietta in his analysis of the process in the USA when he stated that the waves of centralisation coincided with movements of huge liquidity and financial speculation (Aglietta, 1979:197). On the one hand, they coincide with times when capital in general settles in the form of finance capital because it does not find at that time, profitable productive investment, a typical situation of over-accumulation (Boccara, 1973; Marx III,1894: Chapter 15 – "Exposition of internal contradictions of the law [fall in the rate of profit]", as commented in Chapter 1, when there exists excess productive capital functioning and therefore, individual money capital cannot continue converting itself into new productive capital. This is the moment in which the individual capitals that have resources available or that have "fire-power" to obtain credit, acquire the weaker ones, realising the processes of centralisation.

Aglietta analyses these movements in the North American economy, whilst Tavares and Chesnais, commented on above, refer to the global process of the formation and strengthening of global oligopolies. Thus, capital in general uses the money available as financial capital to reorganise all its productive structure under the control of certain individual capitals and of certain states, in a dispute for (political and economic) spaces. It is therefore evident that the relations between political power and the power of money make up the energy-generating nucleus that moves globalisation (Fiori, 1997b:92), that moves its main characteristic, that is the centralisation of capital, and that defines what new structure capital will have, including in relation to the global hegemonic[9] structure.

Now, when one verifies the pressure in the 1980s and 1990s for the liberalisation of the international financial flows that are available in the world, its connection to a strong "dollar" currency, when the central states themselves support liberalisation and deregulation in the sense of the "Washington Consensus" and, at the same time, one observes the wave of mergers and acquisitions that happen simultaneously, clearly related to the dismantling of the productive structures of the national peripheral states – in part by their own will and in part by pressure – it is difficult not to connect these movements. In the process of globalised centralisation, the individual capitals and

---

9 According to Benjamin the policies of liberalisation are contained in a strategy for the recovery of North American hegemony (Benjamin, 2001:81).

the states that survive are strengthened and manage to ensure or conquer the hegemonic position.

Reinforcing this relationship previously described as symbiotic between transnational capital and their states of origin, it is worth underlining the affirmation of Fiori. "None of this ... means that capital and financial markets are autonomous from political power, as an indispensable condition for the multiplication of their profitability. It does mean that inter-capitalist and interstate competition now occurs in an extremely concentrated manner and there will only be room in this game, for a very limited number of competitors" (Fiori, 1997b:144). One can also add to this Benjamin's assertion: "In international economic relations, they obtain advantages the countries that manage to control a larger part of the excess produced in the overall system" (Benjamin, 2001:81).

5.6 Centralisation and the Periphery

It seems, therefore, that there remain no doubts that the 1980s and 1990s marked a strong period of capital centralisation on a global scale, in a broad process of reordering the productive structures of transnational corporations themselves in the world, between, mainly, the central countries themselves. The Latin American countries despite participating in this process up to a certain point in a marginal way, relative to the volume and scale of the process that happens at the centre, suffers perhaps the greatest impact, one of the largest, if not the largest, productive restructuring (de-structuring) in the last 50 years. Its participation in this process was related to detachment from the state and the greater control of transnational capital over its economy. The restructuring of the global economy, as noted, is linked to a contest for hegemony, not only between large transnational groups, but between their states, by the control of currency and of the spaces for accumulation in the world faced with the needs of restructuring that marked the centralisation of capitals on a global scale. In this movement, this periphery, as dependent and associated, with transnational capital dominating its productive structures, is what becomes most vulnerable. Partly by its real loss of capacity to act in an autonomous way in this scenario, but mostly, by the subordinate way that it adhered to this movement of capital restructuring, facilitating the movement by its policies of deliberate and consented liberalisation.

As in any process of capital centralisation, by implying the reduction of the number of individual capitals that take part in accumulation after restructuring, the result is a tendency to de-industrialisation on this periphery and its distancing in relation to the centre, with the intensification of the internal contradictions manifested in unemployment and exclusion and the reinforcement of a certain bloc of power and political control. It is a process that reduces the participation of Latin America in the global accumulation of capital and separates it from its own control. The process of centralisation on this periphery both excludes social groups that before took part in the accumulation, be they capitalists that lose their capital, be it the worker that loses his job, raising the potential of the contradictions that the process of accumulation itself creates, in each space and now in the world. As the Argentine economist Cláudio Katz points out, globalisation, despite its impact on the centre, had a much more devastating impact on the periphery. He states, for example, that the policy of liberalisation that in England, increased poverty, unleashed destruction and destitution in Argentina; what in the USA resulted in a poorer distribution of wealth, exploded into misery and migration in Mexico; the opening of trade that weakened the Japanese economy produced devastation in Ecuador (Katz, 2003). "The chasm [between rich and poor] in the world is not a novelty. But it registered a widening without precedents in recent decades and that is why 20% of the population of the planet currently consumes 80% of the goods produced, a polarisation that is explained also because the emerging markets were the epicentre of the greatest crises ... [resulting from] the opening up of trade..., and of de-industrialisation" (Katz, 2003:41).

For Katz, the worsening social conditions, the unemployment throughout the world,[10] the worsening of income distribution both at the heart of the system and in the periphery (in a more radical way) and the increase in impoverishment, are realities that contrast with the recovery of the rates of profits in the world of a group of privileged transnational corporations. In the words of the author "the offensive perpetrated by neoliberalism registered a recovery in the rates of profit and caused an erosion of spending power" (Katz, 2003: 44–45). Thus, he asks himself, how could this be possible? The explanation proposed here is in the centralisation itself of global capitals that contributes to the elimination of superfluous capitals. The combination of these elements only becomes possible when the increase in the rates of profit results in the processes of the centralisation of capitals. There are fewer capitals operating in a more efficient way – in the real concept of capitalist productivity – in a market, now global and narrower. Thus, this apparent contradiction is part of the logic of the centralisation of capitals. Left to itself, the logic of capital does

---

10   The operations of M&A involve enormous losses in jobs everywhere. In Europe the rate of unemployment reached 11% in 1998 (Gonçalves, 2000:87) being that in the "periphery" (Spain and Italy) unemployment is much greater than this percentage.

not lead to development, on the contrary, it leads to exclusion and to growing impoverishment, to unemployment and to the exclusion of entire peripheral spaces by the destruction or weakening of its productive structure.

5.7   The Forced Disconnection

"In fact, as the global economy became more global and, especially after the collapse of the Soviet region, more purely capitalist and dominated by companies, investors and businessmen discovered that large parts of it had no profitable interest for them..." (Hobsbawn, 1995:355). In this assertion of Hobsbawn one has perhaps the true meaning of the disconnection. For capital some spaces in the world became expendable. Capital does not need all the spaces to continue in its process of accumulation on an extended scale. Appropriate spaces have already been occupied during the periods of capital expansion,[11] and even these run the risk of becoming superfluous to the process of capital accumulation when it centralises itself. Capital may survive and each individual capital may be lucrative (and even increase its profitability) in the midst of exclusion and impoverishment. To this end, by reducing the basis for accumulation relevant to capital, capital itself takes care of destroying the excess of functioning capitals. Companies go broke, obsolete and excess productive structures are eliminated. This is an action of the process of centralisation of capital in order to keep capitals functioning on a smaller basis of accumulation with larger profits for those who remain. This is the qualitative transformation that capital in general constantly experiences in its crises (of over-accumulation that results in over-production or under-consumption), the movement of restructuring to reposition the process of accumulation on new bases, by definition, always narrower, and with a greater volume of excluded people and places. This mechanism of adjustment is known traditionally by the economic theories of the cycles of accumulation, which in fact is about a cycle that never returns to the same point, is always changing; it is about a cycle in which capital overcomes the crisis, it strengthens itself, but comes to reproduce itself in a qualitatively different new environment.

Exclusion is a characteristic process of capital accumulation. Be it by the constant replacement of variable capital (labour) with fixed capital (constant capital) with technological increments, be it by unemployment or the

---

11   With all its particular characteristics, China represents an exception, an important space that had still not been occupied by large transnational capital in the 1990s, but now comes to be included in this logic, but in a specific way: under Chinese state control.

moments of crisis the process of accumulation entails, be it by the destruction of individual capitals that lose their space in accumulation. The result is always the same and "it is measured in jobs destroyed, much more than in new jobs created" (Chesnais, 1996:307). And, according to Amin (2002:85) and Chesnais (1996:306), in the absence of a regulatory state, the market excludes without returning and new mechanisms of re-inclusion are never created automatically by the logic of the accumulation process, by the logic of the market. Those excluded become unnecessary for the market, superfluous, because, faced with the qualitative restructuring through which it passes, the process of capital accumulation may maintain itself with the capitals and workers that remain. "The market activates a regressive system that always excludes more and concentrates the production on the solvent lowered demand" (Amin, 2002:85), which means to say that capital restructures itself to continue its process of accumulation on a smaller base.

In so far that the periphery stops being the "solvent" market, that the contradictions of the accumulation process itself are rooted in the periphery and makes the consumer market that before attracted capital evaporate, and, more importantly, in so far that capital, once that it occupies and controls this space, begins its process of global restructuring, of global centralisation of capital, the result is the de-industrialisation of this periphery at the same time that the flow of accumulation becomes much more dynamic between the countries at the centre. This is the path of disconnection from this periphery, in which it loses relative importance in the process of global capital accumulation, or like Brazil that reinserts itself as yet again a primary-products exporter. Or Mexico subordinated to the USA as a "maquilas" centre. This seems to have been the tendency sketched out in recent years that perhaps formed the first wave of exclusion. "From the Latin American point of view, it does not seem that we are evolving to a situation of a 'new dependency', but to an advanced de-structuring of the international division of labour begun in 1914" (Tavares, 1997 b: 81).

Capital in its process of accumulation on an expanded scale always, by its own logic, is hampered by the contradictions it creates. It expands and shrinks but is always strengthening itself in the processes of inclusion and exclusion, with the latter always stronger than the former. In its movement it needs all the "solvent" spaces in the world. However, as pointed out, these spaces only become attractive to the movements of capital expansion in so far that they had created conditions, market, or they possessed resources that interest capital. This scenario of attractive space for the accumulation of capital in the periphery was constructed by their national states and may lose its attractiveness at the same time in which it makes the action of the local states unfeasible or that it destroys part of its "solvent" market.

So, one falls into a vicious circle. Free capital in its free process of accumulation has an expansive movement and another destructive in its trajectory. If its destructive movement prevails, the continuity of the process of accumulation seems to become unfeasible in that space. Historically, the destructive movements of capital, of exclusion both of the workers and of the individual capitals that do not manage to survive in the struggle for the space of accumulation, were always and up to a certain point compensated by the action of state policy when it occurred in the national space. It was the power of the state in undertaking compensatory policies, at times against the nature of the process of accumulation or compensating for the intrinsic exclusion that result, which permits the continuity of the accumulation of capital.

The problem that is now posed is that the contradictions that exclude come to occur on a world scale and the local states lose power. The result is the exclusion now from spaces, mainly peripheral ones. This makes the traditional state mechanism of compensation much more difficult, if not impossible. If previously the exclusion generated was in the context of local economies, today, if the hypothesis of globalisation with centralisation of capitals is correct, these movements of exclusion would be occurring on a global scale. Or put another way, one is no longer pointing to a district or a city in which new technologies have been adopted and generated a mass of unemployment, a place within a country where companies have crashed or closed because of the processes of centralisation of capitals in a national context. When this occurred in the domestic space, it was considered a social problem and could have been minimised by state social policies. However, when this same mechanism occurs on a global scale, under only the predominance of the logic of accumulation, the logic of capital incorporated in the state-centres, they are not districts or cities that find themselves in this situation, but whole countries that depend on their weak national states submitted to the process of global accumulation. Seemingly their vulnerability and dependency may impede them from acting in a compensatory way, making it much more difficult for this peripheral state to reconstruct the basis for re-inclusion in the process of accumulation. That is the problem when the periphery is submitted to the movement of globalised capital, it suffers the contradictions of the process and becomes impaired from acting with countervailing policies. It thus runs a real risk of exclusion from the process of accumulation itself.

What one wishes to point out here is that this would be the result of the submission of the periphery to the movement of capital according to the logic of the process of accumulation. This submission may mean being excluded from the movement of capital itself. The history of capitalist development itself in Brazil, Argentina and Mexico showed that inclusion in the accumulation had an enormous national state participation, even in a scenario in which the movement of capital was one of expansion. Now, once capital is globalised, at a time when its contradictions acquire a global character, what still remains is the national state to compensate its destructive movement. The contradiction of this movement is that capital itself has taken charge of weakening or destroying the peripheral states, reducing their capacity to act in the sense expounded. That is the big contradiction. The periphery needs its state to survive in globalised capitalism; it needs countervailing actions to the destructive and excluding movement of globalised capital; and it needs a state with capacity for intervention. It cannot submit itself to the movement of capital, to the movement of the market, at the risk of ceasing to exist even as the periphery.

The weakening and de-industrialisation of the Latin American economies are connected to this logic. On submitting itself, voluntarily, to the logic of the process of global capital accumulation, it constructed its own mechanisms facilitating its exclusion. The form of insertion of Latin America in global capitalism, especially Brazil, analysed in more detail in Chapter 4, was politically, deliberately constructed in Latin America itself or in Brazil, by its elites that compose its power bloc, and that now prevents changes. It was therefore not decided exclusively, as a greater external force, by the "machine of capital" that in its process of accumulation invades the spaces of the world. This is true, this is the movement of capital, but on the other side were states, social and political organisation that opted for submission to this natural movement of capital, to the "laws of the movement of capital", of course, with the aid and additional help of the central states. What one wishes to say here is that one cannot disconnect what happens domestically, to the periphery, to its political strategy, from what occurs internationally, of the movement of capital. Both movements are defined, are mutually strengthened through the internal economic and political forces as well the external economic and political forces. It is not mere coincidence the almost simultaneous existence of dictators in Latin American, neither was the way how liberalisation and stabilisation came about in the 1980s and 1990s in Mexico, Argentina and Brazil. Despite the processes being sparked by relatively autonomous states and its power bloc's elites, there are many things in common between them and, mainly, in relation to the interests of large transnational capital. The forms of submission constructed and rooted in the structure of accumulation of the Latin American periphery that industrialised made a real trap for itself, difficult to escape from, given the degree of involvement created with transnational capital, the concrete representative of capital in general.

Liberalisation has a perverse effect on peripheral economies such as Brazil's. On the one hand, the reduction of tariffs and the abolition of import barriers leads to an increase in the import of products, reducing incentives to direct foreign investment into production, given that the foreign corporations may simply export from other plants to the country.[12] On the other hand, it stimulates direct foreign investments in mergers and acquisitions, considering that the companies can restructure their productive strategy according to elements such as markets and cost factors. This allows the large transnational corporation to choose where to produce, close factories in one place and open in another, to reorder its production in a more central and efficient way. Thus, liberalisation may, as in fact occurred in Brazil, incentivise foreign investments to buy companies in Brazil, be they transnational buying competitors installed here, be it buying national companies that did not survive the liberalising strategy allied to the policy of stabilisation (see Chapter 4). On the other hand, when liberalisation comes associated with privatisation, this becomes the main factor of attraction for direct foreign investment, a typical case is Brazil, in that the large transnational corporations come to have control over new sectors that they did not have before, and over sectors in which what is produced is not easily imported, characteristic of the infrastructure sectors.

Thus, one may infer that liberalisation, the opposite of resulting in greater industrialisation, ends up by raising imports and stimulating processes of centralisation. It is for this reason that Brazil experiences liberalisation with a trade deficit and the broad entry of direct foreign investments, in a process of de-industrialisation and rising unemployment, much more in the sense of exclusion. As Reinaldo Gonçalves points out, the result of this is a greater presence of transnational capital in Brazil's industrial structure, associated with greater economic concentration and centralisation, to industrial slowdown, with the modernisation of the industrial structure (Gonçalves, 1999:101).

Brazil submitted itself in a perverse way to the movement of global capital. It became thus much more subordinated and vulnerable to its movement, inserting itself in a process that at best makes it almost impossible to have a strategy of development within this logic, the logic of globalised capital.

---

12 A cut in tariffs on imported North American products may direct a significant part of new direct investment to transnationals to the United States itself, incorporating, when it is might be the case, Mexican labour. Mexico could make itself an export platform for North American transnational companies for markets in South America, strongly inhibiting the creation of a local industrial base (Dupas, 1999:65).

5.8 Final Considerations

The centralisation of capital occurs on a global scale by the fact that capital itself globalised its process of accumulation. The process of accumulation, stemming from the large transnational corporations spreads across the world-space, placing its logic of accumulation in this new scenario. Thus, the real meaning of capital globalisation seems to be that the world has become a single space for capital, a single space for its accumulation. This does not mean that now all spaces are equal in the face of capital as some ideologues of "globalisation" imagine, neither that it might have lost its centre. However, this was never true not even while capital reproduced itself in an expanded way in its local spaces. This idea that fed the liberal rationale of "globalisation" never existed. Capitalism has never been a space for competition between equal economic agents, competitors, not even in the local space and very much less would it be so in the global space. Seemingly, the trend appears to be to reproduce in this new space of accumulation, now occupied, the contradictions, in a similar way to those that were present in the restricted space. This is what seems to happen when one verifies the movements of concentration and centralisation of capital on a global scale. The world-space is, as or more hierarchal in power relations in the hands of some specific central states, also arranged in a hierarchical way and in the hands of some large transnational capitals that act in symbiosis with these states as partners in control of the world-space of accumulation.

Previously, the movements and contradictions of capital as well as the relations of power in which they were involved, as well as its flow of accumulation and movement of growth and crisis, were up to a certain point, much more related to local spaces. Each place possessed its own periphery and created its own excluded, a movement that to a certain point could be compensated for by the actions of the local state. Globalisation seems to recreate these movements on a world scale. Inequality that was already a trend in local spaces now appears in a new form in the global space. The movements of expansion, growth etc., as well as the movements of exclusion and the increase in unemployment etc., now they are global movements that reach the periphery of the system and recreate them in a more dramatic form, within a now global accumulation; if before, contradictions such as unemployment are manifested in certain spaces, excluding districts and cities, it now acts on regions and whole nations in the periphery. The local currency also comes to be questioned by the hegemony of a single global currency, disputed by the countries of the centre, but, still under the hegemony of the dollar, and speculative movements acquire a global character flowing between the spaces as previously they flowed in the national space. Seemingly, the space for capital has expanded and its contradictions reach a world scale. Unemployment is largest in certain places that are de-industrialised more than others because of the strategic movement of capital and on account of the nature of the movement that destroys more jobs than it creates.

When one imagines capital free to move itself according to its needs for accumulation having in the national states its partner, it seems that it is not wholly misplaced the analogy in which countries take on the appearance of corporations, competing with each other, having similar structures of hierarchical oligopolies, where relationships are established of control and power of one country over other, forms of hierarchy in that, some states, like outsourced companies, run the risk of being simply excluded from the process of production, substituted by "another producer". In this scenario, the states of the centre behave like a holding company, like the large centralised groups that concentrate power, power embodied in their capacity for control over the process of global accumulation, through their individual capitals and their currency. It is in these leader states that there is control over technology, processes of production, brands, marketing etc. They have the power of a global oligopoly, as well as the financial power. Certain productive sectors would thus remain concentrated in the centre whilst others could be "outsourced" in the peripheries, those of low technology and that need cheap resources (raw materials or labour), whilst it suits the centre, but under the control of the centre.

Authors of different theoretical lines point to the idea that the world today would be conducted by competition between countries, such as Michelet (1999 and 2002) and Porter (1989). Porter imagines countries as companies competing between each other in the space according to their natural or created comparative advantages. For him, as in companies, each country must create comparative advantages by investments in differentiated products that make the country internationally competitive. (Porter, 1989:754). This author considers the nations as economic agents in a competition in the capitalist "free market". Transposing thus the false relations between free economic agents that compete in their national spaces to the global space, in an analogy of competition that was never true, not even in the local space, never mind in the world. At any rate, it does seem that the logic of accumulation of capital on an extended scale that existed in the local space is now, up to a certain point, transposed to the global-space, with all its contradictions, hierarchised, in a fierce and excluding competition (Michelet, 2002:110) between states, throwing places into "auto-destructive competitions for economic survival, always relinquishing more power to the centre" (Korten, 1995:308).

Capital has occupied the world-space, but seems to have brought with it, as might be expected, all its contradictions and some aggravating ones. In this new space, the contradictions find fertile space to manifest themselves in a more radical way given that the world-space is much more subject to "organisation" undertaken by capital itself, with much more autonomy than that which it had in local spaces. The national states if they act like companies, they act with the same logic of capital. That national state that still has the power to act in the local space, often as organiser, with compensatory policies to the contradictory power of the devastation of capital, cannot act in the same way in the global space. The logic of action of each national state in the world, it seems, comes to be mixed up with the logic of capital in the world. Its role and its interest is to strengthen individual capitals and have them under its wings, as well as the social groups that make up the state, which necessarily, in the competition reflex of capital, excludes other social groups and other spaces. That is why it seems that the contradictions of the process of accumulation, when they reach this global scale, become much more radical and excluding. The contradictions become more acute and complex by the natural anarchic and excluding movement that capital always had in its local space.

In the local spaces, the national states perhaps still have some power of control and regulation over the movement of capital, even though this power might be and continues being constantly questioned and may come to be weakened as a countervailing power to each wave of centralisation and globalisation through which capital passes. Of course, as previously stated, this weakening is more radical in the peripheral states dominated by transnational capital, at the point which capital, acting on a world scale, becomes freer to move, becomes more autonomous in its process of appreciation, a process that creates and strengthens itself by its own centralisation, as well as from the absence of a global regulatory power. Capital is freer to walk on its own feet. More than this, it has its strategy of accumulation embodied in the action of each individual capital in symbiosis with its state of origin which functions as an ally, with the power of imposing certain policies in certain places, with the principal aim of facilitating the movement of capital in these locations. This is the form of confrontation that seems to be present between the states of the centre and the periphery, in a rationale of competition for global power which is won by the one who has most political, economic and financial power available. Therefore, it is the peripheral states that suffer most in this scenario.

"The globalised order affects societies in completely different ways. In the case of the central countries, the economic and technical environment, on the one hand, and the environment of political decisions (here understood that which has military ramifications), on the other hand, they remain closely related, by the strong link between the mega-corporation businesses and powerful national states. In the case of the rest, these environments are dissociated by the geographic dispersion of productive chains, on a global scale, made under the command of business corporations that have no obligations to the weaker states and societies, where they only install subsidiaries" (Benjamin, 2001:83).

The logic of the exclusion of the periphery enters in this way of acting of capital engaged in a process of global centralisation. The hypothesis is that, despite being from very different periods, given its being a specific type of globalised accumulation constructed through history, some of the laws of capital movement seem now to remain on a world scale. Despite the differences, the now globalised capital follows the logic of accumulation on an increased scale, of the concentration and the centralisation and in these processes, the mirror image of what occurred in each place of accumulation occupied by capital, the tendency it seems to reproduce itself on a global scale and, in a certain way, to reproduce some of its contradictions, among them exclusion, now on a global scale, involving places that previously were more engaged in the process of global accumulation, that had an importance perhaps greater in the survival of the system. The centralisation of capital on a global scale seems to put on the agenda a wider form of exclusion, the exclusion of entire areas, the exclusion of the periphery as a relevant space for accumulation. This is not, as it could not be, a linear process as the centralisation of capital is not. As centralisation is a process that occurs by waves in which capital strengthens itself and destroys itself. Impoverishment and the distancing of the periphery from the process of accumulation at the centre also could occur by the same logic. Until now, what one can observe are indications that this is a possible tendency that has already shown signs of its impact on the periphery.

The "dissemination of a spacial standard of growth in the context of a global strategy of large capitals clearly excluded the peripheries, most vulnerable to the neoliberal orthodoxy and the new hierarchization of international political power. Among these are included the European periphery itself ... to Africa and Latin America." (Tavares, 1997b:77)

"In any case, for now, the tendency apparently predominant is that of a system that tends to close in on itself, to settle in a 'dualism', and that its leaders, along with a significant portion of the population, are making an effort to build, at the same time, fortresses to contain the 'barbarians' on the periphery, and barbed wire around their internal ghettos" (Chesnais, 1996:315). To have a vision of this process, it is enough to walk through some peripheral cities and to look at global migration.

The submission of the periphery to the movement of globalised capital creates contradictions on a world scale that seem to explain its distancing in relation to the central countries, the growth of unemployment and the poverty of the periphery. The global process of centralisation of capital appears to demonstrate this trend. The gulf between the centre and periphery seems to be widening faced with the logic of capital accumulation that is now global.

Thus the dependency of Latin American countries is relocated in new terms in the face of the process of global capital accumulation. It has been attempted here to understand these terms to perhaps make it possible to think – as it was partly the aim of Cepal more than 50 years ago –, not how to insert this periphery in this capital movement, but what are the alternatives for its development in a wider sense, given the new contradictions present, given the global movement of capital in this new context, given the form itself of how some countries on the periphery are included in it.

Bibliography

Abreu, M.P. (1992) "Inflação, Estagnação e Ruptura: 1961–64", in M.P. Abreu (org) "A ordem do progresso: cem anos de política econômica republicana" 1889–1989, Edt. Campus, Rio de Janeiro-RJ.

Aglietta, M. (1979) "Regulacion y Crisis Del Capitalismo", México, Ed. Siglo Vintiuno.

Allen, G.C. (1983) "A Economia Japonesa", Edt. Zahar, Rio de Janeiro-RJ.

Almeida, L.F. (1995) "Ideologia Nacional e Nacionalismo", Edt. Educ, São Paulo-SP.

Amin, S. (1990) "Maldevelopment Anatomy of a global failure", United Nations University Press, Tokyo; Zed Books Ltd., London and New Jersey. (http://www.unu.edu/unupress/unupbooks/uu32me/uu32me00.htm).

Amin, S. (2002) "O Capitalismo Senil", Revista da Sociedade de Economia Política n°11, Rio de Janeiro-RJ.

Arbix, G., M. e Laplane (2002) "Estagnação, liberalização e investimento externo na América Latina", in G. Arbix. "Brasil, México, África do Sul, Índia e China: diálogo entre os que chegaram depois", Edt. Unesp/Edusp, São Paulo-SP.

Arrighi, G. (1996) "O Longo Século XX", Edt. Contraponto/Unesp, São Paulo-SP.

Arrighi, G. (1998) "A Ilusão do Desenvolvimento", Edt. Vozes, Petrópolis-RJ.

Arrighi, G. J.B. e Silver (2001) "Caos e Governabilidade", Edt. Contraponto/UFRJ, Rio de Janeiro-RJ.

Assmann, H., T. Dos Santos, N. Chomsky (1979) "A trilateral: nova fase do capitalismo mundial", Edt. Vozes, Petrópolis-RJ.

Baer, W. (2002) "A economia brasileira", Edt. Nobel, São Paulo-SP.

Baran, P., P. e Swezzy (1978) "Capitalismo Monopolista", Edt. Zahar, Rio de Janeiro-RJ.

Barros, J.R.M., L. Goldenstein (1997) "Avaliação do processo de reestruturação industrial brasileiro", Revista de Economia Política, vol. 17, n° 2 (66), abril-junho/1997, São Paulo-SP.

Belluzzo, L.G., J.G. e Almeida (2002) "Depois da queda: a economia brasileira da crise da dívida aos impasses do Real", Edt. Civilização Brasileira, Rio de Janeiro-RJ.

Benjamin, C. (2001) "A nova ordem mundial e o destino do Brasil", Revista Sociedade Brasileira de Econômica Política n°8, Rio de Janeiro-RJ, junho/2001.

Blaug, M. (1984) "The Methodology of Economics", Edt. Cambridge University Press, Cambridge-UK.

BNDES, (1997) "Desempenho do Setor de Autopeças" n°12, set/97, Área de operações industriais.

Boccara, P. (1978) "Estudos Sobre o Capitalismo Monopolista de Estado", Ed. Estampa, Lisboa.

Boron, A.A. (1994) "Estado, Capitalismo, e Democracia na América Latina", Edt. Paz e Terra, Rio de Janeiro-RJ.

Bukhárin, N.I. (1994) "A Economia Mundial e o Imperialismo", Edt. Abril Cultural, São Paulo-SP.

Cardoso, F.H. (1995) "Desenvolvimento: o mais político dos temas econômicos", Revista de Economia Política, vol. 15, n° 4 (60), outubro-dezembro/1995, São Paulo-SP.

Cardoso De Mello, J.M. (1982) "O capitalismo Tardio", Edt. Brasiliense, São Paulo-SP.

Carneiro, D.D., E.M. e Modiano (1992) "Ajuste externo e desequilíbrio interno" in M.P. Abreu (org) "A ordem do progresso: cem anos de política econômica republicana" 1889–1989, Edt. Campus, Rio de Janeiro-RJ.

Carroll, W. (2010) "The making of capitalist class: corporate power in the twenty-fisrt century", Edt. Zed Books.

Castro, A.B., F.E.P. e Souza (1985) "A Economia brasileira em marcha forçada", Edt. Paz e Terra, São Paulo-SP.

CEPAL (2002) "La Inversión extrangera em América Latina y Caribe", Nações Unidas, Chile.

CEPAL (2003) "Balance preliminar de las economías de América Latina y el Caribe", Nações Unidas, Chile, dez/2003.

Chang, H-J. (2002) "Kicking Away the Ladder: development strategy in historical perspective", Edt. Anthem Press, London-UK.

Chesnais, F. (1996) "A Mundialização de Capital", Edt. Xamã, São Paulo-SP.

Chesnais, F. (1999) "A Mundialização Financeira". Edt. Xamã, São Paulo-SP.

Chick, V. (1993) "Macroeconomia após Keynes: um reexame da Teoria Geral", Edt. Forense Universitária, Rio de Janeiro-RJ.

Chomsky, N. (2000) "Democracia e mercados na ordem mundial", in P. Gentili (org) "Globalização Excludente", Edt. Vozes/Clasco/LPP, Petrópolis-RJ.

Chossudovsky, M. (1999) "A Globalização da Pobreza", Edt. Moderna, São Paulo-SP.

Clarke, T. (1996) "Mechanisms of Corporate Rule", in J. Mander, E. e Goldsmith. "The Case Against the Global Economy", Edt. Sierra Club Books, São Francisco-USA.

Comin, A. (1998) "De volta para o futuro: política e reestruturação industrial do complexo automobilístico nos anos 90", Edt. Annablume/Cebrap/Fapesp, São Paulo-SP.

Coriat, B., O. e Weinstein (1995) "Les Nouvelle Théories de L'enterprise", Edt. Le Livre de Poche, França.

Coutinho, L.G., L.G.M. e Belluzzo (1982) "Estado, Sistema Financeiro e Fora de Manifestação da Crise: 1929–74", in L.G. Belluzzo, R. e Coutinho (orgs) "Desenvolvimento Capitalista no Brasil: ensaios sobre a crise.", Edt. Brasiliense, São Paulo-SP.

Cruz, P.D. (1983) "Notas Sobre o Endividamento Brasileiro Externo nos anos Setenta", in L.G. Belluzzo, R. e Coutinho (orgs) "Desenvolvimento Capitalista no Brasil: ensaios sobre a crise n°2", Edt. Brasiliense, São Paulo-SP.

Dicken, P. (1992) "Global Shift: the interantionalization of economic activity", Edt. Paulo Chapman Publishing, London.

Dos Santos, T. (1973) "The Crisis of Development Theory and The Problem of Dependence in Latin America", in H. Bernstein (org) "Underdevelopment and Development: The third World Today" Edt. Peguin Books, England.

Dos Santos, T. (1977) "Imperialismo e Corporações multinacionais", Edt. Paz e Terra, Rio de Janeiro.

Dos Santos, T. (2000) "A teoria da dependência balanço e perspectivas", Edt. Civilização Brasileira, Rio de Janeiro-RJ.

Dupas, G. (1999) "Economia Global e Exclusão Social", Edt. Paz e Terra, São Paulo-SP.

Evans, P.B. (1982) "Autonomia Nacional e Desenvolvimento Econômico: Perspectivas Críticas das Empresas Multinacionais em Países Pobres", in G. Carbalho (org) "Multinacionais: Os Limites da Soberania", Edt. Fundação Getúlio Vargas, Rio de Janeiro-RJ.

Fajnzylber, F. (2000) "Industrialização da América Latina, da caixa preta ao conjunto vazio", in R Bielschowsky. (org) "Cinquenta Anos de Pensamento da Cepal", Edt. Record/Cofeco/CEPAL, São Paulo-SP.

Fiori, J.L. (1995) "Em busca do dissenso perdido: ensaios críticos sobre a festejada crise do Estado", Edt. Insight, Rio de Janeiro-RJ.

Fiori, J.L. (1997) "Os moedeiros falsos", Edt. Vozes, Petrópolis-RJ.

Fiori, J.L. (1997b) "Globalização hegemonia e império", in M.C. Tavares, J.L. e Fiori (orgs) "O Poder do Dinheiro", Edt. Vozes, Petrópolis-RJ.

Fiori, J.L. (2001) "Brasil no Espaço", Edt. Vozes, Petrópolis-RJ.

Fiori, J.L. (2001b) "Para um diagnóstico da 'modernização' brasileira", in J.L. Fiori, C. e Medeiros. "Polarização Mundial e Crescimento", Edt. Vozes, Petrópolis-RJ.

Franco, G.H.B. (1998) "A inserção externa e o desenvolvimento", Revista de Economia Política, vol. 18, nº 3 (71), julho-setembro/1998, São Paulo-SP.

Furtado, C. (1971) "Teoria Política do Desenvolvimento", Edt. Companhia Editora Nacional, São Paulo-SP.

Furtado, C. (1974) "O Mito do Desenvolvimento Econômico", Edt. Paz e Terra, Rio de Janeiro-RJ.

Furtado, C. (1978) "A Hegemonia dos Estados Unidos e o Subdesenvolvimento da América Latina", Edt. Civilização Brasileira, Rio de Janeiro-RJ.

Furtado, C. (1987) "Transformação e Crise na Economia Mundial", Edt. Paz e Terra, São Paulo-SP.

Furtado, C. (2000) "Desenvolvimento e Subdesenvolvimento", R. em Bielschowsky (org) "Cinqüenta Anos de Pensamento da Cepal", Edt. Record/Cofeco/CEPAL, São Paulo-SP.

Gentili, P. (2000) "Globalização excludente", Edt. Vozes/Clacso/LPP, Petrólpolis-RJ.

Giannotti, J.A. (1983) "Trabalho e Reflexão", Ed. Brasiliense, São Paulo-SP.

Gonçalves, R. (1999) "Globalização e Desnacionalização", Edt. Paz e Terra, São Paulo-SP.

Gonçalves, R. (2000) "O Brasil e o Comércio Internacional", Edt. Contexto, São Paulo-SP.
Gonçalves, R. (2003) Revista Teoria e Debate n°52 jan/fev/03 2003.
Heilbroner, R.L. (1963) "A Luta Pelo Desenvolvimento", Edt. Zahar, Rio de Janeiro-RJ.
Hineklammert, F.J. (1979) "O credo econômico da comissão Trilateral", in H. Assmann, T. Dos Santos, N. e Chomsky (orgs) "A Trilateral, nova fase do capitalismo mundial", Edt. Vozes, Petrópolis-RJ.
Hirst, P., G. e Thompson (1998) "Globalização em Questão", Edt. Vozes, Petrópolis-RJ.
Hobsbawm, E. (1995) "A Era dos Extremos", Edt. Companhia das Letras, São Paulo-SP.
Hunt, D. (1989) "Economic Theories of Development: an analysis of competing paradgmas" Edt. Harvester Wheatsheaf, New York.
Hymer, S. (1978) "Empresas Multinacionais: A internacionalização do Capital", Edt. Graal, Rio de Janeiro-RJ.
Ianni, O. (1996) "Estado e Planejamento Econômico no Brasil", Edt. Civilização Brasileira, Rio de Janeiro-RJ.
Ianni, O. (1999) "Teorias da Globalização", Edt. Civilização Brasileira, Rio de Janeiro-RJ.
IEDI – Instituto de Estudos Para o Desenvolvimento Industrial, (2000) "Política Industrial, Empresa Nacional, e Mercado Interno", IEDI, São Paulo-SP.
Katz, C. (2003), Capitalismo Contemporáneo: etapa, fase y crisis. in Ensayos de Economia, Volumen 13, Número 22, pp. 36–68, Universidade Nacional de Colombia. https://revistas.unal.edu.co/index.php/ede/article/view/24975/25520.
Keynes, J.M. (1982) "Teoria Geral do Emprego, do juro e da Moeda". Edt. Atlas, São Paulo-SP.
Keynes, J.M. (1978) "O Fim do Laissez-faire", in T Szmrecsányi. (org) "John Maidard Keynes", Edt. Ática, São Paulo-SP.
Korten, D.C. (1996) "Quando as Corporações Regem o Mundo", Edt. Futura, São Paulo-SP.
Kurz, R. (1992) "O Colapso da Modernização", Edt. Paz e Terra, São Paulo-SP.
Lacerda, A.C. (2004) "Globalização e investimento estrangeiro no Brasil", Edt. Saraiva, São Paulo-SP.
Lago, A.C. (1992) "A retomada do crescimento e as distorções do 'Milagre': 1967–73", in M.P Abreu. (org) "A ordem do progresso: cem anos de política econômica republicana" 1889–1989, Edt. Campus, Rio de Janeiro-RJ.
Lenin, V.I. (1987) "Imperialismo, Fase Superior do Capitalismo", Ed. Global, São Paulo-SP.
Lessa, C. (1982) "15 anos de política econômica", Edt. Brasiliense, São Paulo-SP.
Lessa, C. (1998) "A estratégia de desenvolvimento 1974–1976: sonho e fracasso", Edt. UNICAMP, Campinas-SP.
Lessa, C., S. e Dain (1982) "Capitalismo Associado: algumas referencias para o tema Estado e Desenvolvimento", in L.G. Belluzzo, R. e Coutinho (orgs) "Desenvolvimento Capitalista no Brasil: ensaios sobre a crise.", Edt. Brasiliense, São Paulo-SP.

Lipietz, A. (1987) "O capital e seu Espaço", Edt. Nobel, São Paulo-SP.
Lozardo, E. (1987) "Déficit público brasileiro: política econômica e ajuste estrutural", Edt. Paz e Terra, Rio de Janeiro-RJ.
Lundberg, E., L.P. e Castro (1987) "Desequilíbrio financeiro do setor público e seu impacto sobre o orçamento monetário", in E. Lozardo (org) "Déficit Público Brasileiro: política econômica e ajuste estrutural", Edt. Paz e Terra, Rio de Janeiro-RJ.
Luxemburg, R. (1983) "A Acumulação de Capital", Ed. Zahar, Rio de Janeiro-RJ.
Magdoff, H. (1978) "A Era do Imperialismo", Edt. Hucitec, São Paulo-SP.
Mandel, E. (1982) "Capitalismo Tardio", Edt Abril Cultural, São Paulo-SP.
Marx, K. (1977) "Manifesto do Partido Comunista", K. em Marx, F. Textos, e Engels vol. 3, Edt. Edições Sociais, São Paulo.
Marx, K. (1977b) "O 18 de Brumário de Luís Bonaparte", K. em Marx, F. Textos, e Engels vol. 3, Edt. Edições Sociais, São Paulo.
Marx, K. (1977c) "Trabalho Assalariado e Capital", K. em Marx, F. Textos, e Engels vol. 3, Edt. Edições Sociais, São Paulo.
Marx, K. (1887a) "Capital: a critique of political economy" Volume I Source: First English edition of 1887 (4th German edition changes included as indicated) with some modernisation of spelling; Publisher: Progress Publishers, Moscow, USSR. Proofed: and corrected by Andy Blunden and Chris Clayton (2008), Mark Harris (2010).
Marx, K. (1887b) "Capital: a critique of political economy" Volume II Source: First English edition of 1907; Published: Progress Publishers, Moscow, 1956, USSR; Transcribed: by Doug Hockin and Marxists Internet Archive volunteers in the Philippines in 1997; Proofed: and corrected by Andy Blunden and Chris Clayton (2008), Mark Harris (2010).
Marx, K. (1894) "Capital: a critique of political economy" Volume III, Source: Institute of Marxism-Leninism, USSR, 1959; Publisher: International Publishers, NY, [n.d.]; On-Line Version: Marx.org 1996, Marxists.org 1999; Transcribed: Transcribed for the Internet in 1996 by Hinrich Kuhls and Zodiac, and by Tim Delaney and M. Griffin in 1999. HTML Markup: Zodiac 1996, Tim Delaney and M. Griffin in 1999.
Marx, K. (1985) "A Miséria da Filosofia", Edt. Global, São Paulo-SP.
Marx, K. (1987) "Elementos Fundamentales para la Crítica de la Economia Política" (Grundrisse), Ed. Siglo Veintiuno, 15º edição, México.
Marx, K. (2002) "Manuscritos Econômicos Filosóficos", Edt. Martin Claret, São Paulo-SP.
Mello, A.F. (1999) "Marx e a Globalização", Edt. Boitempo, São Paulo-SP.
Mello, J.M.C. (1982) "Capitalismo tardio", Edt. Brasiliense, São Paulo-SP.
Mészáros, I. (2002) "Para Além do Capital", Edt. Boitempo, São Paulo-SP.
Michalet, C-A. (1983) "O Capitalismo Mundial", Edt. Paz e Terra, Rio de Janeiro-RJ.
Michalet, C-A. (1999) "La Séduction des Nation ou Comment Attirer les investissements". Edt. Economica, Paris-FR.

Michalet, C-A. (2002) "Qu'est-ce que la Mondialisation?", Edt. La Decouverte, Paris.
Miglioli, J. (1981) "Acumulação de Capital e Demanda Efetiva", Ed. T.A. Queiroz, São Paulo-SP.
Nagels, J. (1993) "La tiers-modialization de l'ex-URSS?", Edt. Université de Bruxelles, Bélgica.
Nayyar, D. (2003) "Globalization and Development", in H-J, Chang (org) "Rethinking development economics" edt. Anthem Press, London.
Nolan, P. (2003) "Industrial Policy in the early 21st century: the challenge of the global business revolution", in H-J, Chang (org) "Rethinking development economics" edt. Anthem Press, London.
Oliveira, F. (1977) "A Economia da Dependência Imperfeita", Edt. Graal, Rio de Janeiro-RJ.
Oliveira, F. (1987) "Crítica à Razão Dualista", Edt. Vozes, Petrópolis-RJ.
Oliveira, F. (1995) "Neoliberalismo à Brasileira", in E. Sader, P. e Gentili (orgs), "As Políticas Sociais e o Estado Democrático: Pós-neoliberalismo", Edt. Paz e Terra, São Paulo-SP.
Oliveira, F. (1998) "Os direitos do antivalor: a economia política da hegemonia imperfeita", Edt. Vozes, Petrópolis-RJ.
Oliveira, F. (2003) "O Ornitorrinco", Edt. Boitempo, São Paulo-SP.
Oliveira, F. (2003b) "A Navegação Venturosa: ensaios sobre Celso Furtado", Edt. Boitempo, São Paulo-SP.
Orenstein, L., A.C. e Sochaczewski (1992) "Democracia com Desenvolvimento: 1956–1961" in M.P. Abreu (org) "A ordem do progresso: cem anos de política econômica republicana 1889–1989", Edt. Campus, Rio de Janeiro-RJ.
Palloix, C. (1971) "L'économie Mondiale Capitaliste", Tome 1 e 2, Edt. François Maspero.
Palloix, C. (1989) "La autoexpansíon del Capital a Escala Mundial" El Trimestre Económico, n°30, seleción de René Villareal – Economia Internacional II – Teorias del Imperialismo, La Dependência e sua Evidência Histórica, Fondo de Cultura México.
Porter, M.E. (1989) "A Vantagem Competitiva das Nações", 5° edição, Edt. Campus, Rio de Janeiro-RJ.
Porter, M.E. (1998) "Competitive Advantage: creating and sustaining superior performance", Edt. Free Press, New York.
Possas, M.L. (1983) "Empresas Multinacionais e Industrialização no Brasil", in L.G. Belluzzo, R. e Coutinho (orgs) "Desenvolvimento Capitalista no Brasil: ensaios sobre a crise n°2", Edt. Brasiliense, São Paulo-SP.
Poulantzas, N. (1975) "As Classes Sociais no Capitalismo de Hoje", Edt. Zahar, Rio de Janeiro-RJ.
Poulantzas, N. (1985) "O Estado, O Poder, O Socialismo", Edt. Graal, Rio de Janeiro-RJ.

Prebisch, R. (2000) "O desenvolvimento econômico da América Latina e alguns de seus problemas", R, em Bielschowsky (org) "Cinquenta Anos de Pensamento da Cepal", Edt. Record/Cofeco/CEPAL, São Paulo-SP.

Ricardo, D. (1985) "Princípios de Economia e Política e Tributação", Edt. Nova Cultural, São Paulo-SP.

Robinson, J. (1964) "Filosofia Econômica", Edt. Zahar, Rio de Janeiro-RJ.

Rodriguez, O. (1981) "Teoria do Subdesenvolvimento da Cepal", Edt. Forense Universitária, Rio de Janeiro-RJ.

Rodrik, D. (2002) "Estratégias de desenvolvimento para o novo século", in G. Arbix (org) "Brasil, México, África do Sul, Índia e China: diálogo entre os que chegaram depois", Edt. Unesp/Edusp, São Paulo-SP.

Rosdolsky, R. (1989) "Génesis y Estructura de El Capital de Marx", Ed. Siglo Veintiuno, México.

Rostow, W.W. (1978) "Etapas do Desenvolvimento Econômico", Edt. Zahar, Rio de Janeiro-RJ.

Rubin, I.I. (1980) "A Teoria Marxista do Valor", Ed. Brasiliense, São Paulo-SP.

Santos, M. (2000) "Por uma outra globalização: do pensamento único à consciência Universal", Edt. Record, São Paulo-SP.

Santos, M. (2002) "Por uma nova geografia", Edt. Edusp, São Paulo-SP.

Sawaya, R.R. (2001) "Social Democracia e a humanização do capital", Anais, VI Encontro Nacional de Economia Política, SEP, EAESP, São Paulo-SP.

Schoultz, L. (1999) "Estados Unidos: poder e submissão – uma história da política norte-americana em relação à América Latina", Edt. EDUSC, Bauru-SP.

Schumpeter, J.A. (1961) "Capitalismo, Socialismo e Democracia", Edt. Fundo de Cultura, Rio de Janeiro-RJ.

Serra, J. (1982) "Ciclos e Mudanças Estruturais na Economia Brasileira do Pós-guerra", in L.G. Belluzzo, R. e Coutinho (orgs) "Desenvolvimento Capitalista no Brasil: ensaios sobre a crise", Edt. Brasiliense, São Paulo-SP.

Simonsen, M.H. (1982) "O Brasil e as multinacionais", G. Carvalho (org) "Multinacionais: os limites da soberania", Edt. Fundação Getúlio Vargas, Rio de Janeiro-RJ.

Singer, P. (1985) "A crise do Milagre: interpretação crítica da economia brasileira", Edt. Paz e Terra, Rio de Janeiro-RJ.

Stiglitz, J.E. (2002) "A Globalização e Seus Malefícios", Edt, Futura, São Paulo-SP.

Sunkel, O. (1972) "Capitalismo trasnancional y desintegracion nacional en América Latina", Edt. Nueva Visión SAIC, Buenos Aires, Argentina.

Sunkel, O., P. e Paz (1975) "Um ensaio de interpretação do desenvolvimento latino-americano" Edt. DIFEL/FORUN, São Paulo/Rio de Janeiro.

Suzigan, W. (1986) "Indústria Brasileira: origem e desenvolvimento", Edt. Brasiliense, São Paulo-SP.

Sweezy, P.M. (1973) "Teoria do Desenvolvimento Econômico", Rio de Janeiro, Ed. Zahar.

Sweezy, P.M., P.A. e Baran (1978) "Capitalismo Monopolista", Edt. Zahar, Rio de Janeiro-RJ.

Tavares, M.C. (1982) "Da Substituição de Importações ao Capitalismo Financeiro", Edt. Zahar, Rio de Janeiro-RJ.

Tavares, M.C. (1997) "A Retomada da Hegemonia Norte-americana", in M.C. Tavares, J.L. e Fiori (orgs) "O Poder do Dinheiro", Edt. Vozes, Petrópolis-RJ.

Tavares, M.C. (1998) "Acumulação de capital e industrialização no Brasil", Edt. UNICAMP, Campinas-SP.

Tavares, M.C., J.C. e Assis (1986) "O grande salto para o caos", Edt. Jorge Zahar, Rio de Janeiro-RJ.

UNCTAD (2000) "Cross-Border Mergers and Aquisitions and Development", World Development Report 2000, United Nations, New York and Geneva.

UNCTAD (2003) "Capital Accumulation, Growth and Structural Change", United Nations, Hew York and Geneva, Trade and Development Report.

UNCTAD (2003b) "FDI Polices For Development: National and International Perspectives", World Development Report 2003, United Nations, New York and Geneva.

Wallerstein, I. (2004) "O Declínio do Poder Americano", Esd. Contraponto, Rio de Janeiro-RJ.

Werneck, R.F. (1987) "Crise financeira do setor público", in E. Lozardo (org) "Déficit Público Brasileiro: política econômica e ajuste estrutural", Edt. Paz e Terra, Rio de Janeiro-RJ.

Williamson, O.E. (1985) "The Economic Institutions of Capitalism", Edt. The Free Press, New York.

Index

Abreu, M.P.   132, 135, 139
accumulation   4–5, 24, 25, 27, 29, 33, 43, 44, 45–48, 55, 59–66, 72–78, 92–95, 176, 178
   continuity of   2, 5, 64, 69, 80, 179
   cycles of   112, 199
   effects of   51, 90
   ensuring   9, 15, 49
   expanded   23, 26, 28, 42, 48, 61, 73, 78, 79, 180, 183, 186
   expansion of   18, 49, 86
   flow of   33, 35, 42, 60, 84, 89, 91, 101, 184, 200, 204
   global   2, 3, 4, 7, 8, 94, 97, 98, 102, 103, 106, 119, 149, 176, 177
   global process of   155, 180, 181
   globalised   113, 155, 207
   logic of   7, 56, 57, 77, 93, 102, 114, 176, 193, 201, 204, 207
   national   119, 125
   process of   3, 4, 9, 36, 37, 41, 42, 43, 50, 58, 68, 183, 187, 200, 201
   processes of   3, 5, 7, 9, 20, 51, 54, 81, 87, 94, 106
   progressive   25, 61
   space for   3, 41, 57, 63, 64, 98, 178, 197, 207
   strategy of   102, 193, 206
accumulation and concentration   27, 43, 44, 48, 59, 65, 74, 181
Aglietta, M.   5, 15, 16, 27, 28, 41, 42, 43, 44, 46, 75, 76, 186, 187, 196
Almeida, L.F.   121, 122, 132, 150, 152, 153
American countries and Brazil   7, 184
Amin, S.   56, 59, 73, 200
apparatus, productive   70, 141, 151
appropriation   13, 14, 15, 22, 23, 24, 26, 43, 92
Arbix, G.   164
Argentina   57, 81, 85, 98, 104, 105, 109, 113, 167, 168, 189, 192, 198, 202
Arrighi, G.   6, 55, 66, 72, 113
Asian countries   113, 116, 119, 130
autonomous capitals   16, 45, 56, 75, 154
autonomous development   91, 92, 142
autonomy of capital   10, 19, 20, 53, 57

Baer, W.   129, 130
Baran, P.   49, 56, 60, 64
Barros, J.R.M   163, 164
Belluzzo, L.G.   150, 152, 166
Benjamin, C.   190, 195, 196, 197, 207
Blaug, M.   158
block   7, 8, 66
Boccara, P.   41, 45–46, 186, 196
Boron, A.A.   134, 151
Brazilian development   116, 118, 121, 131, 146, 147, 156, 161
   characterised   152
Brazilian elites   155, 175
Brazilian industrialisation   117, 121, 128, 144
Brazilian state   110, 117, 122, 145, 149, 152, 154, 160, 161
Brazilian state apparatus   152
Brazilian state companies   139
Brazil-United States Joint Commission   123
Brzezinski, Z.   148, 149

capital
   accumulating   86
   centralisation characterises   48
   centralised   9, 48, 49, 50
   centralises   78
   commodity   16, 21, 24, 34, 36, 37
   constant   34, 35, 68, 199
   expropriation of   48, 74
   individual fragmented   18, 20, 22
   industrial   16, 41, 59, 77, 78, 121, 122, 126
   international   100, 115, 124, 131, 133, 134, 136, 152, 156
   large   5, 44, 64, 72, 73, 102, 160, 188, 207
   laws of the movement of   202
   monopoly   53, 60
   national/transnational   135
   new industrial   128
   oligopolistic transnational   170
   process of accumulation and concentration of   32, 40
   processes of concentration and centralisation of   53, 86, 110
   strengthened transnational   148
   superfluous   73, 74, 191, 198

capital (*cont.*)
  variable   33, 37, 199
  working   38, 39, 41, 45
capital accumulation   2, 4, 5, 17, 21, 23, 24, 25, 35, 40–41, 54, 55, 60, 69, 72–73
  expanded   24
  increased   82
  increasing scale   62
  international   83
  process of   86, 95
  uninterrupted   188
capital concentration   2, 20, 33, 55, 61, 111, 177
capital control   15
  national   168
capital destruction   46, 183
capital expansion   43, 56, 62, 66, 69, 83, 94, 100, 199, 200
capital gains   7, 9, 73
capital goods   35, 87, 100, 107, 108, 123, 142, 143, 171, 177
capital internationalises   53, 179
capital movement   10, 23, 33, 47, 64, 158, 161, 176, 184, 207, 208
capital turnover   34, 35, 36, 40, 67, 68, 70
  cycle of   24, 69
capital valorisation   2, 3, 9–10, 23, 31, 33, 35, 36, 41, 52, 61, 67, 70, 75
  process of   16, 23
Capital's Globalisation   115, 117, 119, 121, 123, 125, 127, 129, 131, 133, 135, 137, 139, 141, 143
capitalism   10, 11–16, 21, 24, 53, 55, 71, 82, 85, 86, 88, 90, 115–16, 187, 188
  associated   125, 131
  centralised   48
  globalised   84, 202
  international   119, 133, 136
  introduction of   104, 106, 115
  monopoly   49, 66
  national   125, 142
  peripheral   98, 108
capitalist accumulation   85, 90, 91, 93, 95
  global   104, 106, 146
  process of   14, 91, 92
capitalist development   53, 82, 86, 116, 122, 136, 149, 201
  centre's   90
capitalist expansion   121
capitalist flows   87, 92, 186
  dynamic   86, 105

capitalist process   12, 23
  historic   48
capitalist production   13, 18, 20, 26, 27, 45, 64
  development of   24, 40, 47, 61
  immanent laws of   25, 61
  methods of   30, 63
  mode of   48, 59, 67
  motive of   26, 62
capitalist productivity   198
capitalist relations   14, 21
capitalist reproduction   23, 128
Cardoso, Fernando Henrique   95, 96, 97, 121, 125, 127, 160, 161
Carneiro, D.D.   110, 150
Carroll, W.   55, 57, 104, 156, 194
Castro, A.B.   145, 151, 153
central countries   72, 83, 84, 90, 92, 98, 100, 112, 155, 167, 190, 192, 194, 206, 207
central states   57, 66, 71, 72, 101, 182, 190, 191, 195, 196, 202, 204
central thread   103, 116
centralisation   2, 9, 20, 42–61, 74, 75, 76, 78, 79, 179, 181, 182, 187, 193, 207
  global   3, 5, 8, 180, 181, 182, 185, 186, 187, 188, 189, 191, 192, 194, 195
  movement of   44, 59, 74, 186, 187
  new wave of   74, 78
  process of   5, 6, 7, 44, 45, 47, 52, 53, 74, 75, 76, 78, 79, 80, 183
  processes of   47, 50, 79, 135, 196, 203
  wave of   77, 186, 187, 188, 193, 196, 206
centralisation of capital   4, 5, 10, 42, 43, 44, 45, 47, 48, 79, 178, 192, 197, 198, 207
  global   114, 149, 176, 182, 185
  movement of   42, 71
  process of   2, 4, 42, 56, 57, 73, 75, 178, 179, 180, 181, 182, 189, 197, 199
  processes of   10, 117, 134, 201
Centralisation of Space   78
centralise   44, 78, 183, 199
centralising power   57
centre   4, 55, 78–82, 90, 91, 93, 94, 113, 114, 176, 177, 182, 190, 195, 205
centre-periphery   70
centre-periphery type   69
centre-states   66, 114, 182
Cepal   82, 83, 84, 86, 88, 89, 91, 93, 94, 95, 96, 101, 103, 106, 166
Cepal strategy   83, 91, 179, 180

INDEX 219

Cepal's thinking 88, 90, 92, 93
Chang, H.-J. 119
character, social 11, 13, 14, 16, 19
Chesnais, F. 64, 65, 66, 67, 70, 71, 78, 79, 80, 183, 184, 188, 192, 196, 200
Chick, V. 60
China 81, 166, 175, 194, 199
Chinese state control 199
Chomsky, N. 133, 148
Chossudovsky, M. 110
circuit 20, 36, 37, 39
circulation 22, 37, 39, 67
class 6, 58, 59, 86, 131, 137, 141
    Clarke 110
command 10, 17, 18, 44, 70, 73, 112, 113, 121, 135, 144, 158, 166, 207
commission 82, 123, 124, 148
commodities 10, 11, 12, 13–17, 19, 20, 21–24, 34, 35, 36, 37, 39, 40, 67, 68
    exchange of 21, 67
    flow of 70
    new 22, 34, 35
    owners of 12, 14, 17
    representatives of 10, 13
    sale of 34, 35, 39
commodity production 10, 17
companies 49, 62, 65, 75, 77, 80, 135, 137, 152, 168, 192, 193, 194, 203, 205
    capitalised 194
    central 192
    domestic 163, 168
    international 108, 126, 163
    large 64, 74, 79, 134, 135, 187, 190
    large capitalist 193
    largest 141, 165, 190, 194
    leader 193
    multinational 70, 72, 78, 118, 141, 142, 143, 162, 185
    outsourced 192, 193, 205
    productive 149, 154
    single capitalist 51
    state electricity 123
    state oil 123
    state-owned 139
competition 25, 26, 27, 28, 29, 47, 48, 63, 64, 65, 78, 119, 166, 177, 205
competitiveness 64, 77, 78, 107, 108, 162, 166, 188
competitors 29, 62, 166, 197, 203, 204

concentration 27, 28, 29, 30, 32, 33, 42–44, 48, 52, 53, 60, 63, 73, 178, 193
    absolute 134
    characterises 43
    economic 203
    greatest 189
    growing 32
    increased 56
    indefinite 92
    international 76
concentration and centralisation 9, 11, 19, 20, 21, 33, 34, 35, 41, 42–43, 47, 51, 52–53, 59, 179
    processes of 9, 10, 20, 176
concentration and centralisation of
    capital 2, 3, 7, 37, 52, 53, 54, 60, 61, 76, 86, 87, 93, 110, 204
concentration enlarges 2
concentration movement 65
conglomerates, large transnational 85, 154
consumer 25, 37, 61, 82, 88, 125, 126, 135, 137, 138, 142, 157, 158
consumer market 88, 89, 127, 200
consumption 22, 35, 37, 41, 59, 64, 69, 89, 92, 106, 137, 138
context 10, 11, 19, 41, 44, 88, 90, 120, 123, 156, 166, 167, 168, 187, 194
continuity 9, 23, 36, 44, 45, 61, 62, 73, 74, 78, 79, 84, 85, 86, 201
contracts 10, 44, 65, 75, 138
contradictions 4, 5, 9, 32, 51, 56, 73, 74, 75, 76, 78, 178, 202, 204, 205–7
    central 32
    internal 41, 45, 76, 119, 166, 196, 198
control 19, 50, 51, 52, 71, 102, 106, 117–19, 190, 191, 192, 194, 195, 197, 205
    centralised 193
    national 58, 143, 164, 168
    productive 114
cooperation 31, 33, 143, 146
Coriat, B. 49
corporations 49, 50, 53, 62, 65, 66, 72, 74, 100, 104, 113, 114, 190, 192, 195
    large 3, 6, 10, 16, 20, 50, 52, 53, 88, 104, 119, 120, 183
    large capitalist 9, 16
countries 1–2, 5, 54, 59, 73, 80, 109, 113, 118–19, 130, 159, 167, 179, 189–94, 205
countries in development 192

coup   132, 133, 136, 174
coup d'état   133, 174
Coutinho, L.G.   128
creation   21, 22, 32, 82, 85–86, 88, 90, 91, 92, 93, 96, 99, 107, 108, 109
credit   47, 135, 137, 139, 150, 152, 172, 173, 195, 196
crises   3, 40, 41, 42, 46, 61, 68, 75, 89, 134, 135, 145, 158, 186, 199
   circumstantial   42, 67, 75, 76
Cruz, P.D.   139, 151, 152
currency   171, 173, 195, 197, 205
Current Brazilian Central Bank data   129
cycle   39, 41, 107, 109, 112, 128, 131, 134, 137, 139, 140, 156, 164, 166, 199

Dain, S.   121, 122
debt   110, 151, 153
decision-making centres   106, 129
   strategic   109
de-industrialisation   166, 176, 181, 183, 185, 195, 197, 198, 200
   process of   166, 167, 174, 193, 203
denationalisation   116, 131, 134, 165
dependency   85, 97, 98, 102, 104, 105, 106, 107, 108, 109, 111, 112, 113, 116, 117
dependent economies   100, 124
   peripheral   100
depreciation   42, 45, 48
destruction   5, 19, 44, 45, 46, 58, 69, 73, 74, 76, 77, 118, 178, 199, 200
destruction of local capitals   183
developed centres   91, 113
developed countries   58, 90, 96, 109, 112, 189, 192
development   1–2, 76, 82, 85–102, 106, 109, 112, 115, 122, 124, 125–26, 128, 129, 138, 166
development processes   1, 124
development strategy   7, 83
Developmental state   157
developmentalist   111, 136, 159
Dicken, P.   80, 193
dictatorship   105, 147, 148, 152
direct foreign investment   114, 117, 130, 157, 159, 194, 203
direct investment   26, 59, 65, 69, 70, 79, 99, 156, 164, 166, 185, 189, 190
   foreign   70, 72, 79, 96, 98, 100, 125, 129, 164, 188

direction   33, 34, 59, 60, 73, 77, 79, 80, 87, 89, 120, 122, 124, 128, 131
domestic capital   163, 171
domestic market   127, 128, 171
Dos Santos, T.   78, 88, 92, 99, 107, 108, 111, 134, 148, 149
Dupas, G.   105, 109, 193, 203
dynamic centre   85, 101, 103, 112, 128
dynamic flow   82, 83, 87, 89, 92, 99, 103, 104, 105, 111
dynamic sectors   1, 7, 99, 101, 102, 114, 119, 125, 126, 131, 136, 138, 141, 146, 165

economic crisis   67, 131, 132
economic development   88, 90, 92, 99, 101, 115, 116, 135, 136, 159, 160
economic growth   82, 85, 86–89, 109, 110, 137, 140, 141, 157, 166, 167, 171, 172, 173, 174
   national   140, 143, 146, 151, 168
economic growth strategies   149
Economic Miracle   1, 5, 134, 135, 136, 137, 156
economic policies   94, 96, 97, 98, 110, 130, 131, 135, 136, 156, 157, 158, 162, 163, 165
   governmental   101, 102
economic power   57, 72, 114, 170
economic relations   11, 21, 142
economic structure   96, 128, 130, 131, 132, 135, 169
economies   31, 37, 38, 83, 89, 91, 102, 105, 107, 108, 136, 138, 143, 165, 173
   central   83, 90, 99, 102, 105, 149, 194
   coffee   121
   global   67, 111, 121, 142, 175, 187, 197, 199
   underdeveloped   89, 97, 106
elites, peripheral   100, 114
Enlarged accumulation and concentration   56
European countries   140, 189
Evans, PB.   112
excess capacity   190–91
exchange   14, 21, 22, 67, 153, 157, 171, 172
   relation of   21, 86
exchange rates   119, 126, 153, 157, 171, 172, 173
   overvalued   162, 171, 172
exchange value   14, 22, 24, 34
exclusion   4, 14, 53, 54, 55, 56, 58, 59, 77, 78, 183, 199, 200, 201, 207
   movements of   201, 204
   process of   5, 32, 167

INDEX

expansion 2, 3, 23, 43, 55, 56, 60, 64, 71, 73, 84, 128, 133, 178, 188
  continuous 19, 25, 26, 27
expansion process 128

Fajnzylber, F. 113
Fernando Henrique Cardoso 154, 160
finance capital 47, 77, 195, 196
  international 136, 150
  national 141, 152
financial capital 53, 98, 155, 196
financial flows 156, 157, 195
financial markets 139, 153, 172, 173, 197
financial power 195, 205, 206
financial system 64, 117, 137, 138, 139, 150
financing 139, 145
Fiori, J.L. 57, 115, 118, 122, 132, 145, 151, 152, 155, 156, 161, 196, 197
fixed capital 5, 38, 39, 41, 199
  new 39
Forced Disconnection 176, 177, 179, 181, 183, 184, 185, 187, 189, 191, 193, 195, 197, 199, 201
forces 27, 29, 64, 78, 86, 115, 116, 155
  productive 25, 26, 41, 42, 46, 76, 86, 87, 126
  productive capitalist 87
foreign capital 1–5, 7, 102, 116, 117, 122, 124, 126, 127, 128, 132, 134, 144, 145–49, 161
  attracted 184
  benefited 132
  favoured 139
  junior partner of 134, 156
  large 1, 101, 158
  new 127
  speculative 162
foreign companies 105, 110, 111, 112, 125, 127, 132, 135, 139, 144, 145, 146, 162, 163, 165
  large 127, 135
foreign debt 85, 107, 109, 131, 139, 141, 142, 149, 150, 151, 152, 153, 154, 162
foreign direct investment (FDI) 63, 64, 70, 81, 98, 140, 164, 188–92, 194
  movement of 189
foreign investments 99, 104, 111, 117, 121, 140, 152, 164, 166, 203
foreign resources 137, 138, 139, 145, 151, 163
Franco, G.H.B. 154, 157, 159, 160, 163
Free capital 77, 201
Furtado, C. 88, 91, 92, 93, 97, 106, 107, 118, 154

GDP per capita 167
geographic spaces 46, 58, 176
Getúlio Vargas 117, 118, 122, 123, 124, 125, 126
Giannotti, J.A. 20
global capital 2, 3, 103, 111, 112, 114, 115, 116, 117, 118, 119, 120, 165, 179, 180
global capital accumulation 1, 7, 81, 84, 85, 91, 94, 102, 111, 113, 115, 117, 200, 202, 208
global capitalism 7, 80, 83, 91, 95, 97, 102, 103, 116, 133, 143, 175, 181, 202
globalisation 20, 58, 59, 60, 61, 63, 64, 66, 67, 160, 161, 176, 177, 185, 204
  movement of 66, 79
  process of 57, 71, 79, 106, 116, 154, 155, 180
  process of capital 5, 60, 104, 178, 181
globalisation of capital 5, 7, 53, 56, 60, 61, 64, 70, 72, 149, 178, 186, 187, 188, 189
globalised capital 1, 66, 114, 115, 117, 118, 142, 155, 166, 168, 177, 182, 203, 207
  interests of 104, 166
  movement of 2, 66, 111, 112, 114, 156, 169, 201, 202, 207
Goldenstein, L. 163, 164
Gonçalves, R. 165, 168, 184, 198, 203
government bonds 150, 169, 172, 173
growth 34, 69, 79, 87, 88, 89, 127, 131, 134, 137–42, 149, 153, 159, 164, 172
  peripheral 107
growth cycle 137, 138–41, 164, 172

hard currency 96, 107, 108, 109, 151, 162
head offices 85, 110, 156, 160, 162, 164, 168
  central 163, 177
hegemonic centres 55, 57, 66, 78
Heilbroner, R.L. 98
Hirst, P. 108
Hobsbawn, E. 56, 64, 188, 199
Hunt, D. 90, 92, 97
Hymer, S. 65

Ianni, O. 101, 102, 107, 122, 123, 126, 128, 129, 131, 133, 135, 141, 142, 187, 190
imperialism 53, 66, 71, 72, 76
import substitution 84, 85, 93, 94, 96, 97, 101, 103, 104, 106, 107, 108, 110, 113, 119
  logic of 100, 103

import substitution (*cont.*)
  policies of   2, 5, 84, 85, 94, 96, 99, 101, 105, 107, 111, 168
  process of   7, 96, 98, 107, 123, 125, 143
  strategy of   1, 84, 143, 179
impoverishment   14, 32, 86, 87, 169, 181, 183, 198, 199, 207
income concentration   111
income distribution   61, 132, 137, 138, 171, 174, 198
income per capita   113
individual capitalist   18, 19, 20, 33, 37, 38, 40, 43, 48, 49, 50, 52, 54, 61, 65
  hands of   29, 63, 178
individual capitals   2, 28, 35, 39, 43, 44, 45, 46, 47, 63, 74, 75, 177, 178, 182
  autonomous   16
  autonomy of   27, 48
  centralised   54
  concentrated   42
  large   56
Individual capitals and local industrial structures   78
industrial development   99, 116, 162
  dependent   133
industrial policies   96, 174
industrial structure   32, 33, 82, 84, 85, 90, 92, 93, 99, 101, 103, 104, 105, 181, 203
industrialisation   82, 84, 85, 86, 93, 95, 99, 100, 101, 104, 111, 121, 122–26, 179, 180
industrialised countries, peripheral   70
industrialising   98, 107, 111, 112, 181
industrialising effort   83, 99, 100
industrialising strategy   1, 94, 128
industry   31, 82, 84, 88, 89, 90, 92, 105, 106, 107, 108, 127, 129, 168, 169
  basic   97, 127, 137, 138, 144, 145
  heavy capital goods   126
  manufacturing   166, 167
  nascent   97, 119, 121
infrastructure   97, 127, 137, 140, 144, 145, 161, 186
innovations   47, 88, 90
installation, productive   105, 184
Institute of Studies for Industrial Development (IEDI)   117, 162, 164, 168
institutions   104, 151, 158
  financial   169, 170, 172, 196
interest rates   157, 169, 170, 171, 173
  high   110, 150, 172, 173

interests   5, 6, 94, 95, 99, 100, 101, 134, 141, 142, 153, 155, 173, 181, 185
internal market   77, 93, 111, 121, 132
international crisis   145, 146, 147
International Monetary Fund (IMF)   85, 96, 98, 104, 110, 150, 151, 152, 156, 158
internationalisation   26, 27, 40, 42, 56, 60, 67, 68–69, 71, 72, 116, 121, 131, 159, 161–62
  commercial   67, 68, 71, 72, 84, 93, 176
  degree of   141, 142, 146, 165
  movement of   60, 179
  process of   7, 20, 42, 60, 69, 130, 159, 165
internationalisation of capital   4, 67, 68, 102, 105, 128, 130, 142
intervention   38, 98, 117, 118, 122, 148, 159, 181, 182, 187, 202
investments   35, 60, 61, 84, 89, 109, 137, 139–40, 144, 145, 152, 157, 163, 168, 189
  public   140, 157

jobs   51, 52, 77, 80, 89, 166, 183, 198, 200, 205
Juscelino Kubitschek   1, 124, 125, 129

Keynes, J.M.   19, 35, 37, 40, 60, 61, 76, 80, 87, 88, 89
Korten, D.   104, 110, 205
Kurz, R.   76

labour   11, 13, 14, 15, 21, 22, 23, 24, 26–33, 35, 37–38, 43, 48, 51, 52
  capital expropriates   74
  cost of   30
  dead   22, 24, 28, 32, 33, 51
  human   13, 21
  individual   15
  international division of   64, 91, 97, 100, 124, 200
  live   24, 51
  new international division of   143
  organisation of   31
  products of   11, 48
  share of   41, 42
  social   28, 29, 33
Labour Party   173, 174
labour productivity   28, 29, 31, 51, 90, 93
labour-power   17, 21, 22, 30, 31, 32, 33, 36, 37, 48, 86
labourer   17, 31, 32, 37, 76
Lacerda, A.C.   162, 165

Lago, A.C.   136, 140
Laplane, M.   164
large transnational capital   1, 99, 112, 132, 134, 135, 139, 148, 155, 158, 189, 190, 199, 202, 204
large transnational corporations   6, 98, 99, 149, 158, 190, 191, 193, 203, 204
Latin America   1–3, 57, 81, 82, 84, 94, 96, 97, 98, 100, 101–2, 108, 113, 167, 202
Latin American   1–2, 83, 84, 85, 93, 94, 97, 98, 101, 102, 103, 112, 113, 166, 202
Lenin, V.   53, 56, 60, 64, 67, 71, 76
Lessa, C.   118, 121, 122, 124, 125, 126, 127, 131, 144–47
liberalisation   71, 73, 77, 154, 155, 156, 163, 181, 182, 191, 192, 195, 196, 202, 203
liberalising policies   2, 81, 114, 117, 118, 159, 167, 168, 192
liberty   30, 183–84
Lipietz, A.   79
local capitals   115, 183
local space   3, 4, 5, 64, 65, 69, 70, 71, 73, 176, 178, 179, 204, 205, 206
logic   2, 3, 7, 58, 82, 85, 87, 93, 94, 97, 98, 103, 159, 200, 206
  centre's   94
  primary-exporter   91, 180
loss   19, 46, 47, 64, 108, 119, 120, 140, 162, 164, 165, 166, 168, 185, 198
Lula, Luiz Inácio   8, 170, 173, 174
Lundberg, E.   151
Luxemburg, R.   40, 68, 69, 70, 71, 75, 84

machinery   31–33, 35, 37, 96, 170, 177, 186
machines   22, 31, 32, 108
  new   30, 31
Magdoff, H.   56
manufactured products   83, 91, 105
  finished   107, 108
market value   28
markets   12, 21, 22, 50, 51, 52, 64, 69, 92, 140, 157, 158, 191, 200, 203
  free   9, 19, 86, 154, 157, 158, 161, 205
  global   51, 70, 71, 160
  new   26, 36, 46, 55, 68, 69, 84, 105, 164
  solvent   200
Marx, K.   3, 4, 10–34, 36, 37, 39, 44, 45, 46–52, 60, 61–63, 68, 76, 86, 186
Marx capitalism   17

Marx states   40, 74, 195
Marx Wage Labor and Capital in Marx-Engels Collected   27
Marx-Engels   11, 12, 17, 26, 38, 41, 46, 49, 58, 59, 169
Marx's logic   87
Marx's statement   12
Marxist   60, 62
material relations   13, 14
Mello, A.F.   95, 96, 97, 121, 125, 127, 187
mergers   42, 44, 77, 162, 164, 181, 183, 184, 185, 189, 190, 191, 193, 194, 196
mergers and acquisitions (M&As)   185, 189, 190, 191, 192, 198
Mészáros, I.   18, 19, 54, 74
Mexico   85, 98, 104, 109, 166, 167, 189, 198, 200, 202, 203
Michalet, C-A.   4, 56, 57, 58, 60, 64, 66, 67, 77, 80–81, 85, 166
middle   125, 137, 138, 194
military government   1, 118, 135, 136, 141, 142, 143, 149
military power   69, 71
Miracle, Economic   136, 138–40, 142, 144, 145, 147, 149, 164
modernisation   76, 90, 104, 105, 108, 109, 113, 123, 127, 133, 137, 140, 163, 164, 169
  process of   83, 103, 139
money capital   16, 21, 24, 34, 36, 37, 38, 39
movement of accumulation   54, 57, 59, 61, 77, 83
multinational capital   118, 126, 130, 133, 135, 136, 137, 143, 148, 165
multinationals   80, 136, 142, 143

Nagels, J.   54, 113
national capital   6, 7, 77, 102, 122, 127, 134, 135, 139, 148, 164, 168
  private   104, 129, 135, 138, 139, 144, 156, 165
national companies   105, 127, 135, 142, 144, 145, 147, 164, 168, 203
  medium-sized   127, 135
national development   101, 112, 118, 123, 145, 146, 152, 159, 166, 179
national integrated productive state   142
national productive structure   123, 125
national states   3, 119, 122, 126, 128, 136, 142, 149, 183, 192, 200, 202, 205, 206
nation-state   148, 149, 178

nation states 1, 6, 7, 58, 66, 77, 83, 88, 112, 117, 120, 151, 182
  peripheral 112, 181
nations 38, 58, 61, 76, 82, 86–87, 90, 193, 204, 205
nature of accumulation 50, 64, 73
nature of capital 50, 55, 65
nature of capital accumulation 10, 54, 58, 72
Nayyar, D. 14
neoliberal 149, 156, 157, 158, 170
neoliberalism 170, 174, 175, 198
new cycle 35, 134, 137, 138, 157, 159
new cycle of accumulation 25, 92
new dependency 200
new spaces of accumulation 27, 63, 204
Nolan, P. 193, 194
North-Atlantic countries 85, 156

occupation 25, 27, 58, 60, 62, 65, 70, 71, 76, 78, 100, 102, 125, 176, 177
  productive 147, 177
oligopolies 50, 55, 135, 161, 171, 179
Oliveira, F. 100, 102, 105, 107, 109, 110, 111, 115, 116, 122, 124, 130, 132, 134, 142
Orenstein, L. 124, 129
over-accumulation 41, 42, 44, 45, 51, 52, 75, 178, 196, 199
over-accumulation of capital 46, 68
over-production 40, 41, 42, 45, 68, 199
ownership 14, 15, 24, 25, 48, 49, 78, 164

Palloix, C. 35, 40, 55, 56, 65, 66
patents 106, 108
payments, balance of 99, 131–32, 139, 145, 150, 151
period of growth 109, 131, 138, 139, 141
peripheral countries 1, 55, 72, 80, 83, 108, 112, 151, 160, 166, 177, 179, 184, 191, 194
  new industrialised 81
peripheral development 86, 89, 98, 103
peripheral economies 85, 87, 90, 91, 92, 96, 97, 99, 106, 108, 109, 110, 111, 112, 113
  independent 103
  industrialised 7
peripheral Latin American economies 104, 107
peripheral Latin American state 97
peripheral productive structure 95, 102

peripheral states 3, 6, 7, 57, 58, 59, 66, 72, 94, 95, 98, 100, 103–4, 201, 202
  national 196
peripheral subnational capitalist systems 109
Peripheralisation 54, 113
periphery 1–8, 57, 70–73, 81–85, 88, 89–114, 120, 176, 177, 180, 181, 184, 198, 200, 207–8
  economic 95
  included 4
  industrialised 77, 120, 190
periphery undertaking policies 181
Philosophic Manuscripts 11, 12, 38, 48, 49
PND (National Development Plan) 118, 122, 135, 142, 143, 144, 145, 146, 147, 148, 149, 150, 151
policies 98, 99, 110, 111, 117, 131, 137, 138, 149, 151–57, 163, 165, 166, 171–74, 191
  developmentalist 148, 160, 182
  neoliberal 169, 172
  pro-capital 120
  restrictive 150, 151
  social 152, 174, 183, 201
  strategic 114, 130
political action 87, 97, 112, 135, 182
political power 53, 134, 158, 182, 194, 195, 196, 197
Porter, M.E. 62, 75, 109, 205
Possas, M.L. 125, 128
Poulantzas, N. 57
power blocs 6, 170, 171, 172, 173, 174, 175, 202
power relations 72, 204
power structure 170, 171, 172, 175
Prebisch, R. 83, 88, 90, 99
private banks 173, 174
private capital 95, 97
  national 141, 146, 147
private companies 153
  domestic 162, 163
private property 14, 15, 24, 48
privatisation 105, 117, 152, 153, 154, 160, 165, 170, 174, 188, 191, 203
process
  de-industrialising 183
  economic 92
  historic 13, 53
  industrialisation 84, 125, 175
  social 10, 12, 16, 17

INDEX

production 10, 11, 12, 14, 15, 17, 22–31, 33, 34–41, 45, 52, 86, 92, 103, 138
  centralising 5
  global 163, 193
  industrial 87, 105, 172, 187
  local 6, 69, 77, 79, 127
  organisation of 29, 30
  technological 146, 147
productive bases 137, 145
  state-owned 123
productive capacity 29, 117, 125, 140, 188, 189
productive capital 16, 20, 24, 34, 35, 36, 38, 39, 47, 77, 127, 130, 182, 196
  foreign 121, 129
  international 171
  new 45, 47, 49, 196
productive chains 87, 92, 137, 156, 190, 207
  domestic 152
productive internationalisation 83, 84, 100, 101, 102, 114, 116, 120, 123, 147, 148, 180, 181, 183, 186
productive investments 3, 56, 64, 65, 72, 129, 137, 180, 189
  direct 77, 101
productive plants 72, 156, 177
  new 140, 164
productive power 31, 47, 145
  increased 31
productive processes 65, 89, 92, 98, 152, 191
  global 5
  new 106
productive scale 27, 51
productive sectors 38, 118, 140, 205
productive structure 43, 113, 116, 117, 147, 148, 156, 183, 184, 186, 189, 194, 196, 197, 199
  global 4, 191, 193, 194
Productive transnational capital 174
productiveness 31, 33, 45
productivity 20, 24, 27, 29, 30, 31, 32, 33, 37, 92, 95, 99, 102, 118, 142
  increasing 30, 31, 92, 178
  low 96, 113
products 11, 28, 29, 30, 35, 36, 38, 40, 41, 47, 48, 59, 108, 152, 192
  chemical 97, 130
  final 51, 190

imports of 120, 203
  primary 83, 91, 108, 175
profitability 74, 75, 76, 77, 78, 115, 126, 150, 153, 172, 197, 199
profits 30, 32, 46, 47, 63, 70, 76, 89, 199
  rate of 41, 53, 63, 74, 75, 76, 80, 134, 196, 198
projects 10, 42, 96, 123, 124, 125, 129, 142, 144, 145, 151
  national 133, 145, 146, 160
property 12, 15, 22, 24, 44, 74, 191, 192, 193
public debt 110, 149–50, 152, 153, 162, 169, 170, 172, 175

raising productivity 31, 32, 99
realisation 34, 35, 37, 38, 39, 40, 41, 61, 67, 68, 69, 70, 71, 75, 103
  crises of 32, 39, 40, 41, 51, 68, 69, 75
  crisis of 40
  process of 34, 39, 177
realisation of surplus value 70
recessive policies 110, 134, 136, 153
reconversion 34, 35, 62
recovery 30, 124, 136, 138, 171, 196, 198
reforms 125, 137, 138, 139, 160, 161
reinvestment 23, 24, 34, 60
  continuous 24
relationship
  centre-periphery 106
  social 17, 18, 19, 55
rentiers 169, 170, 172, 173, 174
restrictions 62, 107, 108, 117, 139, 151
  external 110, 111, 122, 147, 150
restructuring 3, 4, 42, 53, 55, 182, 183, 184, 186, 187, 190, 191, 194, 195, 197
resumption 131, 132, 136, 137, 183
Robinson, J. 14, 61
Rodriguez, O. 88, 93, 95, 113
Rodrik, D. 157
Rostow, W.W. 90, 91, 113

salaries 89, 111, 137, 138
Santos, M. 6, 78, 88, 92, 99, 107, 108, 111, 134, 148, 149, 188
Schoultz, L. 72, 98, 99, 129
Schumpeter, J.A. 51, 88
scrapping 149, 151, 152
Second National Development Plan 118, 142, 143

sectors 38, 39, 40, 64, 92, 96, 102, 105, 112, 129, 135, 138, 168, 190, 191
  food 129
  manufacturing 166, 167
  petrochemical 144
  private 139, 141, 152, 153, 160
  public 126, 149, 151, 153
sectors of consumer durables 126, 129, 130, 135, 138
Serra, J. 127, 138, 142, 143, 144, 145
services, public 152, 153, 154
Simonsen, M.H. 143
Singer, P. 136, 137, 142, 143
Sochaczewski, A.C. 124, 129
social capital 20, 35, 43, 46, 51, 62
social development 86, 87, 167
social inclusion 18, 86, 87, 88, 89, 140, 142
social relations 11, 12–14, 16, 17, 19, 52, 86
  centre of 10, 12
social relations of production 11, 16
spaces 4, 6, 43, 56, 57, 59, 64, 69, 71, 72, 79–80, 177, 178, 199–202, 204
  capital denies 57
  central 78, 97
  global 3, 5, 7, 55, 58, 59, 60, 62, 67, 164, 179, 195, 204, 205, 206
  national 54, 58, 68, 195, 201, 204, 205
  new 4, 5, 25, 26, 33, 53, 55, 56, 60, 78, 100, 177, 178, 179, 181
  peripheral 71, 92, 93, 177, 184, 199
  regional 67, 78
  restricted 4, 43, 61, 178, 204
spending, public 132, 173, 174
stages, state company centre 144
state action 83, 89, 112
state apparatus 128, 155
state-centres 201
state companies 97, 117, 137, 141, 142, 144, 145, 146, 147, 151–53, 161, 163, 165, 174
  forbade 152
  healthy 146
  large 144, 146
  largest 136
  privatisation of 151, 156
State Development Bank 163
state intervention 143, 181
state investments 135, 137, 140, 144
state-owned productive structure, strong 145
state participation 94, 123, 136, 141

state planning 87, 144
state policies 130, 135, 201
  national 137
state power 148
state strategy 115
state structure 124, 126
states 6, 57, 58–59, 65, 72, 89, 98, 122, 136, 145, 147, 151, 153–54, 161, 182
  autonomous 143, 202
  developmentalist 149, 154, 156
  local 200, 201, 204
  regulatory 157, 200
  weaker 66, 72, 182, 207
Stiglitz, J. 110, 156, 158
strategy 80, 84, 85, 93, 99, 102, 103, 104, 109, 115, 118, 119, 124, 125, 179–82
  deliberate 155, 156
  economic 131, 164
  national 155, 164, 166
  productive 203
structural problems 42, 107, 108, 116
submission 1–2, 8, 70, 101, 111, 112, 114, 115, 117, 118, 120, 158, 159, 201, 202
submitting 1–3, 8, 9, 10, 11, 18, 49, 73, 94, 155, 156, 158, 202
subordination 6, 7, 94, 103, 112, 115, 118, 120, 131, 142, 168, 175, 176, 183
subsidiaries 65, 77, 80, 105, 108, 120, 139, 140, 162, 177, 190
Sunkel, O. 101, 105, 107
super-production 32
surplus labour 18, 28, 30
surplus value 2, 22, 23, 24, 25, 26, 28, 32, 39, 49, 51, 55, 60, 61, 63, 69, 70, 74
  absolute 30
  increasing 28, 49
  producing 31
  relative 31
Suzigan, W. 121, 129
Sweezy, P.M. 14, 34, 49, 56, 60, 64
system centre-periphery 95

Targets Plan 122, 123, 124, 125, 126, 128, 129, 130, 131, 133, 135, 140, 143, 145, 156
Tavares, M.C. 92, 93, 96, 97, 121, 126, 128, 131, 134, 135, 136, 138, 195, 196, 200
technological development 134, 146
  national 146
technology 50, 51, 96, 99, 106, 108, 109, 112, 113, 115, 118, 126, 127, 144, 146

transnational capital   4, 6–7, 83, 84–85, 94, 98–106, 111, 112, 134, 135–36, 169, 179, 194, 195, 197
Transnational Capital & Exclusion   55, 57, 59, 61, 63, 65, 67, 69, 71, 73, 75, 77, 79, 81
transnational companies   59, 63, 70, 74, 77, 99, 108, 109, 113, 137, 139, 143, 146, 183, 188
  large   50, 107, 183, 185
  world oil   174
transnational corporations   7, 8, 54, 64, 66, 80, 81, 85, 94, 98, 105, 163, 164, 191, 195
  productive structures of   183, 197
transnationals   52, 57, 104, 105, 109, 112, 113, 114, 119, 159, 160, 164, 181, 182, 203
Triad   54, 55, 66, 79, 81, 114, 196
Triad countries   55, 56, 57
Tripod of Accumulation   105, 117, 122, 126, 141, 147, 149, 152, 153, 156
turnover   36, 38, 41, 165

UNCTAD   2, 3, 10, 79, 109, 113, 164, 166, 167, 185, 186, 189, 190, 191, 192
underdevelopment   1, 83, 88, 90, 91, 97, 99, 101, 113
unemployment   36, 41, 61, 86, 89, 157, 162, 163, 169, 174, 198–99, 201, 204, 205, 207
United States   101, 119, 128, 129, 132, 133, 140, 148, 159, 203

valorisation   2, 5, 9, 10, 16, 17, 19, 28, 33, 34, 36, 45, 46, 52, 178
  process of   3, 4, 9, 10, 12, 15–18, 20, 25, 26, 41, 51, 52, 55, 56, 177–78
value   13, 15, 16, 20, 21, 22, 23, 24, 26, 28, 29, 32, 34, 35–38, 177
  mass of   33, 177
  process of valorisation of   60, 62, 100, 184
  production of   86, 177
  realisation of   26, 27, 34, 51, 64, 67, 69, 84, 178

revolution in   20, 28, 47
  social   14, 29, 32, 34, 47
value chain   109, 111, 126, 184, 191, 192
value of independent existence   16, 59
Vargas   121, 122, 123, 124, 130, 145
Vargas government   122, 130
vulnerability   101, 104, 116, 118, 119, 120, 156, 180, 201

Wallerstein, I.   72
Washington Consensus   149, 155, 156, 157, 159, 161, 166, 182, 191, 196
Weaker individual capitals   179
wealth   11, 12, 13, 14, 15, 21, 28, 37, 38, 82, 172
  concentration of   29, 63
wealth accumulation   13
Werneck, R.F.   153
Williamson, O.   44, 155
work   13, 14, 15, 18, 22, 48, 49, 50, 55, 58, 86, 88, 116, 185, 188
workers   9, 10, 16, 17, 18, 19, 23, 24, 30, 31, 32, 37–38, 86, 89, 90
working day   30, 31, 32
world accumulation   118, 180
World Bank   104, 149, 156, 158
world capital   5, 6, 115, 128, 130, 131
  movement of   1
world capital accumulation   2, 83, 164
world capitalism   7, 158
world capitalist system   131
world centralisation   20
world economy   1, 4, 125, 136, 148, 160
world hegemonic centre   133
World Investment Report   3, 79
world market   27, 41, 59, 68
world scale   5, 6, 73, 179, 181, 182, 183, 187, 189, 193, 201, 204, 205, 206, 207
world-space   4, 5, 56, 61, 62, 70, 176, 179, 204, 205–6

www.ingramcontent.com/pod-product-compliance
Lightning Source LLC
Chambersburg PA
CBHW071157070526
44584CB00019B/2823